Lecture Notes in Computer Science 12257

More information about this series at http://www.springer.com/series/7408

Raghunath Nambiar · Meikel Poess (Eds.)

Performance Evaluation and Benchmarking for the Era of Cloud(s)

11th TPC Technology Conference, TPCTC 2019
Los Angeles, CA, USA, August 26, 2019
Revised Selected Papers

 Springer

Editors
Raghunath Nambiar
Advanced Micro Devices (United States)
Santa Clara, CA, USA

Meikel Poess
Oracle Corporation
Redwood Shores, CA, USA

ISSN 0302-9743   ISSN 1611-3349 (electronic)
Lecture Notes in Computer Science
ISBN 978-3-030-55023-3   ISBN 978-3-030-55024-0 (eBook)
https://doi.org/10.1007/978-3-030-55024-0

LNCS Sublibrary: SL2 – Programming and Software Engineering

This Springer imprint is published by the registered company Springer Nature Switzerland AG
The registered company address is: Gewerbestrasse 11, 6330 Cham, Switzerland

Preface

The Transaction Processing Performance Council (TPC) is a non-profit organization established in August 1988. Over the years, the TPC has had a significant impact on the computing industry's use of industry-standard benchmarks. Vendors use TPC benchmarks to illustrate performance competitiveness for their existing products, and to improve and monitor the performance of their products under development. Many buyers use TPC benchmark results as points of comparison when purchasing new computing systems.

The information technology landscape is evolving at a rapid pace, challenging industry experts and researchers to develop innovative techniques for evaluation, measurement, and characterization of complex systems. The TPC remains committed to developing new benchmark standards to keep pace with these rapid changes in technology. One vehicle for achieving this objective is the TPC's sponsorship of the Technology Conference Series on Performance Evaluation and Benchmarking (TPCTC) established in 2009. With this conference series, the TPC encourages researchers and industry experts to present and debate novel ideas and methodologies in performance evaluation, measurement, and characterization.

This book contains the proceedings of the 11th TPC Technology Conference on Performance Evaluation and Benchmarking (TPCTC 2019), held in conjunction with the 44th International Conference on Very Large Data Bases (VLDB 2019) in Los Angles, USA, during August 26–29, 2019.

The hard work and close cooperation of a *number of people have contributed to the success* of this conference. We would like to thank the members of TPC and the organizers of VLDB 2019 for their sponsorship; the members of the Program Committee and Publicity Committee for their support; and the authors and the participants who are the primary reason for the success of this conference.

June 2020

Raghunath Nambiar
Meikel Poess

Organization

General Chairs

Raghunath Nambiar   AMD, USA
Meikel Poess   Oracle, USA

Program Committee

Daniel Bowers	Gartner, USA
Michael Brey	Oracle, USA
Alain Crolotte	Teradata, USA
Paul Cao	HPE, USA
Ajay Dholakia	Lenovo, USA
Karthik Kulkarni	Cisco, USA
Manoj Kumar	INFLIBNET, India
Dhabaleswar Panda	The Ohio State University, USA
Tilmann Rabl	TU Berlin, Germany
Reza Taheri	VMWare, USA

Publicity Committee

Meikel Poess	Oracle, USA
Andrew Bond	Red Hat, USA
Paul Cao	HPE, USA
Gary Little	Nutanix, USA
Raghunath Nambiar	AMD, USA
Reza Taheri	VMware, USA
Michael Majdalany	L&M Management Group, USA
Forrest Carman	Owen Media, USA
Andreas Hotea	Hotea Solutions, USA

About the TPC

Introduction to the TPC

The Transaction Processing Performance Council (TPC) is a non-profit organization focused on developing industry standards for data centric workloads and disseminating vendor-neutral performance data to the industry. Additional information is available at http://www.tpc.org/.

TPC Memberships

Full Members

Full Members of the TPC participate in all aspects of the TPC's work, including development of benchmark standards and setting strategic direction. The Full Member application can be found at http://www.tpc.org/information/about/app-member.asp.

Associate Members

Certain organizations may join the TPC as Associate Members. Associate Members may attend TPC meetings but are not eligible to vote or hold office. Associate membership is available to non-profit organizations, educational institutions, market researchers, publishers, consultants, governments, and businesses that do not create, market, or sell computer products or services. The Associate Member application can be found at http://www.tpc.org/information/about/app-assoc.asp.

Academic and Government Institutions

Academic and government institutions are invited join the TPC and a special invitation can be found at http://www.tpc.org/information/specialinvitation.asp.

Contact the TPC

TPC
Presidio of San Francisco
Building 572B (surface)
P.O. Box 29920 (mail)
San Francisco, CA 94129-0920
Voice: 415-561-6272
Fax: 415-561-6120
Email: info@tpc.org

How to Order TPC Materials

All of our materials are now posted free of charge on our website. If you have any questions, please feel free to contact our office directly or by email at info@tpc.org.

Benchmark Status Report

The TPC Benchmark Status Report is a digest of the activities of the TPC and its technical subcommittees. Sign-up information can be found at the following URL: http://www.tpc.org/information/about/email.asp.

TPC 2019 Organization

Full Members

Actian
Alibaba
AMD
Cisco
Dell EMC
DataCore
Fujitsu
Hewlett Packard Enterprise
Hitachi
Huawei
IBM
Inspur
Intel
Lenovo
Microsoft
Nutanix
Oracle
Pivotal
Red Hat
SAP
Teradata
Transwarp
TTA
VMware

Associate Members

IDEAS International
University of Coimbra, Portugal
China Academy of Information and Communications Technology, China

Steering Committee

Michael Brey (Chair), Oracle
Matthew Emmerton, IBM
Jamie Reding, Microsoft
Ken Rule, Intel
Nicholas Wakou, Dell EMC

Public Relations Committee

Paul Cao, HPE
Gary Little, Nutanix
Raghunath Nambiar, AMD
Meikel Poess (Chair), Oracle
Reza Taheri, VMware

Technical Advisory Board

Paul Cao, HPE
Matt Emmerton, IBM
Gary Little, Nutanix
Jamie Reding (Chair), Microsoft
Da-Qi Ren, Huawei
Ken Rul, Intel
Nicholas Wakou, Dell EMC

Technical Subcommittees and Chairs

TPC-C: Jamie Reding, Microsoft
TPC-H: Meikel Poess, Oracle
TPC-E: Matthew Emmerton, IBM
TPC-DS: Meikel Poess, Oracle
TPC-VMS: Reza Taheri, VMware
TPC-DI: Meikel Poess, Oracle
TPCx-HS: Tariq Magdon-Ismail, VMware
TPCx-IoT: Meikel Poess, Oracle
TPCx-BB: Chris Elford, Intel
TPCx-V: Reza Taheri, VMware
TPCx-HCI: Reza Taheri, VMware
TPC-Pricing: Jamie Reding, Microsoft
TPC-Energy: Paul Cao, HPE

Working Groups and Chairs

TPC-AI: Hamesh Patel, Intel
TPC-LDBC: Meikel Poess, Oracle
TPC-OSS: Andy Bond, IBM
Reza Taheri, VMware

Contents

Benchmarking Elastic Cloud Big Data Services Under SLA Constraints

Nicolas Poggi[1,2](✉), Víctor Cuevas-Vicenttín[1], Josep Lluis Berral[1,2],
Thomas Fenech[1], Gonzalo Gómez[1], Davide Brini[1], Alejandro Montero[1],
David Carrera[1,2], Umar Farooq Minhas[3], Jose A. Blakeley[3],
Donald Kossmann[3], Raghu Ramakrishnan[3], and Clemens Szyperski[3]

[1] Barcelona Supercomputing Center (BSC), Barcelona, Spain
{nicolas.poggi,victor.cuevas,josep.berral,thomas.fenech,gonzalo.gomez,
davide.brini,alejandro.montero,david.carrera}@bsc.es
[2] Universitat Politècnica de Catlalunya (UPC - BarcelonaTech), Barcelona, Spain
[3] Microsoft Corporation, Microsoft Research (MSR), Redmond, USA
{ufminhas,joseb,donaldk,raghu,clemens}@microsoft.com

Abstract. We introduce an extension for TPC benchmarks addressing the requirements of big data processing in cloud environments. We characterize it as the Elasticity Test and evaluate under TPCx-BB (BigBench). First, the Elasticity Test incorporates an approach to generate real-world query submissions patterns with distinct data scale factors based on major industrial cluster logs. Second, a new metric is introduced based on Service Level Agreements (SLAs) that takes the quality of service requirements of each query under consideration.

Experiments with Apache Hive and Spark on the cloud platforms of three major vendors validate our approach by comparing to the current TPCx-BB metric. Results show how systems who fail to meet SLAs under concurrency due to queuing or degraded performance negatively affect the new metric. On the other hand, elastic systems meet a higher percentage of SLAs and thus are rewarded in the new metric. Such systems have the ability to scale up and down compute workers according to the demands of a varying workload and can thus save dollar costs.

Keywords: Benchmarking · Big data · Databases · Cloud · SLA · QoS

1 Introduction

BigBench [1] was standardized by the Transaction Processing Performance Council (TPC) as TPCx-BB. It is the first reference and implemented benchmark for Big Data Analytics. BigBench addresses important aspects in Big Data such as variety (considering structured and semi-structured data), volume (through large and varying scale factors), and velocity (through a policy of interspersing inserts, deletes, and updates with query streams).

N. Poggi—Contribution while at the BSC-MSR Centre, currently at Databricks Inc.

R. Nambiar and M. Poess (Eds.): TPCTC 2019, LNCS 12257, pp. 1–18, 2020.
https://doi.org/10.1007/978-3-030-55024-0_1

However, BigBench does not fully address some of the aspects relevant to data analytics services operating in cloud infrastructures. For instance, the benchmark runs for a single database size tied to a scale factor, while in real-life, we can expect queries processing varying amounts of data at the same time. Furthermore, in BigBench queries are run in n concurrent streams (where n is defined by the user), while the sequence of queries to be executed for each particular stream is specified in a placement table. Thus, the system load is constant in terms of the number of queries under execution e.g., queries start only when the previous from the stream has finished and do not queue in the system.

Such an approach is adequate to replicate a homogeneous workload with aggregate performance considerations. It is inappropriate, however, when the workload is expected to vary with time in response to real user demands, and when users can have specific performance or isolation expectations for each query i.e., for batch, interactive, and streaming queries. Moreover, elastic services such of a database or query as-a-service (DBaaS or QaaS) provide the ability to scale up or down compute resources to either process more rapidly or to save costs i.e., in periods of low intensity. We address these problems by introducing a new test, which we call the Elasticity Test and incorporating it into the existing TPCx-BB benchmark. We test the approach in TPCx-BB here, while the test could be applied directly to other TPC benchmarks, in particular, TPC-DS and TPC-H.

Our extension is built from three main components. First, we design and implement a workload generation approach that produces workloads that are more representative of what we can expect in a highly dynamic environment such as the cloud (Sect. 2). Second, we implement a driver capable of executing such workloads. Third, we propose a new benchmark metric based on Service Level Agreements (SLAs) (Sect. 3), which enables to measure the compliance with the performance expectations of the user and thus the quality of service (QoS) of the system under test.

In Sects. 4 and 5, we present and analyze the results of experiments that use our extended TPCx-BB benchmark to evaluative Apache Hive and Spark running on three major cloud platforms. Subsequently, we present related work and the conclusions.

2   Workload Characterization and Generation

2.1   Analyzing Cloud Services Workloads

We present how we generate realistic workloads based on the analysis of data obtained from a real-world production cluster, the Cosmos cluster [4] operated at Microsoft. The dataset analyzed consists of about 350,000 job submissions sampled from the period between January 2 to February 9, 2017.

Modeling the Arrival Rate. To implement a benchmark that reflects the workloads that real-world Big Data computing infrastructures face, a fundamental aspect is to understand the arrival rates of jobs, i.e. the number of jobs that arrive for each unit of time, and to model it adequately. With this purpose in mind, we analyzed the job submissions in the Cosmos sample dataset.

Identifiable trends in the arrival rate of jobs, such as peaks in usage during working hours and a decline in activity on the weekends, led us to conclude that the periodicity and variability of the job submission rate cannot be captured through a simple approach. For instance, if we were to define a single cumulative distribution function (CDF), this CDF would conflate all of the data irrespective of the particular patterns observed. Instead we need to adopt a more sophisticated approach capable of temporal pattern recognition.

A technique capable of modeling temporal patterns in the arrival rate is Hidden Markov Models (HMMs). A HMM enables us to take into account the transition between busy and quiet periods. In practice, the arrival rate varies continuously, but it can be modeled using a series of n discrete levels associated with states. At a given point in time, the arrival rate is represented by a series of parameters, describing the probability of being in each level (1 to n), along with the probabilities of transitioning to each of the other levels. In our case, we found that a model consisting of four levels was sufficient to capture the fluctuations in activity over the period in the dataset.

Once the model has been trained with the reference data, it can be used to produce a synthetic randomized sequence of job arrivals, which possesses similar statistical characteristics to the reference data. The generated arrival sequence can then be scaled in terms of the range of arrival rates and the period, which makes the model a useful part of a realistic workload simulator. The output model is expected to have periods of a high number of job submissions (*peaks*), as well as periods of low (*valleys*) or even no submissions where the system might be *idle*.

To validate the capability of the model to produce an arrival rate whose properties match those of the reference dataset, but adding variability and avoiding being fully deterministic, we can generate synthetic sequences of job submissions and then compare their distributions. Example synthetic distributions of arrival rates are shown in Fig. 1. Kernel density estimation (KDE) is used to approximate the distribution of each data series. These data series correspond to the generated job arrival data with the original states and with newly generated states (a distinction explained below). KDE is a non-parametric technique to estimate probability density functions that yields a result closely related to histograms, hence it is an adequate technique to perform this comparison. The lines are close to one another but not equal, indicating a close match between the sequences generated and a degree of non-determinism.

The aforementioned HMM is encapsulated in a script that receives the following parameters: *dataset, max jobs*, minutes/hours, keep the original state sequence. The dataset parameter corresponds in our experiments to the Cosmos dataset. The *max jobs* parameter denotes the maximum number of jobs that can be generated for each time unit, which in turn is defined to be in seconds (or fractions of a second) by the third parameter. A sequence of states has to be generated by the algorithm to produce the HMM, this same sequence can

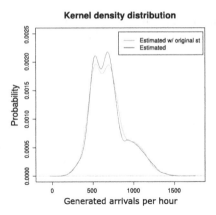

Fig. 1. Comparison between two arrival rate sequences generated by the model.

then be used to produce the output data, or alternatively, a new sequence can be generated. This is specified by the last parameter that takes a boolean value.

Input Data Size. Another fundamental aspect of modeling a realistic workload is the complexity of the submitted jobs. In this paper we address data complexity, related to the size of the database; whereas query type or complexity, related to the query expression, forms part of future work.

We investigated the presence of temporal and periodic effects on the size of the job input data sizes, which can occur in particular cases. For example, we can expect that some users will prefer to run numerous short jobs during business hours followed by a few data-intensive jobs during the night shift. However, we did not find evidence that such a pattern holds across all of the data. Therefore, while the job arrival rate varies significantly, as stated earlier, the distribution of the corresponding input data sizes is not subject to similar temporal patterns. Consequently, we take an aggregate view of job input data sizes. For benchmarking, the effects of our analysis are reflected only on the scale factors that the BigBench queries are subject to.

We present the cumulative distribution function for the input data sizes of the sampled Cosmos dataset in Fig. 2; it is a discrete CDF with the data sizes axis expressed in log scale and with data points corresponding to the usual units of measuring data. The size of the input data varies from a few bytes to up to near a petabyte. Almost 60% of the jobs have less than 1 GB of data as input and very few more than 10 TB. Recall that we are dealing with sampled data, so such outliers may not be representative of the full dataset.

From the CDF we can generate random variates representing the input data sizes of the jobs in the workload simulation. The generated input data sizes are then matched to scale factors in the BigBench database. We consider only a few representative scale factors in factors of 10 i.e., 1 GB, 100 GB, 1 TB, 10 TB.

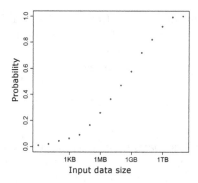

Fig. 2. CDF of the input data sizes of the jobs in the Cosmos sample dataset.

We next show how our model derived from the analysis of the Cosmos dataset enables us to generate a workload suitable for our BigBench extension, experimental results for this workload are presented in Sect. 4.

2.2 Workload Generation for Cloud Services

Our goal for the Elasticity Test is to create a realistic workload that can be integrated with existing TPC metrics. We explain this integration to TPCx-BB in Sect. 3, although the Elasticity Test can also be run in stand-alone manner. With that goal in mind, we adapted the notion of streams employed in TPC benchmarks, where for a given number of streams n, one instance of each query appears in the stream. Thus, the number of streams defines the total number of queries in the workload, namely, n times the number of different queries in the benchmark.

Once the total number of queries in the workload is defined, these are assigned randomly to time-slots (batches) whose size is determined by the HMM, subject to a maximum $n - 1$ streams. Setting the maximum limit to $n - 1$ makes the Elasticity Test compatible with the Throughput Test, as it is expected that n is a user-defined threshold where the system is expected to complete all the queries. Also, it prevents introducing a new parameter into the benchmark, simplifying adoption. Repetition of queries is not allowed within a single batch but can occur among different batches. The query batches can be viewed as the static specification of the workload, which is then made dynamic during execution by a batch interval, λ_{batch}, optionally defined by the user and that determines the time interval between the submissions of each batch of queries (defaults to 60 s.). Having a smaller value of λ_{batch} means that the driver will submit the batches faster i.e., put more load on the System Under Test (SUT), while a larger value results in longer waiting times between query batches. Having a lower interval could produce lower test times to improve the final score if the system is able to run the queries without SLA-penalties.

For the experiments, as we increase the data scale factor from 1 TB to 10 TB, to compensate for the corresponding increase in system load, the number of streams is lowered. Specifically, we use: from $n = 4$ at 1 TB we lower the number of streams to $n = 2$ at 10 TB. We also increase the batch interval λ_{batch}, to account for the higher time taken to complete queries for larger data sizes as the systems failed to meet the SLAs with lower values.

At 1 TB, the above parameters result in the workload presented in Fig. 3 (left). The blue line on the chart (left axis) shows the total number of queries that have been submitted to the system. The green impulses (right axis) show the size of each batch of jobs, up to a maximum of 3 (always less than or equal to $n = 4$). The sizes of the batches increase at around half of the timeline, implying that a statically-provisioned system with sufficient capacity to handle the maximum batch size is over-provisioned for the first part of the test, so the total cost of the execution may be higher than that of an elastic system.

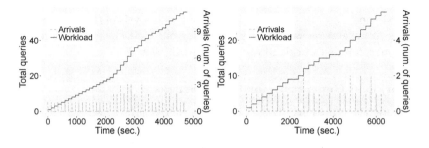

Fig. 3. Workloads for the 1 TB (left) and 10 TB (right) scale factors.

For the workload in Fig. 3 (left) we consider only the 14 SQL queries from BigBench, which means that the total number of queries is $n \cdot M = 56$, reached at the top right corner of the graph. We note that although in this workload all of the queries that form part of a batch arrive at the same time, our driver provides the option of evenly distributing the queries of every individual batch across their corresponding batch interval. In that case, we would observe much lower green lines (of height 1, in fact), but there would be a much higher number of them in the chart.

Figure 3 (right) depicts the workload for the 10 TB scale factor. With the number of streams being reduced to $n = 2$, the only possible batch sizes are 0, 1 and 2. The batch interval λ_{batch} is 240 s and the total number of queries is 28. Note that some batches have zero queries, representing the low-workload periods that occur in systems like Cosmos.

For dynamic workloads as exemplified above, it is highly desirable to measure not only the query execution times, but also how well these execution times meet the user requirements, particularly when the system is subject to higher loads. For this purpose, we introduce in the next section a SLA-aware performance metric.

3   New SLA-Aware Metric for Big Data Systems

A shortcoming of the current TPCx-BB specification is that the quality of service (QoS) per query is not measured. This means that a system can achieve a high score by completing parts of the execution quickly while neglecting others. In a real-world business use case, workloads have deadlines and an expected QoS, so a system operating at scale must be able to maintain a reasonable response time for individual queries.

In this section, we present a new Elasticity Metric to be incorporated into TPCx-BB, which assesses the ability of a system to deliver a consistent quality of service at a per-query level. The metric is based on the concept of each query having a completion deadline, i.e., a Service Level Agreement (SLA). We define a per-query SLA, and to achieve the maximum score, the system must execute each query within its SLA. The system is penalized for the number of queries that fail to meet their SLA, and by how much time the deadline was missed. Recall that in the Elasticity Test, we submit queries to the system according to fluctuating batch arrivals, generated using the HMM model presented in Sect. 2.1, which can produce a queuing effect where more queries are running concurrently than in the previous Throughput Test.

We begin this section by giving a brief overview of the performance metric used in TPCx-BB. We then describe how to calculate the score corresponding to our proposed metric. Finally, we conclude this section by proposing a means of integrating the Elasticity Test into the TPCx-BB.

Existing Performance Metric. We first revisit the existing formula used to calculate the score in TPCx-BB. The overall Performance Metric is defined as

$$BBQpm@SF = \frac{SF \cdot 60 \cdot M}{T_{LD} + \sqrt[3]{T_{PT} \cdot T_{TT}}} \tag{1}$$

The three variables T_{LD}, T_{PT} and T_{TT} are derived, as described below, from the time taken to run the Load Test, Power Test, and Throughput Test, respectively. SF is the scale factor and M is the total number of queries in the benchmark. The Performance Metric is designed to represent the number of queries per minute that a system can execute, which decreases as the various test times increase. The square root of $T_{PT} \cdot T_{TT}$ is the geometric mean of the two values, which is more suitable than the more commonly-used arithmetic mean, in situations where values are associated with different scales.

The Load Test measures the time taken to prepare the data for the benchmark. The details of this test vary, depending on the SUT, but the total time T_{Load} is multiplied by a constant factor of 0.1 to reduce the weight of this score, i.e.,

$$T_{LD} = 0.1 \cdot T_{Load} \tag{2}$$

The Power Test measures the raw performance of the system, running the full suite of queries serially. It is calculated as follows

$$T_{PT} = M \cdot \sqrt[M]{\prod_{i=1}^{M} t_i} \tag{3}$$

where t_i is the time taken to execute query i, measured in seconds.

The Throughput Test measures the ability of the system to execute multiple streams in parallel, defined as

$$T_{TT} = \frac{1}{n} \cdot T_{Tput} \tag{4}$$

where n is the total number of streams, chosen by the user, and T_{Tput} is the elapsed time between the start of the Throughput Test and the completion of all streams, measured in seconds.

New Performance Metric. Complementing the existing T_{LD}, T_{PT} and T_{TT}, we introduce a new performance metric, T_{ET}, which is defined as

$$T_{ET} = \lambda_{batch} \cdot \Delta_{SLA} \cdot \rho_{SLA} \cdot T_{el} \tag{5}$$

Each of the terms is described below. In all cases, n refers to the maximum level of concurrency during the test. By default, the value of n used in the Elasticity Test will be the same as the total number of streams used in the Throughput Test. The number of streams is used to reduce the number of user-defined parameters in the new test, also due to n usually corresponding to the maximum concurrency of the SUT and scale factor intended by the user. Again, M is the number of queries in the benchmark.

- λ_{batch} is the time interval between job batch submissions. This is the only additional optional parameter for the user. Defaults to 60 s.
- Δ_{SLA} is the SLA distance, which is the average failure ratio of queries that do not complete within their SLA, and is defined as

$$\Delta_{SLA} = \frac{1}{n \cdot M} \cdot max\left(1, \sum_{i=1}^{n \cdot M} max\left(0, \frac{t_i - SLA_{Q(i)}}{SLA_{Q(i)}}\right)\right) \tag{6}$$

where t_i is the time taken to run query i from the schedule and $SLA_{Q(i)}$ is the SLA for query i. The inner max ensures that queries which complete within their SLA do not contribute to the sum. The outer max means that when all queries pass their SLA, $\Delta_{SLA} = 1$.

- ρ_{SLA} is the *SLA factor*, which is defined as

$$\rho_{SLA} = \frac{1}{n \cdot M} \cdot max\left(1, \frac{N_{fail}}{0.25}\right) \tag{7}$$

where N_{fail} is the number of queries that fail to meet their SLA. $\rho_{SLA} < 1$ when under 25% of the queries fail their SLAs, which reduces (improves) the value of the metric T_{ET}. Conversely, failing more than 25% of the queries results in $\rho_{SLA} > 1$, which has a negative impact on T_{ET}. As in the definition of Δ_{SLA}, a max is applied to prevent ρ_{SLA} from reaching zero, limiting the minimum value to $1/(n \cdot M)$.

– T_{el} is the total elapsed time of the Elasticity Test.

The score from the Elasticity Test is incorporated into the existing TPCx-BB formula as follows

$$BB + +Qpm@SF = \frac{SF \cdot 60 \cdot M}{T_{LD} + \sqrt[3]{T_{PT} \cdot T_{TT} \cdot T_{ET}}} \tag{8}$$

That is, the geometric mean is extended to include the score from the Elasticity Test. Since the range of scores in the Power Test, the Throughput Test, and the Elasticity Test are all different, scores obtained using this new metric cannot be compared directly with older results. However, it is possible to calculate the new metric using the existing Load Test, Power Test and Throughput Test results, provided that the Elasticity Test is run with the same number of streams n. The next section presents experiments in which we apply this new metric.

4   Experimental Evaluation

We now present the results of executing the workloads derived from our model based on the analysis of the Cosmos dataset and evaluated by our SLA-based metric. As discussed in Sect. 3, the computation of our benchmark score requires, in addition to the Elasticity Test metrics, also the metrics of the current Big-Bench tests; namely for the Data Loading, the Power, and the Throughput tests. We present the results of our experiments in regards to each of these next. Due to failures and scalability problems of the non-SQL queries, all the presented experiments were limited to the 14 SQL-only queries.

The SUTs considered are Apache Hive and Apache Spark running on three major cloud providers. We avoid identifying the particular providers and refer to them only through pseudonyms: ProvA, ProvB, and ProvC. On the three providers, Hive was either version 2.2 or 2.3 and Spark with 2.1 or 2.2.

We considered 1 TB and 10 TB scale factors, although not all configurations for the latter. In some cases, failures at a particular test prevent us from presenting the corresponding test scores and also to compute the global metrics. The configurations of the different SUTs were defined in such a way that they include 32 worker nodes, with 16 virtual cores (512-vcpus in total), and 64 GB of RAM each (2 TB total).

4.1 Data Loading Test

We present the measured loading times for the 1 TB scale factor in Fig. 4 (left).
Hive outperforms Spark in ProvA and ProvB, but the opposite is true for ProvC.
Also, ProvB and ProvC achieve lower loading times than ProvA. We note that
for Hive and Spark the data were stored using the ORC columnar storage format.

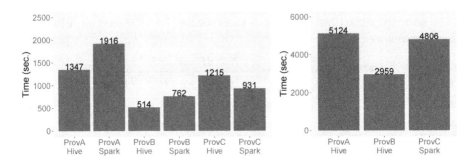

Fig. 4. Data loading times for the 1 TB (left) and 10 TB (right) scale factors.

The second scale factor that we considered is 10 TB, which involved only
some of the SUTs and whose results are illustrated in Fig. 4 (right). The data
loaded is used for both Hive and Spark. The lowest load time overall corresponds
to Hive on ProvB, followed by Spark on ProvC, whose value is close to the results
of ProvA.

4.2 Elasticity Test

An extension of the TPCx-BB driver was required to execute the Elasticity Test.
The structure of the driver we implemented enables the execution of queries by
independent threads and at various data sizes within the same run. Additionally,
it facilitates incorporating new data engines, since the functionality to interoper-
ate with a given engine is encapsulated in a wrapper that adopts a standardized
interface.

We now present the experiments that we carried out with the workloads
described in Sect. 2.2 and limiting the TPCx-BB query set to the SQL queries
only. For each run, we produce a chart that shows for the individual queries in
the Elasticity Test, which of them satisfied their corresponding SLA and which
ones violated it. In turn, the SLAs were defined by averaging the running times
of a given query at the Power Test (thus, in isolation) for each system and adding
a 25% percent margin. We present next results for the 1 TB and 10 TB scale
factors.

For the 1 TB scale factor, we limit the number of query streams to 4, resulting
in a total of 56 queries (14 × 4). The time interval between each batch of queries
was set to 120 s. In relation to execution times and SLA satisfaction, Fig. 5

shows the behavior of the different SUTs. Hive on ProvA reflects a relatively poor performance by a significant proportion of SLA violations. Concretely, the result for ProvA Hive is 71% SLA violations. The results are slightly worse for Hive on ProvB, for which 80% of the SLAs are violated. In both cases, the fact that execution times increase as the test progresses indicates that a significant backlog of queries is built as shown in Hive charts at 1 TB in Fig. 5.

In contrast, in the Spark results no SLAs were violated on any of the platforms. Furthermore, through the execution significant slack is left after the query is completed, as indicated by the gray areas in the charts. Similar execution times at the beginning and end of the test also indicate that a query backlog is not formed.

The largest data sizes considered in our experiments correspond to the 10 TB scale factor. Taking the smaller 1 TB scale factor as its precedent, the number of streams is now reduced from 4 to 2, resulting in a total of 28 $(14 * 2)$ queries. The time between batches is doubled from 120 to 240 s as the cluster are not scaled with the increased data size. The workload generated for these experiments has the peculiarity that some batches have zero queries to be submitted, as depicted in Fig. 6.

The experiments for only two of the SUTs considered completed successfully: Hive and Spark on ProvA; the result charts for these systems are presented in Fig. 6, respectively. Spark violated the SLAs of only 3 queries, which represent 11% of the total in this experiment. Furthermore, these violations were not severe in terms of the additional time required to complete the queries, consequently, the SLA distance value for the run is low at 0.04. Hive missed the SLAs for 39% of the queries, 11 out of the 28 queries, to be exact. The SLA distance is 0.28 for Hive, due to many queries requiring significant time to complete.

4.3   Power Test

We now present the summarized results of the TPCx-BB Power Test for the 1 TB, and 10 TB scale factors. Recall that the Power Test involves the consecutive execution of each of the queries in the specified list, in their sequential order. Thus, there is no concurrency, making this test useful to determine how efficient a system is to evaluate a particular query.

Figure 7 (left) presents the results for the 1 TB scale factor. A noteworthy observation is that the performance of Spark surpasses that of Hive for ProvB and ProvC, while ProvA exhibits the opposite result. The best performance corresponds to Spark on ProvB, while Hive on ProvC shows the poorest performance.

The results for the 10 TB scale factor are illustrated in Fig. 7 (right). The best results correspond again to Spark but his time for ProvA. Hive on ProvA obtains the second-best results. Hive on ProvB shows a slightly poorer performance than Hive on ProvA. Finally, Spark on ProvC shows the poorest performance.

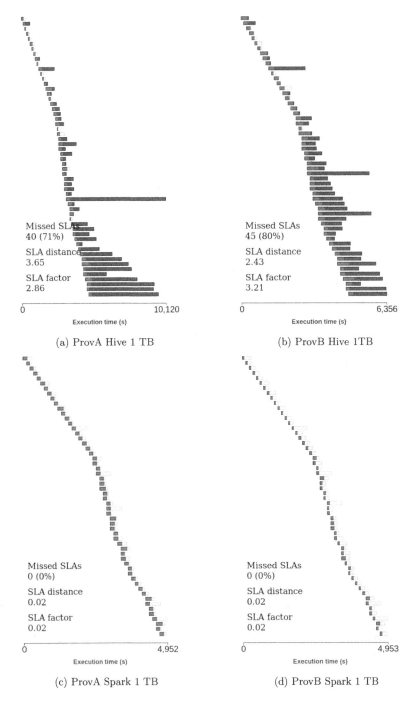

Fig. 5. Elasticity Test results at 1 TB of Hive and Spark of 56 total queries. Queries in red have missed the SLA.

4.4   Throughput Test

We next present the results of the TPCx-BB Throughput Test. This test consists of issuing queries through a series of streams. The queries of a particular stream have to be completed serially, and according to an order established in the benchmark. Thus, in contrast with the Elasticity Test, the number of streams bounds the overall concurrency. Again, the 1TB and 10TB scale factors were used in these experiments, which were also limited to the 14 SQL queries. In the following charts, the times given correspond to the metric discussed in Sect. 3. Essentially, this metric is calculated by taking the time to complete the Throughput Test and dividing it by the number of streams.

The results for the 1 TB scale factor Throughput Test are presented in Fig. 8 (left). The test used four query streams at this scale factor. Spark showed adequate performance, clearly surpassing Hive for all providers. Particularly, the results Spark obtains with ProvB and ProvC represent the best among the SUTs; Spark with ProvA shows a completion time that is not much larger.

We present the results for the 10 TB scale factor in Fig. 8 (right), which consisted of two query streams. Spark shows again the best performance, with ProvB beating ProvA. In the case of Hive, the system relying on ProvA shows a better performance than that on ProvB, but both lag behind the Spark systems.

Based on the results of these tests, in the next section, we derive full benchmark metrics and also examine the corresponding costs.

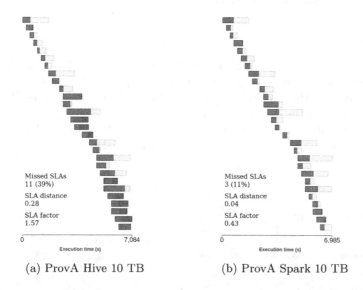

(a) ProvA Hive 10 TB   (b) ProvA Spark 10 TB

Fig. 6. Elasticity Test results at 10 TB for ProvA Hive and Spark of 28 total queries.

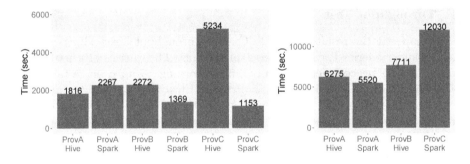

Fig. 7. Power Test times for the 1 TB (left) and 10 TB (right) scale factors.

5   Results Analysis

In this section, we present the final performance scores for each system. We compare the result of the original TPCx-BB metric with the score obtained using the Elasticity Test introduced in Sect. 3. As in the TPCx-BB specification, we also consider the Price/Performance Metric, which is obtained by dividing the total cost of executing the benchmark by the performance metric. However, we present results based only of relative costs, since as stated earlier the providers are not identified and additionally, costs have exhibited a downward trend that makes the exact amounts less relevant.

5.1   BBQ++ Metric

In Fig. 9 (left) we present the results obtained using our new BB++Qpm metric at 1 TB, alongside with the original BBQpm score. We emphasize that the two values are not directly comparable and that the purpose of presenting them side by side is to see how the differences between systems and potentially the rankings change as a result of introducing the Elasticity Test. We can see that Spark on all providers achieves significantly higher scores than Hive at this scale factor,

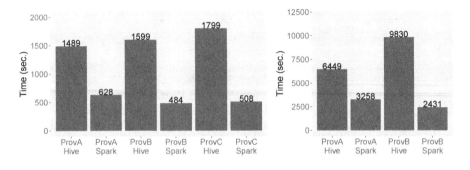

Fig. 8. Throughput Test times for the 1 TB (left) and 10 TB (right) scale factors.

once elasticity is considered. Furthermore, for Hive we witness an enormous drop in performance for the new metric.

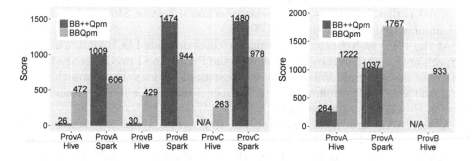

Fig. 9. BB++Qpm and BBQpm scores for the 1 TB (left) and 10 TB (right) scale factors.

In Fig. 9 (right) we show the results at 10 TB. Hive struggled to meet the SLAs at this data scale. On the other hand, Spark on ProvA obtained a much better score because of its score in the Elasticity Test.

5.2   Costs

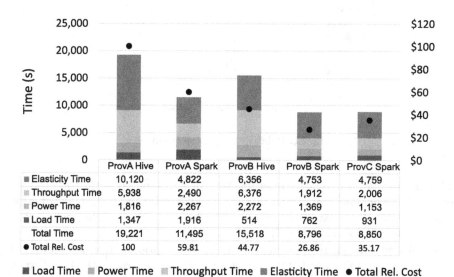

Fig. 10. Total BigBench times and relative costs at 1 TB.

For our cost analysis, the benchmark execution is broken down into separate parts, the times of the individual tests of the benchmark are then added up to obtain the total time, then a total cost is calculated as a function of the total time. The cost calculation depends on the characteristics of each system. Since, as stated earlier, we present only relative costs, a cost of $100 represents the maximum actual cost among the SUTs.

At the 1 TB scale factor, we obtain the costs presented in Fig. 10. The costs of Spark are lower than those of Hive, with the ProvB and ProvC systems having the lowest costs overall. We also observe that the Elasticity Test plays the most significant role in determining the total execution time for most systems, with Hive on ProvB being the exception.

At the 10 TB scale factor, we were able to generate complete results only for Hive and Spark on ProvA. Due to space limitations, we omit a full time and cost breakdown and report only the total relative costs. For Hive the total relative cost was (as defined) $100, whereas it was $79 for Spark. Thus Spark turned out to be about 21% cheaper than Hive.

5.3   Price/Performance Score

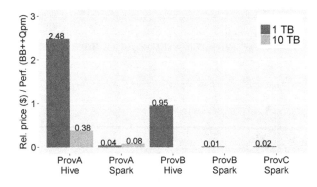

Fig. 11. Relative price/performance.

In Fig. 11, we show the relative price/performance, computed as the total relative cost of the benchmark execution in dollars, divided by the BB++Qpm performance metric. Where available, results are shown at each of the scale factors that were tested. On this chart, lower is better.

We observe that there is a significant range in the price/performance at 1 TB. There is a large difference between Hive (worse) and Spark (better) on ProvA. Overall at 1 TB, Spark dominates, achieving very low price/performance on all providers. ProvA with Spark provides the best price/performance at 10 TB, the difference with respect to Hive on ProvA is significant but not as large as for the 1 TB scale factor.

6   Related Work

A methodology to measure the elasticity of cloud services under varying work-loads is presented in [2], we adopt similar techniques but also integrate our approach into a full benchmark. SLAs have been applied in many contexts. For instance, their specification (through step-wise functions) and associated optimization problems are addressed for Service Oriented Architectures in [5]. Those and other alternative methods to define SLAs could be incorporated into our approach. Similar to our work, TPC-DS V2 is presented in [3], where the authors extend TPC-DS to consider data integration and multiple user aspects.

7   Conclusions

The Elasticity Test takes into consideration dynamic workloads and QoS aspects that are crucial in cloud environments i.e., fluctuating query submissions and multiple scale factors. We evaluate this extension by experiments on the cloud platforms of three major vendors and at two different scale factors, using two popular open-source big data processing systems. The analysis of the results of these experiments yields information of practical interest and validates our approach.

In particular, experiments show how certain configurations of the systems and platforms fail to meet SLAs under concurrency, scoring differently than the current TPCx-BB metric and reflecting poor resource isolation or scheduling. In contrast to the Throughput Test, which waits until a query finishes per concurrent stream to issue the next, our Elasticity Test summits queries following a more realistic pattern. This fact creates either high-intensity periods or queues, as well as low-intensity or even no new query arrivals. In this way testing more system components i.e., the scheduler and workload manager. Modern elastic services such of database or query as-a-service (DBaaS or QaaS) which can scale up a down compute nodes can benefit by saving in costs in low insensitive periods while adding more resources to prevent missing query SLAs. We believe an extension such as the Elasticity Test can complement current data TPC benchmarks to evaluate cloud analytical services.

References

1. Ghazal, A., et al.: Bigbench: towards an industry standard benchmark for big data analytics. In: Proceedings of the 2013 ACM SIGMOD International Conference on Management of Data, SIGMOD 2013, pp. 1197–1208. ACM, New York (2013)
2. Islam, S., Lee, K., Fekete, A., Liu, A.: How a consumer can measure elasticity for cloud platforms. In: Proceedings of the 3rd ACM/SPEC International Conference on Performance Engineering, ICPE 2012, pp. 85–96. ACM, New York (2012)
3. Poess, M., Rabl, T., Jacobsen, H.A.: Analysis of TPC-DS: the first standard benchmark for SQL-based big data systems. In: Proceedings of the 2017 Symposium on Cloud Computing, SoCC 2017, pp. 573–585. ACM, New York (2017)

4. Ramakrishnan, R., et al.: Azure data lake store: a hyperscale distributed file service for big data analytics. In: Proceedings of the 2017 ACM International Conference on Management of Data, SIGMOD 2017, pp. 51–63. ACM, New York (2017). https://doi.org/10.1145/3035918.3056100
5. Zhang, L., Ardagna, D.: Sla based profit optimization in autonomic computing systems. In: Proceedings of the 2Nd International Conference on Service Oriented Computing, ICSOC 2004, pp. 173–182. ACM, New York (2004)

Efficient Multiway Hash
Join on Reconfigurable Hardware

Rekha Singhal[1,2]([⊠]), Yaqi Zhang[1], Jeffrey D. Ullman[1], Raghu Prabhakar[1],
and Kunle Olukotun[1]

[1] Stanford University, Stanford, CA, USA
{rekhas2,yaqiz,ullman,raghup17,kunle}@stanford.com
[2] Tata Consultancy Services Research, Mumbai, India

Abstract. We propose the algorithms for performing multiway joins
using a new type of coarse grain reconfigurable hardware accelerator –
"Plasticine" – that, compared with other accelerators, emphasizes high
compute capability and high on-chip communication bandwidth. Joining
three or more relations in a single step, i.e. multiway join, is efficient when
the join of any two relations yields too large an intermediate relation. We
show at least 130x speedup for a sequence of binary hash joins execution
on Plasticine over CPU. We further show that in some realistic cases,
a Plasticine-like accelerator can make 3-way joins more efficient than a
cascade of binary hash joins on the same hardware, by a factor of up to
45X.

1 Motivation

Database joins involving more than two relations are at the core of many modern
analytics applications. Examples 1 and 2 demonstrate two scenarios that require
different types of joins involving three relations.

Example 1 (Linear 3-way join). Consider queries involving the Facebook
"friends" relation F. One possible query asks for a count of the "friends of
friends of friends" for each of the Facebook subscribers, perhaps to find people
with a lot of influence over others. There are approximately two billion Facebook users, each with an average of 300 friends, so F has approximately 6×10^{11}
tuples. Joining F with itself will result in a relation with approximately 1.8×10^{14}
tuples.[1] However, the output relation only involves 2 billion tuples, or 1/90000th
as much data.[2] Thus, a three-way join of three copies of F might be more effi-

---

[1] Technically, there will be duplicates, because if x is a friend of a friend of y, then there
will usually be more than one friend that is common to x and y. But eliminating
duplicates is itself an expensive operation. We assume duplicates are not eliminated.

[2] There is a technical difficulty with answering this query using parallel processing:
we must take the union of large, overlapping sets, each produced at one processor.
We cannot avoid this union if we are to get an exact count of the number of friends
of friends of friends. However, we can get an asymptotically correct approximation
to the size of the union using a very small amount of data to represent each set. One
method to do so is the algorithm of Flajolet-Martin [7,16].

© Springer Nature Switzerland AG 2020
R. Nambiar and M. Poess (Eds.): TPCTC 2019, LNCS 12257, pp. 19–38, 2020.
https://doi.org/10.1007/978-3-030-55024-0_2

cient, if we can limit the cost of the input data replication as we execute the three-way join.

Example 2 (Cyclic 3-way join). Consider the problem of finding triangles in relation F. That is, we are looking for triples of people who are mutual friends. The density of triangles in a community might be used to estimate its maturity or its cohesiveness. There will be many fewer triangles than there are tuples in the join of F with itself, so the output relation will be much smaller than the intermediate binary joins.

Afrati and Ullman [3] showed that in some cases, a multiway join can be more efficient than a cascade of binary joins, when implemented using MapReduce. But multiway joins are superior only when the intermediate products (joins of any two relations) are large compared to the required replication of the input data at parallel workers, and the output is relatively small; that is the case in each of the Examples 1 and 2. The limitation on the efficiency of any parallel algorithm for multiway joins is the degree to which data must be replicated at different processors and the available computing capacity. The performance benefits of multiway joins over cascaded binary joins could be perceived on hardware architectures facilitating cheap data replication.

Spatially reconfigurable architectures [24], such as Coarse-grained reconfigurable architecture (CGRA), have gained traction in recent years as high-throughput, low-latency, and energy-efficient accelerators. With static configuration and explicitly managed scratchpads, reconfigurable accelerators dramatically reduce energy and performance overhead introduced by dynamic instruction scheduling and cache hierarchy in CPUs and GPUs. In contrast to field-programmable gate arrays (FPGAs), CGRAs are reconfigurable at word or higher-level as opposed to bit-level. The decrease in flexibility in CGRA reduces routing overhead and improves clock frequency, compute density, and energy-efficiency compared to FPGAs.

Plasticine [20] is a recently proposed tile-based CGRA accelerator. As shown in Fig. 1, Plasticine has a checkerboard layout of compute and memory units connected with high bandwidth on-chip network. Plasticine-like architectures offer several advantages to enable efficient multiway join acceleration. First, it has peak 12.3 FLOPS throughput designed for compute-intensive applications, like multiway join. Second, the high-bandwidth static network can efficiently broadcast data to multiple destinations, which makes replication very efficient.

1.1   Contributions

In this paper, we study algorithms to efficiently perform multiway joins on Plasticine-like accelerator. We show an advantage of such accelerators over CPU-based implementation on a sequence of binary hash joins, and additional performance improvement with 3-way joins over cascaded binary joins. Although we describe the algorithms with Plasticine as a potential target, the algorithms can also be mapped onto other reconfigurable hardware like FPGAs by overlaying

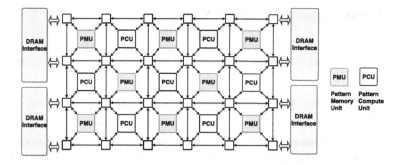

Fig. 1. Plasticine-like coarse grain reconfigurable hardware accelerator.

Plasticine structure on top of the substrate architecture. The contributions of the paper are summarized below.

- Algorithms and efficient implementations for both linear and cyclic 3-way join operations for Plasticine-like accelerators. These algorithms are significantly different from the algorithms of [3] for the MapReduce implementation of the same joins.
- Analysis of the cost of running these algorithms in terms of the number of tuples that are read onto an accelerator chip.
- Performance comparison of a sequence of binary hash-join implementation on a Plasticine-like accelerator to state-of-the-art CPU hash-join on Postgres [21].
- Evaluation of the 3-way join algorithms compared to the cascaded binary hash-join implementation on the same accelerator.

1.2 Simplifying Assumptions

In our analyses, we shall assume a uniform distribution of join-key values. This assumption is unrealistic because there is typically *skew*, where some values appear more frequently than others. Small amounts of skew can be handled by leaving some components of the accelerator chip to handle "overflow" of other components. However, large amounts of skew require a modification to the algorithms along the lines of [19], which we do not cover in detail due to space limitation.

The rest of this paper is organized as follows: Sect. 2 presents some background and related work. Sections 3 discuss the challenges for multiway join algorithm implementation on Plasticine-like accelerator. Sections 4 and 5 present our algorithms for linear and cyclic multiway joins respectively. Section 6 compare the performance results of a sequence of binary hash joins on Plasticine-like accelerator and CPU. Further, we also compare the performance of the accelerated multiway join algorithms to an accelerated sequence of binary join approach on Plasticine-like accelerator. Finally the paper concludes with the future work in Sect. 7.

2   Background and Related Work

This section provides a brief background and reviews relevant related work on multiway join algorithms, hash-join acceleration, and spatially reconfigurable architectures.

2.1   Multiway Joins

Efficient join algorithms are usually based on hashing [4]. Parallelism can be exploited by the parallel processing of a tree of several binary joins [17], an approach that is unsuitable for joins generating large intermediate relations, as is the case for our two introductory examples. The focus of such approaches has been to find optimal plans for parallel execution of binary joins. Henderson et al. [12] presented a performance comparison of different types of multiway-join structures to two-way (binary) join algorithm.

A leapfrog approach [23] has been used to join multiple relations simultaneously by parallel scanning of the relations that are sorted on the join key. Aberger et al. [2] have accelerated the performance of leapfrog triejoin using SIMD set intersections on CPU-based systems. The algorithm is sequential on the number of join keys and requires the relations to be preprocessed into trie data structures.

2.2   Hash-Join Acceleration

A hash-join algorithm on large relations involves three key operations - partitioning of relations, hashing of the smaller relation into a memory (build phase) followed by the probing of the second relation in the memory. Kara et al. [14] present an efficient algorithm for partitioning relations using FPGA-based accelerator. Onur et al. [15] use on-chip accelerator for hash index lookup (probing) to process multiple keys in parallel on a set of programmable 'walker' units for hashing. Robert et al. [10,11] use FPGA for parallelizing hashing and collision resolution in the building phase. Huang et al. [13] have explored the use of open coherent accelerator processor interface (OpenCAPI)-attached FPGA to accelerate 3-way multiway joins where the intermediate join of two relations is pipelined with a partition phase and join with the third relation.

2.3   Spatially Reconfigurable Architectures

Spatially reconfigurable architectures are composed of reconfigurable compute and memory blocks that are connected to each other using a programmable interconnect. Such architectures are a promising compute substrate to perform hardware acceleration, as they avoid the overheads in conventional processor pipelines, while retaining the flexibility. Recent work has shown that some spatially reconfigurable architectures achieve superior performance and energy efficiency benefits over fine-grained alternatives such as FPGAs and conventional CPUs [20].

Several spatially reconfigurable architectures have been proposed in the past for various domains. Architectures such as Dyser [9] and Garp [5] are tightly coupled with a general purpose CPU. Others such as Piperench [8], Tartan [18], and Plasticine [20] are more hierarchical with coarser-grained building blocks. Plasticine-like accelerator is not limited to databases alone but can efficiently accelerate multiway joins. Q100 [26] and Linqits [6] are accelerators specific to databases.

3   Accelerating Multiway Joins

We present algorithms for accelerating both linear $(R(AB) \bowtie S(BC) \bowtie T(CD))$ and cyclic $(R(AB) \bowtie S(BC) \bowtie T(CA))$ multiway joins on a Plasticine-like accelerator using hashing. There may be other attributes of relations R, S, and T. These may be assumed to be carried along as we join tuples, but do not affect the algorithms. Also, A, B, C, and D can each represent several columns of the relations and by symmetry, assume that $|R| \leq |T|$.

A naive approach to map the Afrati et al. [3] algorithm on Plasticine-like architecture will be bottlenecked by DRAM bandwidth and limited by the size of on-chip memory. The proposed multiway hash-join algorithms exploit the pipeline and parallelism benefits in a Plasticine-like architecture to improve the performance while eliminating the limitations mentioned above.

We partition one or more relations using hash functions, one for each of the columns used for joining, such that the size of potentially matching partitions of the three relations is less than or equal to the size of on-chip memory. The loading of a partition of a relation from DRAM to on-chip memory is pipelined with the processing of the previously loaded partition(s) on the accelerator. Further, to squeeze more processing within the given on-chip memory budget, at least one of the relations is streamed, unlike batch processing in Afrati et al. [3].

3.1   Notations

In what follows, we use $|R|$ to represent the number of records of a relation R. A relation $R(AB)$'s tuple is represented as $r(a,b)$ and the column B's values is accessed as $r.b$. We use the name of hash functions–h, g, f, G, and H (or h_{bkt}, g_{bkt}, f_{bkt}, G_{bkt}, and H_{bkt}) in certain equations to stand for the number of buckets produced by those functions. U is the number of distributed memory and compute units, and we assume there is an equal number of each. M is the total on-chip memory capacity.

4   Linear 3-Way Join

For the linear, three-way join $R(AB) \bowtie S(BC) \bowtie T(CD)$, we partition the relations at two levels in a particular way, using hash functions as shown in Fig. 2. The relations are partitioned using robust hash functions [25] on the columns involved in the join, which, given our no-skew assumption, assures uniform sizes for all partitions. We can first configure the accelerator to perform the needed partitioning. Since all hash-join algorithms require a similar partitioning, we shall not go into details regarding the implementation of this step.

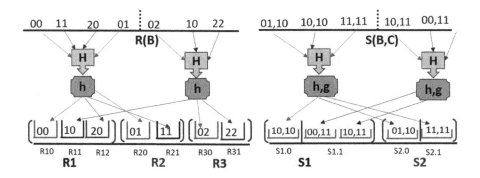

Fig. 2. Partitioning of Relation R and S. Relation R is partitioned using radix hashing on the first digit, $H(B)$, to create subpartitions R_1, R_2, and R_3. Each R_i is further partitioned using radix hashing, $h(B)$, on the second digit of B. S is partitioned using radix hashing similar to R, on both the B and C columns.

The relations R and T are similar, each having one join column, while relation S has two columns to join with relations R and T. The relative sizes of the three relations affect our choice of algorithm. The largest relation should be streamed to the accelerator to optimize the on-chip memory budget. When S is largest, relations R and T must either be small enough to fit on the on-chip memory (discussed in detail as a "star" 3-way join in Sect. 6) or they should be partitioned, based on the values of attributes B or C, respectively, each of them having L sub-partitions. Then each pair of sub-partitions is loaded on to the accelerator iteratively and matched with the corresponding one of the L^2 partition of the streamed relation S. In the case of larger R and T relations, one of them is streamed and the other one is partitioned as discussed in detail below.

4.1   Joining Relations on Plasticine-Like Accelerator

Consider the case where S is no larger than R or T. For the first level partitioning of the relations R and S on attribute B, we choose a number of partitions for the hash function $H(B)$ so that a single partition of R (that is, the set of tuples of R whose B-value hashes to that partition) will fit comfortably in one pattern memory unit (PMU) of the Plasticine. The second level of partitioning serves two purposes and involves two hash functions. First, we use hash function $h(B)$ to divide a single partition of R and S into U buckets each, one bucket per PMU. We use hash function $g(C)$ to divide C into a very large number of buckets.

Algorithm 1: Pseudo-code for $R(AB) \bowtie S(BC) \bowtie T(CD)$

Data: Relations R(A,B), S(B,C) and T(C, D). Memory grid, MemGrid[], on accelerator. Column B values hashed using $H()$ and $h()$, and Column C hashed using $g()$. #Rpart denotes the number of partitions of relation R

Result: Tuples from R, S and T joined on common values of B and C.

1 $T_i \leftarrow$ Partition T(C,D) using hash function g(C) [#Tpart];
2 $S_{ij} \leftarrow$ Partition S(B,C) using hash function H(B) and g(C) (Sij partitions are ordered first on H(B) and then on g(C) within each Si partition, [#$S_i$part]) ;
3 $R_i \leftarrow$ Partition R(A,B)using hash function H(B) [#Rpart];
4 **for** Each partition $R_{i=H(B)}$ of R till #Rpart **do**
5   **for** All records of R_i **do**
6          $h_b \leftarrow h(r_i.b)$;
7          $MemGrid[h_b] \leftarrow r_i(*, b)$;
8   **end**
9   **for** Each partition $S_{i=H(B)}$ of S till #Spart **do**
10   **for** Each partition $S_{ij=g(C)}$ till #$S_i$part **do**
11   **for** All records of S_{ij} **do**
12                  $h_b \leftarrow h(s_{ij}.b)$;
13                  $MemGrid[h_b] \leftarrow s_{ij}(b, c)$;
14   **end**
15              $MemGrid[*] \leftarrow t_j(c, *)$ [broadcast or send to all Memory units where S_{ij} was sent];
16   Join tuple from R_i, S_{ij} and T_j;
17   Discard tuples from S_{ij} and T_j;
18   **end**
19   **end**
20   Discard tuples of R_i
21 **end**

Each partition of S is further partitioned into sub-partitions that correspond to a single value of $g(C)$. Each $g(C)$ bucket of S's partition may be organized by increasing values of $h(B)$ as shown in Fig. 2. Likewise, the entire relation T is divided into buckets based on the value of $g(C)$.

We shall describe what happens when we join a single partition of R, that is, the set of tuples of R whose B-values have a fixed value $H(B) = i$, with the corresponding partition of S (the set of tuples of S whose B-values also have $H(B) = i$. Call these partitions R_i and S_i, respectively.

1. Bring the entire partition of R onto the chip, storing each tuple $r(a, b)$ in the PMU for $h(b)$.
2. For each bucket of $g(C)$, bring each tuple $s(b, c)$ from that bucket from S_i onto the chip and store it in the PMU for $h(b)$.
3. Once the bucket from S_i has been read onto the chip, read the corresponding bucket of $T - t(c, d)$ with the same hash value $g(C)$ – onto the chip. Since tuple $t(c, d)$ can join with tuple $r(a, b)$ and $s(b, c)$ having any value of B, we must route each $t(c, d)$ tuple to every PMU.

4. Once the buckets with a given value $g(C)$ have arrived, PCUs joins the three tiny relations at each PMU using optimized cascaded binary joins. Recall we assume the result of this join is small because some aggregation of the result is done, as discussed in Example 1. Thus, the amount of memory needed to compute the join at a single memory is small.[3]

The formal representation of the algorithm is presented in Algorithm 1.

4.2   Analysis of the Linear 3-Way Join

Each tuple of R and S is read onto an accelerator chip exactly once. However, tuples of T are read many times – once for each partition of R. The number of partitions produced by the hash function $H(B)$ is such that one partition of R fits onto the entire on-chip memory with capacity M. Thus, the number of partitions into which R is partitioned is $\frac{|R|}{M}$. Therefore, the number of reads for tuples of T is $\frac{|R||T|}{M}$. This function is symmetric in R and T, so it seems not to matter whether R is the smaller or larger of the two relations. However, we also have to read R once, so we would prefer that R be the smaller of R and T. That is, the total number of tuples read is $|R| + |S| + \frac{|R||T|}{M}$.

Thus, the number of tuples read onto the chip is greater than the sizes of the three relations being joined. However, using a cascade of two-way joins may also involve an intermediate relation whose size is much bigger than the sizes of the input relations. Thus, while we cannot be certain that the three-way join is more efficient than the conventional pair of two-way joins, it is at least possible that the algorithm proposed will be more efficient.

Example 3. Consider again the problem of getting an approximate count of the friends of friends of friends of each Facebook user, as was introduced in Example 1. We estimated the number of tuples in the friends relation F as 6×10^{11}. This value is thus the sizes of each of R, S, and T. If we take the three-way join, then the number of tuples read onto an accelerator chip is $6 \times 10^{11} + 6 \times 10^{11} + 3.6 \times 10^{23}/M$. In comparison, if we use two two-way joins, then we need to output first the join of F with itself, which involves producing about 1.8×10^{14} tuples, and then reading these tuples back in again when we join their relation with the third relation. The three-way join will involve reading fewer tuples if $6 \times 10^{11} + 6 \times 10^{11} + 3.6 \times 10^{23}/M < 3.6 \times 10^{14}$. That relationship will hold if $M > 1.003 \times 10^9$. That number is far more than can be expected on

---

[3] For just one example, if R, S, and T are each the friends relation F, and we are using the Flajolet-Martin algorithm to estimate the number of friends of friends of friends for each individual A in the relation R, then the amount of data that needs to be maintained in memory would be on the order of 100 bytes for each tuple in the partition R_i, and thus would not be more than proportional to the size of the data that was read into the memory from outside. In fact, although we do not want to get into the details of the Flajolet-Martin algorithm [16], if we are willing to assume that everyone has at least some small number of friends of friends of friends, e.g., at least 256, then we can reduce the needed space per tuple to almost nothing.

a single chip with today's technologies, even assuming that a tuple is only eight bytes (two 4-byte integers representing a pair of user ID's). However, for somewhat smaller databases, e.g., the 300 million Twitter users and their followers, the on-chip memory requirements are feasible, in that case, the chip needs to hold approximately 150 million tuples.[4]

5   Cyclic 3-Way Join

Consider the cyclic three-way join $R(AB) \bowtie S(BC) \bowtie T(CA)$. The cyclic join is symmetric in all three relations. We shall therefore assume that R is the smallest of the three, for reasons we shall see shortly. Similar to the linear three-way join, we shall partition R such that it's one partition fits conveniently into on-chip memory. However, in this case, since both A and B are shared by other relations, we will partition R using hash functions $H(A)$ and $G(B)$ into H, and G buckets, respectively. The correct values of H and G are to be determined by considering the relative sizes of the three relations. However, we do know that $\frac{|R|}{HG} = M$.

In addition to partitioning R into HG pieces, each of size M, we use $H(A)$ to partition T into H pieces, each of size $\frac{|T|}{H}$, and we use $G(B)$ to partition S into G pieces, each of size $\frac{|S|}{G}$. The partitioning scheme is depicted in Fig. 3.

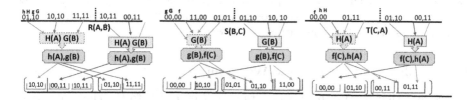

Fig. 3. Partitioning of Relation R, S and T. Relation R is partitioned using radix hashing on the first digit of column A and B using $H(A), G(B)$ respectively. Each R_i is further partitioned using radix hashing, $h(A), g(B)$, on the second digit of A, B. Similarly, S and T are partitioned using radix hashing on B and A columns respectively. Column C is hashed using $f(C)$.

As before, we are assuming that there is no significant skew in the distribution of values in any column, and we also are assuming a sufficient number of different values that hashing will divide the relations approximately evenly. In what follows, we shall only describe the join of a single partition from each of R, S, and T. These three partitions are determined by buckets of H and G. That is, for a fixed value of $H(A) = i$ and a fixed value of $G(B) = j$, we join those tuples

---

[4] In fact, as a general rule, we can observe that the minimum memory size M needed for any social-network graph is very close to half the number of nodes in the graph, regardless of the average degree of the graph (number of friends per user) and size of the relation.

$r(a, b)$ of R such that $H(a) = i$ and $G(b) = j$ with the tuples $s(b, c)$ of S such that $G(b) = j$ and the tuples $t(c, a)$ of T such that $H(a) = i$. In what follows, we shall refer to these partitions as R', S', and T', respectively. Each set of three partitions is handled the same way, either sequentially on one accelerator chip or in parallel on more than one such chip.

5.1   Joining Relations on Plasticine-Like Accelerator

Now, let us focus on joining R', S', and T'. Assuming the chip has U memories arranged in a square $\sqrt{U}$ on a side, we shall use lower-level hash functions $h(A)$, $g(B)$, and $f(C)$. Hash functions h and g each map to $\sqrt{U}$ buckets, while f maps to a very large number of buckets – a sufficient number of buckets so that S' and T' can be partitioned on the basis of their C-values into pieces that are sufficiently small that we can neglect the memory space needed to store one piece from one of these two relations.

Begin the join by bringing onto the chip all the tuples $r'(a, b)$ of R'. Each of these tuples is routed to only one of the U PMUs – the PMU in row $h(a)$ and column $g(b)$. Then we bring onto the chip each of the tuples $s'(b, c)$ of S' that have $f(c) = k$. These tuples are each stored in every PMU in the column $g(b)$. Thus, this tuple will meet at one of these memories, all the tuples of R' that share the same hash value $g(B)$. Finally, we pipe in the tuples $t'(c, a)$ of T' that have $f(c) = k$. Each of these tuples is read into each of the memories in row $h(a)$, where it is joined with the possibly matching tuples $r'(a, b)$ and $s'(b, c)$. Any matches are sent to the output of the chip.

5.2   Analysis of Cyclic Three-Way Join

Notice first that every top-level partition of R is read onto the chip only once. However, a top-level partition of S is read onto chip H times, once for each bucket of $H(A)$. Also, every top-level partition of T is read G times, once for each bucket of $G(B)$. The total number of tuples read onto an accelerator chip is thus $|R| + H|S| + G|T|$. Recall also that $GH = \frac{|R|}{M}$, so previous function can be expressed as $|R| + H|S| + \frac{|R||T|}{MH}$. To minimize this function, set its derivative with respect to H to 0, which gives us $H = \sqrt{\frac{|R||T|}{M|S|}}$. For this value of H, the cost function becomes $|R| + 2\sqrt{\frac{|R||S||T|}{M}}$. Notice that the second term is independent of the relative sizes of the three relations, but the first term, $|R|$, tells us that the total number of tuples read is minimized when we pick R to be the smallest of the three relations.

Example 4. Suppose each of the three relations is the Facebook friends relation F; that is, $|R| = |S| = |T| = 6 \times 10^{11}$. Then the total number of tuples read onto the chip is $6 \times 10^{11}(1 + \sqrt{6 \times 10^{11}/M})$. If we assume as in Example 3 that the binary join of F with itself has about 0.8×10^{14} tuples, we can conclude that the total number of tuples read by the three-way join of F with itself is less than the number of tuples produced in the intermediate product of two copies of a cascade of two-way joins as long as $6 \times 10^{11}(1 + \sqrt{\frac{6 \times 10^{11}}{U}}) < 1.8 \times 10^{14}$. This condition is satisfied for M as small as seven million tuples.

6 Performance Evaluation

In this section, we evaluate the algorithms proposed in the Sects. 4, on Plasticine-like accelerator using a performance model. First, we show the advantage of accelerating a sequence of binary join operators by comparing its execution time on Postgres database on CPU to our simulation on the accelerator. Next, we show additional performance improvement of 3-way join (an instance of multiway join) over a cascade of two binary hash joins on the acccelerator.

We consider two categories of multiway joins in this evaluation: self-join[5] of a big relation of size N, where N does not fit on-chip; and star-join[6] of two small relations (R and T) each of size K with a large relation, S, of size N, where $N >> K$ and $2K <= M$. The self join algorithm described in Sect. 4 is a generic algorithm for any linear join, whereas the algorithm used for star join is a variant of the generic algorithm that specialize for better locality when the dimension relations fit on the on-chip memory.

For a given set of relations, we observe that the proposed algorithms execution time on the accelerator is sensitive to the number of buckets and DRAM bandwidth. We first evaluate the selection of hyperparameters of the algorithms, i.e. bucket size for the cascaded binary and 3-way joins. With best bucket sizes, we compare the performance advantage of 3-way join over a cascade of binary joins for different selectivity of join columns and DRAM-bandwidths. For all experiments, we do not materialize the final output of the join in memory (refer Example 1). Instead, we assume the final results will be aggregated on the fly. Therefore, in our study, we only materialize the intermediate result of the first binary join, and the final output is immediately aggregated (e.g. perform count operation on the number of friends of friends relation).

6.1 Target Systems

The CPU system, used for performance evaluation of cascaded binary join, is Intel Xeon Processor E7-8890 v3 with 143 processors and 1 TB of DDR4 RAM with 1 TB/s memory bandwidth. For performance evalutaion on hardware accelerator, we use performance model for the Plasticine-like architecture. It has DDR3 DRAM technology with 49 GB/s read and write bandwidth, Number of PMUs(PCUs), $U = 64$ and a peak of 12.3 TFLOPS compute throughput with 16 MB on-chip scratchpad.

---

[5] Self 3-way join is joining of a relation with two instances of itself e.g. Friends of friends.

[6] Star 3-way join is joining of a large fact relation with two small dimension relations e.g. TPCH [1] benchmark having join of *lineitem* fact relation with *order* and *supplier* dimension relations.

6.2   Accelerator's Performance Model

The performance model is built by simulating the logic of the proposed algorithm on the hardware specification of the accelerator given in Sect. 6.1. We observed that the performance advantage of the proposed 3-way join over cascaded binary join depends on the number of records in the joining relations and the selectivity of the join column - lower selectivity (i.e. higher duplicates) favors multiway join. The performance model needs two inputs for simulation - the number of records of R, S and T and the maximum distinct values over all joining columns (represented as d).

The performance model accounts for how an application is spatially parallelized and data is streamed across compute and memory units of the accelerator. The model does considers DRAM-contention while loading multiple data streams concurrently on the chip. For higher DRAM bandwidth utilization and to hide the DRAM latency, we overlap execution of the algorithm with prefetching of the data. This requires to split the on-chip memory into two buffers (double buffering) to store both the current and prefetched data. The performance model uses only half of the on-chip memory to include this optimization.

For cascaded binary join, once the intermediate result does not fit in DRAM, the performance model simulates the flushing of the intermediate data to the underlying persistent storage with much lower bandwidth (around 700 MB/s from the latest SSD technology). Appendix A explains the performance model in detail.

6.3   Performance Analysis of Cascaded Binary Join

A cascaded binary-join is a sequence of two binary joins- the first join is $R(AB) \bowtie S(BC)$ which outputs intermediate relation $I(ABC)$ and second join is $I(ABC) \bowtie T(CD)$. For uniform distribution, the intermediate size for a cascaded binary join is $|I| = |R \bowtie S| \leq \frac{|R||S|}{d}$ [22].

Both the joins are executed on the accelerator similar to the 3-way join discussed in Sect. 4. The first join $R(AB) \bowtie S(BC)$ involves loading and matching of partitions of R and S using $H(B), h(B)$ on the chip. The intermediate relation I is stored back to DRAM. The second join $I(A, B, C) \bowtie T(C, D)$ is identical except the output results are no longer materialized in DRAM. For the second join, we also load partitions of relation T on-chip while streaming previous join intermediate result, since $|R \bowtie S| >> |T|$. The bucket sizes of the second level hash functions for both the joins are fixed to the number of PMUs, i.e. $h = g = U$.

Figure 4 (a) shows the breakup of the execution time of a cascaded binary self join of three relations with a varying number of buckets i.e. H_{bkt}. The orange region shows time spent in partitioning the relations for both the joins, which is dominated by the second join due to large size of the intermediate relation. Clearly, the first join is bounded by DRAM-bandwidth, varying H_{bkt} has no impact on the performance. Fig. 4 (b) shows variation of the execution time of

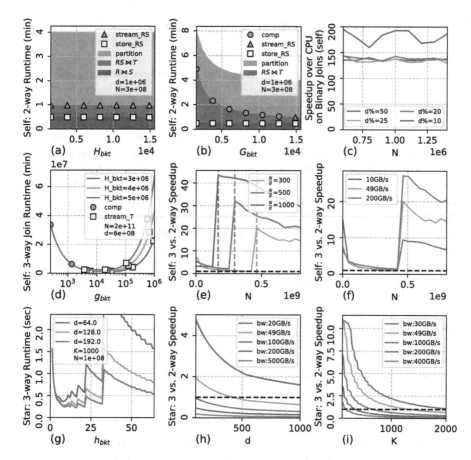

Fig. 4. Performance Evaluation of 3-way join vs. cascaded binary joins. (a,b) 2-way self linear join execution time with breakup. Red, green, and yellow region indicate execution time for the first join, the second join, and partitioning time for both. Marker indicates performance bottleneck in computation (comp), streaming in $R \bowtie S$ relation in second join (stream_RS), or storing $R \bowtie S$ in first join (store_RS). (c) Speedup on Plasticine over CPU for cascaded binary self joins. (d) 3-way linear self join performance. Marker indicates bottleneck of performance in computation (comp) or streaming in T relation (stream_T). (e) Speedup of 3 vs. binary join on linear self join with DDR3 and SSD bandwidth at 49 GB/s and 700 MB/s. The vertical dashed lines indicate when intermediate results do not fit in DRAM for binary join. The horizontal dashed line indicates speedup of 1. (f) Speedup of Self linear 3-way join vs. cascaded binary join with different off-chip memory bandwidth. (g) Performance of Star 3-way join with varying d and h_{bkt}. (h,i) Speedup of 3-way join vs.cascaded binary joins with d and K at different off-chip memory bandwidth. (Color figure online)

the second join varying G_{bkt}. The second join is compute-bound at small G_{bkt}, as the total amount of data loaded is $|R \bowtie S| + |T|$, whereas the total comparison is $\frac{|R\bowtie S||T|}{d}$.

Comparison with Postgres. We compare the performance of cascaded binary join on CPU to that on the accelerator using configuration given in Sect. 6.1. For CPU-based implementation, we follow a COUNT aggregation immediately after the cascaded binary joins, which prevents materializing the final output in memory. Postgres is configured to use a maximum of 130 threads. At runtime, we observe only 5 threads are used at 100% for our problem size.

Figure 4 (c) shows the speedup of binary self join on the accelerator over the CPU with varying sizes of the relations and distinct values in joining columns (d). Although the CPU has much higher memory bandwidth, our experiments show >130x speedups from the accelerator. We observe a limited improvement or even worse when parallelizing a single join on CPU compared to the single-threaded execution. The parallel execution can be bottlenecked by communication on shared last-level cache and overhead from full system database like Postgres. On the other hand, the total amount of parallelism on the accelerator is the product of the number of PCUs with SIMD computation (a vector of size 16) within each PCU, which is $64 \times 16 = 1024$. Furthermore, the static on-chip network provides $384\,\text{GB/s}$ bandwidth between the nearest neighbor CUs. The high compute density and on-chip memory and network bandwidth shift the performance bottleneck to DRAM for streaming in the intermediate relation on Plasticine. Fig. 4 (c) shows that smaller percentage of unique values, $d\%$ are associated with increasing speedup (up to 200x) due to the large-sized intermediate relation in the cascaded binary join, which also increases the computation and communication in the second cascaded binary join.

6.4   Performance Analysis of Linear Self Join

We consider $R(AB) \bowtie S(BC) \bowtie T(CD)$, where R, S, T are copies of the friend-friend relations with N records and d distinct users (column values).

Hyper-parameter Selection. We shall discuss the evaluation of hyperparameter selection of algorithm described in Sect. 4. Figure 4 (d) plots the execution time of 3-way join varying with H_{bkt} and g_{bkt} (h_{bkt} = number of PMUs). It shows that the algorithm achieve higher speedup for larger size partition of R partition (i.e. small H_{bkt}) while exploiting DRAM prefetching. For small g_{bkt}, the algorithm is compute-bound for joining buckets from three relations within PMUs (3-level nested loop). As g_{bkt} increases, the compute complexity reduces with smaller of size T buckets and the performance bottleneck shifts to DRAM bandwidth for streaming in T records. For large values of g_{bkt}, the S_{ij} bucket within each PMU becomes very small (i.e. $\frac{|S|}{Hhg}$), resulting in very poor DRAM performance for loading S_{ij}. Although some PCU might have empty S_{ij} bucket, the algorithm has to wait for completion from other PCUs with non-empty S_{ij} buckets because all PCUs shares the streamed T records. This synchronization and poor DRAM performance on S_{ij} bucket eventually increases execution time dramatically when g_{bkt} becomes too large.

3-Way Join vs. Cascaded Binary Joins. Figure 4 (e) and (f) shows the speedup of 3-way join over cascaded binary joins with varying average friends per person ($f = \frac{N}{d}$), and DRAM bandwidth on the accelerator. When relation size (N) is small, 3-way join achieves up to 15x performance advantage over binary-join because the latter is heavily IO-bound compared to compute-bound 3-way join, and the accelerator favors compute bound operations. However, the speedup decreases with increase in relation size, N. Because the compute complexity of 3-way join increases quadratically with N, whereas, size of intermediate relation of the cascaded binary joins increases quadratically with N. When the intermediate relation fails to fits in DRAM, the off-chip bandwidth drops from $49\,\mathrm{GB/s}$ to $700\,\mathrm{MB/s}$, which is shown as a step increase in the speedup of 3-way over the binary join in Fig. 4 (e) and (f). With more friends per person, the performance cliff happens at smaller relation size. (f) shows that the advantage of 3-way join is more significant when intermediate result fit as binary-join will be more DRAM-bandwidth bounded for smaller DRAM; and less significant when the intermediate result does not fit, at which point, binary-join will be SSD bandwidth-bounded, whereas 3-way join can still benefit from higher DRAM bandwidth.

6.5   Performance Analysis of Linear Star 3-Way Join

Now we consider a special case of linear join where R and T relations are small enough to fit on-chip[7]. Now we only need one level of hash functions on both columns B and C, naming $h(B)$ and $g(C)$. The only difference between cascaded binary joins and 3-way join is that binary join only performs one hash function at a time, which allow $h = g = U$. For 3-way join, we map a $(h(b), g(c))$ hash value pair to each PMU, which restricts number of buckets to $hg = U$. For both 3-way and cascaded binary joins, we first load R and T on-chip, compute hash functions on the fly, and distribute the records to PMUs with corresponding assigned hash values (in binary join) or hash value pairs (in 3-way join). Next, we stream S, compute hash values and distribute to the corresponding PMUs, where the inner join is performed.

Figure 4 (g) shows the execution time of the 3-way join with varying h_{bkt} (Note, h_{bkt} must be dividable by U to achieve the maximum hg). Figure 4 (h) and (i) shows the speedup of 3-way join over a cascade of binary star join. We can see that with increasing DRAM-bandwidth, the advantage of 3-way join eventually disappears since storing and loading intermediate results in binary join becomes free, when they fit on the chip. 3-way join can also be slower than binary join for larger number of buckets (ie. less computation), where number of buckets is $hg = U^2$ for binary and $hg = U$ for 3-way join[8]).

---

[7] With plasticine, this means the dimensions relations are on the order of millions of records.

[8] Total amount of comparison in cascaded binary join roughly equals to $\frac{|R||S|}{h} + \frac{|R\bowtie S||T|}{g} = \frac{|R||S|}{h} + \frac{|R||S||T|}{dg}$.

7   Conclusions

Multiway join involves joining of multiple relations simultaneously instead of traditional cascaded binary joins of relations. In this paper, we have presented algorithms for efficient implementation of linear and cyclic multiway joins using coarse grain configurable accelerator such as Plasticine, which is designed for compute-intensive applications and high on-chip network communication. The algorithms have been discussed with their cost analysis in the context of three relations (i.e. 3-way join).

The performance of linear 3-way joins algorithms are compared to the cascaded binary joins using performance model of the Plasticine-like accelerator. We have shown 130x to 200x improvements for traditional cascaded binary joins on the accelerator over CPU systems. We have concluded that 3-way join can provide higher speedup over cascaded binary joins in a DRAM bandwidth-limited system or with relations having low distinct column values (d) (which results in large size intermediate relation). In fact, the effective off-chip bandwidth will dramatically reduce when the intermediate size does not fit in DRAM, in which case binary join will provide a substantial improvement over 3-way join. We have shown that a Self 3-way join (e.g, friends of friend query) is 45X better than a traditional two cascaded binary joins for as large as 200 million records with 700 thousand distinct users. A data-warehouse Star 3-way join query is shown to have 11X better than that of cascaded binary joins.

In future work, we would like to explore additional levels of hashing beyond two levels, and exploring new algorithms, such as set value join [2], within on-chip join to speedup multi-way join. We plan to extend the algorithms for skewed data distribution in relations and analyze the improvements in the performance and power of the algorithms on Plasticine accelerator.

A   Performance Model of Plasticine

In this section, we provide more details on the analytical performance model used for algorithm performance estimation on Plasticine-like accelerator. The performance model analyzes the loop structures of each algorithm, takes into account how applications are spatially parallelized and pipelined on hardware resource, and provides a cycle-level runtime estimation given data characteristics and architectural parameters as inputs. Figure 6 shows the loop structures of 3-way and cascaded binary self and star join algorithms on the accelerator. To avoid confusion, we use $\langle hash \rangle_2$ and $\langle hash \rangle_3$ for hash functions of binary and 3-way joins- they do not need to be the same.

In Fig. 5 (a), the circles indicate one-level of loop nest, and the hierarchy indicates the nest levels between loops. #par[P] in Fig. 5 (b) suggests a loop parallelized by P. #pipeline in Fig. 5 (c) indicates overlapping execution of the inner loops across iterations of the outer loop, e.g. B can work on the second iteration of A while C is working on the first iteration of A. The pipeline construct is commonly used when a tile of data is reused multiple times on-chip, in which we can overlap prefetching of future tiles with execution of the current tile. In contrary, `#streaming` in Fig. 5 (d) indicates fine-grain pipelining between producer and consumer loops, where the consumer loop only scans the data once without any reuse. In such case, C can execute as soon as B produces the first chunk of data, without waiting for B to finish on one entire iteration of A.

On Plasticine-like acelerator, an example of the streaming construct is streaming data from DRAM directly to PCUs without storing to PMUs. To compute execution time (or run time), we need the throughput (thrpt) and latency (lat) of which B and C produces/consumes data chunks. For DRAM, throughput and latency can be derived from DRAM bandwidth and response time, respectively. For loops executed on Plasticine, throughput is the amount of allocated parallelism between (U) and within PCUs (L). We used $U = 64$ PCUs and SIMD vector width $L = 16$ in our evaluation. The latency is the sum of network latency (we used the worst diagonal latency on a 16×8 chip, which is 24 cycles) and pipeline latency of the PCU (6 cycles). The overall runtime of the outer loop is bounded by the stage with minimum throughput.

Finally, for data-dependent execution in Fig. 5 (d), we compute runtime by associating a probability to each branch. For example, in Fig. 6 (a), the branch on $SC == TC$ indicates comparisons on S records with streamed T records. Only matches records will be compared with R records. The probability of this branch is the expected size of $S \bowtie T$, which is $\frac{|S||T|}{d}$, over the total number of comparisons performed between S and T records. The number of comparison is the product of loop iterations enclosing the branch, which is $H_3 h_3 g_3 \frac{|T|}{g_3} \frac{|S|}{H_3 g_3 h_3} = \frac{|S||T|}{g_3}$. This gives the probability of $\frac{g_3}{d}$ on the branch hit.

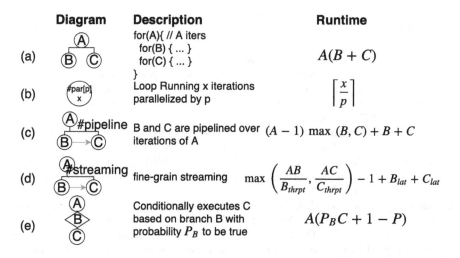

Diagram	Description	Runtime

(a)	for(A){ // A iters
	  for(B) { ... }
	  for(C) { ... }
	}
		$A(B + C)$

(b)	Loop Running x iterations parallelized by p	$\left\lceil \dfrac{x}{p} \right\rceil$
(c)	B and C are pipelined over iterations of A	$(A - 1) \max (B, C) + B + C$
(d)	fine-grain streaming	$\max \left(\dfrac{AB}{B_{thrpt}}, \dfrac{AC}{C_{thrpt}} \right) - 1 + B_{lat} + C_{lat}$
(e)	Conditionally executes C based on branch B with probability P_B to be true	$A(P_B C + 1 - P)$

Fig. 5. Runtime model for different loop schedule.

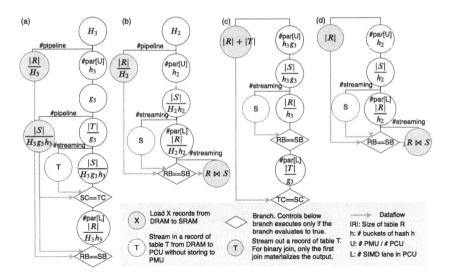

Fig. 6. Loop structure of (a, b) 3-way and cascaded binary self join and (c, d) 3-way and cascaded binary star join. Data reorganization is not shown. Only one of the join in cascaded binary join is shown in (b) and (d).

Using a similar approach, we can derive probabilities of all data-dependent branches. The runtime of each algorithm in Fig. 6 is recursively evaluated at each loop level using equations shown in Fig. 5. The exact model is open-source and can be found at https://github.com/yaqiz01/multijoin_plasticine.git.

References

1. TPC-H: a decision support benchmark. http://www.tpc.org/tpch/
2. Aberger, C.R., Tu, S., Olukotun, K., Ré, C.: Emptyheaded: a relational engine for graph processing. In: Proceedings of the 2016 International Conference on Management of Data, SIGMOD 2016, pp. 431–446. ACM, New York (2016). https://doi.org/10.1145/2882903.2915213
3. Afrati, F.N., Ullman, J.D.: Optimizing multiway joins in a map-reduce environment. IEEE Trans. Knowl. Data Eng. **23**, 1282–1298 (2011)
4. Balkesen, C., Alonso, G., Teubner, J., Özsu, M.T.: Multi-core, main-memory joins: sort vs. hash revisited. Proc. VLDB Endow. **7**(1), 85–96 (2013). https://doi.org/10.14778/2732219.2732227
5. Callahan, T.J., Hauser, J.R., Wawrzynek, J.: The garp architecture and c compiler. Computer **33**(4), 62–69 (2000). https://doi.org/10.1109/2.839323
6. Chung, E.S., Davis, J.D., Lee, J.: Linqits: big data on little clients. In: Proceedings of the 40th Annual International Symposium on Computer Architecture, ISCA 2013, pp. 261–272. ACM, New York (2013). https://doi.org/10.1145/2485922.2485945
7. Flajolet, P., Martin, G.N., Martin, G.N.: Probabilistic counting algorithms for data base applications (1985)

8. Goldstein, S.C., et al.: Piperench: a co/processor for streaming multimedia acceleration. In: Proceedings of the 26th Annual International Symposium on Computer Architecture, ISCA 1999, pp. 28–39. IEEE Computer Society, Washington, DC (1999). https://doi.org/10.1145/300979.300982

9. Govindaraju, V., Ho, C.H., Nowatzki, T., Chhugani, J., Satish, N., Sankaralingam, K., Kim, C.: Dyser: unifying functionality and parallelism specialization for energy-efficient computing. IEEE Micro **32**(5), 38–51 (2012). https://doi.org/10.1109/MM.2012.51

10. Halstead, R.J., Absalyamov, I., Najjar, W.A., Tsotras, V.J.: FPGA-based multi-threading for in-memory hash joins. In: CIDR (2015)

11. Halstead, R.J., et al.: Accelerating join operation for relational databases with FPGAs. In: 2013 IEEE 21st Annual International Symposium on Field-Programmable Custom Computing Machines, pp. 17–20. IEEE (2013)

12. Henderson, M., Lawrence, R.: Are multi-way joins actually useful? In: ICEIS (2013)

13. Huang, K.: Multi-way hash join based on FPGAs. Master's thesis, Delft University (2018)

14. Kara, K., Giceva, J., Alonso, G.: FPGA-based data partitioning. In: Proceedings of the 2017 ACM International Conference on Management of Data, SIGMOD 2017, pp. 433–445. ACM, New York (2017). https://doi.org/10.1145/3035918.3035946

15. Kocberber, O., Grot, B., Picorel, J., Falsafi, B., Lim, K., Ranganathan, P.: Meet the walkers: accelerating index traversals for in-memory databases. In: Proceedings of the 46th Annual IEEE/ACM International Symposium on Microarchitecture, pp. 468–479. ACM (2013)

16. Leskovec, J., Rajaraman, A., Ullman, J.D.: Mining of Massive Datasets, 2nd edn. Cambridge University Press, Cambridge (2014)

17. Lu, H., Shan, M.C., Tan, K.L.: Optimization of multi-way join queries for parallel execution. In: Proceedings of the 17th International Conference on Very Large Data Bases, VLDB 1991, pp. 549–560. Morgan Kaufmann Publishers Inc., San Francisco (1991). http://dl.acm.org/citation.cfm?id=645917.672161

18. Mishra, M., Callahan, T.J., Chelcea, T., Venkataramani, G., Goldstein, S.C., Budiu, M.: Tartan: evaluating spatial computation for whole program execution. In: Proceedings of the 12th International Conference on Architectural Support for Programming Languages and Operating Systems, ASPLOS XII, pp. 163–174. ACM, New York (2006). https://doi.org/10.1145/1168857.1168878

19. Myung, J., Shim, J., Yeon, J., Lee, S.G.: Handling data skew in join algorithms using mapreduce. Expert Syst. Appl. **51**(C), 286–299 (2016). https://doi.org/10.1016/j.eswa.2015.12.024

20. Prabhakar, R., et al.: Plasticine: a reconfigurable architecture for parallel patterns. In: Proceedings of the 44th Annual International Symposium on Computer Architecture, ISCA 2017, pp. 389–402. ACM, New York (2017). https://doi.org/10.1145/3079856.3080256

21. Stonebraker, M., Rowe, L.A.: The Design of Postgres, vol. 15. ACM, New York (1986)

22. Swami, A., Schiefer, K.B.: On the estimation of join result sizes. In: Jarke, M., Bubenko, J., Jeffery, K. (eds.) EDBT 1994. LNCS, vol. 779, pp. 287–300. Springer, Heidelberg (1994). https://doi.org/10.1007/3-540-57818-8_58

23. Veldhuizen, T.L.: Leapfrog triejoin: a worst-case optimal join algorithm. CoRR abs/1210.0481 (2012)

24. Wang, C., et al.: Reconfigurable hardware accelerators: opportunities, trends, and challenges. CoRR abs/1712.04771 (2017). http://arxiv.org/abs/1712.04771

25. Wang, Z., He, B., Zhang, W.: A study of data partitioning on OPENCL-based FPGAs. In: 2015 25th International Conference on Field Programmable Logic and Applications (FPL), pp. 1–8, September 2015. https://doi.org/10.1109/FPL.2015.7293941
26. Wu, L., Lottarini, A., Paine, T.K., Kim, M.A., Ross, K.A.: Q100: the architecture and design of a database processing unit. SIGARCH Comput. Archit. News **42**(1), 255–268 (2014). https://doi.org/10.1145/2654822.2541961

Challenges in Distributed MLPerf

Miro Hodak[(⊠)] and Ajay Dholakia[(⊠)]

Lenovo, Data Center Group, Morrisville, NC, USA
{mhodak,adholakia}@lenovo.com

Abstract. MLPerf has emerged as a frontrunner in benchmarking AI performance by having support of main players in the industry. At the same time, official scores uncover challenges for measuring distributed AI performance: a 2/3 throughput loss at a large scale and longer number of epochs needed to reach the required accuracy. Furthermore, no distributed scored have been submitted for Tensorflow, the most popular AI framework. Our work investigates these issues and suggests ways for overcoming challenges facing benchmarking at scale. Focusing on Tensorflow, wee show how efficient distributed scores can be obtained with appropriate software and hardware choices. Results for various Lenovo servers and Nvidia GPUs (V100 and T4) are also presented. Finally, we examine the utility of MLPerf for evaluating scale-up hardware and propose augmenting the main MLPerf score by an additional score that takes into account computational efficiency. Several options for the score are explored and analyzed in detail.

Keywords: MLPerf · Tensorflow · Deep Learning · GPU · Distributed computing · Performance

1 Introduction

MLPerf benchmark suite [1] is a frontrunner to become a standard AI performance evaluation tool. Forty-one companies are currently listed as supporters with eight academic institutions also contributing to the effort. The latest iteration, v0.5, was released in December 2018. Results for this version have been submitted by Google, Intel, and Nvidia for seven AI benchmark categories.

Prior to MLPerf most of the performance data was published in terms of throughput, such as images per second in case of Deep Learning (DL) training using image-based datasets. While throughput provides a measure of computational efficiency, it does not make a connection to the ultimate goal of DL training – generating an accurate model. MLPerf addresses this issue by making the accuracy the main goal and only specifying the basic training parameters such as network type (ResNet-50 v1) and dataset (ImageNet) while leaving the rest of the parameters up to submitters. The measured quantity is time-to-train, an easy-to-understand metric that can be used for comparison across different hardware types. Overall, MLPerf is an elegant solution to a problem that is complex in both hardware and software.

AI workloads, especially those involving Deep Learning, are known to be computationally intensive. For this reason, they often rely on accelerators such as GPUs or

© Springer Nature Switzerland AG 2020
R. Nambiar and M. Poess (Eds.): TPCTC 2019, LNCS 12257, pp. 39–46, 2020.
https://doi.org/10.1007/978-3-030-55024-0_3

those made specially AI such as Google's TPUs. AI-centric hardware usually contains several accelerators to speed up calculations and clusters of several such machines can be employed to further decrease computational time. Thus, AI frameworks need to be able to handle both scale up (intra-node parallelization) and scale out (inter node parallelization) parallelizations. The current state is that scale up is much easier to use – usually a single switch when launching an application, while scale out is a much more complex involving parallel launching the framework (over MPI or directly) and specifying several additional switches. Additionally, fast interconnect also needs to be present for efficient parallelization. This asymmetry has led to hardware vendors favoring scale up and creating machines integrating large numbers of accelerators such as 8 or 16 GPU servers. However, for maximum performance and lowest possible times, as prescribed by MLPerf, scale out is still needed.

Importantly, there are costs to MLPerf score's simplicity. One is that the scores do not carry information about computational efficiency and it is difficult to determine how well is the hardware utilized. Second, given that vendors can use different AI frameworks, which can differ considerably in AI primitives implementations, the scores are not reliable characteristics of hardware platforms. Finally, large scale distributed runs need more epochs to reach the desired accuracy than smaller scale ones and thus MLPerf is not a strong scaling benchmark, as one might assume. This variation in computational size of the problem is not reflected in MLPerf score. (The reason for this is that in the commonly used parallelization approach - data parallelization with parameter servers - computing units are running independently and only synchronize after they process their assigned batches of data. With more computing units, the synchronization becomes less frequent per epoch and consequently, large scale distributed runs can exhibit convergence problems and need more epochs to reach the accuracy target).

In this work, we focus on analyzing MLPerf Deep Learning benchmarks in distributed computational environment. We analyze published scores, perform our own experiments and use our insights to propose additional metrics to augment MLPerf's main score.

2   Related Work

While performance evaluation of AI workloads has been an active area of research, benchmark development has been a more recent trend. DeepBench [2] from Baidu Research was one of the early projects and targeted low-level operations such as matrix multiplications and convolutions that are key parts of deep learning algorithms. The goal of DeepBench was to characterize hardware designs best suited for these low-level operations, including communication tasks. DAWNBench [3] is another project lead by Stanford University that aims to evaluate end-to-end deep learning including training and inference stages. MLPerf [1], the topic of this paper, expanded the scope by defining more metrics for a benchmark run to collect and report. A survey of such recent benchmarking initiatives and evaluation of associated requirements from metrics and system parameters is given in Ref [4].

3   Distributed MLPerf Analysis

Here we limit ourselves to only one category – Image Classification. This is a popular AI workload that has received most MLPerf entries and thus provides a wealth of data for analysis.

Furthermore, we only consider the runs on GPUs, as these are most practical for this problem. This leaves us with entries listed in Table 1, where we have done the following changes to the official MLPerf data:

1. Column 6: Speedup over reference time was converted to the time it takes to train. This is easier to understand than the speedup relative to a baseline.
2. Column 8: Number of epochs was added. This data is not listed in the spreadsheet on the MLPerf website, but can be extracted from log files for submitted runs.
3. Column 9: Estimated computational throughput, in terms of Images/second/GPU. This metric is not part of MLPerf submissions, but we estimate it as follows:

$$\frac{Number\_of\_epochs * Number\_of\_Imagenet\_Images}{Time\_to\_train[seconds] * Total\_GPUs}$$

where the *Number_of_Imagenet_Images* is 1,281,167. This metric is very important because it provides an easy way to compare computational efficiency across all published data.

Table 1. MLPerf entries for GPU-based image classification.

MLPerf index	Submitter	Nodes	GPU/node	Total GPUs	Time-to-train [min]	Software	Epochs	Images/sec/GPU
5	Google	1	8	8	138	TF	60	1162
12	Nvidia	1	8	8	135	MXNet	62	1229
20	Nvidia	1	16	16	70	MXNet	63	1201
18	Nvidia	1	16	16	74	MXNet	63	1138
17	Nvidia	80	8	640	6.2	MXNet	81	436
25	Nvidia	32	16	512	7.4	MXNet	81	456

The data in the Table 1 encompass both single node and distributed runs. The comparison between 8 GPU runs submitted by Google and Nvidia shows that there is only a small performance difference between Tensorflow and MxNet in single node runs on the same type of GPU. Similarly, scale-up results within a single node are consistent between all entries where number of epoch is close to 60 and throughput per GPU is around 1200 images/s.

The situation is different for scale-out runs. While times require to train are impressive compared to the single node runs (6 or 7 min compared to 1 or 2 h), the computational throughput decreases dramatically by about two thirds from 1,200 images/s to

400 images/s. This makes these runs highly inefficient and GPUs are idle most of the time. The source of this inefficiency cannot be identified from the published data, but we assume that it is due to parameter server communication cost – this communication is global (All-to-All) and thus increases dramatically with the number of training nodes. It should be emphasized that this metric is not listed in MLPerf results and thus this in

Another important thing to note is that distributed runs required more epochs: ~80 compared to ~60 for single node runs. Digging into the log files shows that the accuracy goal, 74.9%, becomes hard to reach at this scale: In the run #17, an accuracy of 73.4 was reached at epoch 61 after which accuracy improvement slowed down and it took additional 20 epochs to reach the criterion. The same effect is observed in run 25, where accuracy of 73.5 is reached after 61 epochs and after that accuracy almost levels off. This shows that the choice of accuracy criterion is very important and that even small changes can have dramatic effect on benchmark results.

4   Distributed Tensorflow in MLPerf

4.1   General Considerations

Tensorflow [5] is currently the most popular DL tool and even provides a popular and easy-to-use benchmarking script that can perform MLPerf Image Classification. Surprisingly, this combination was only used for one entry – a single node 8 GPU run by Google. Note that Google has submitted distributed Tensorflow scores, but those ran on TPUs and utilized a different training script based on ResNet50 model rather than the high performance benchmarking script.

4.2   Generating Unofficial MLPerf Scores Using Distributed Tensorflow

At last year's TPC conference, we have presented distributed benchmarking using Tensorflow and the high performance benchmarking script [6]. After MLPerf v0.5 results were published, we have tried to use it to obtain internal MLPerf scores for Lenovo machines. However, we ran into two types of difficulties: First, most of the MLPerf specific features added to the benchmarking script were coded for single node runs only and throw an error when used in distributed runs. These options include logic for stopping the run when a required accuracy is reached as well as code to skip frequent accuracy testing that is the default behavior and only do so towards the end of the run. While these issues can be worked around, the other difficulty we ran into prevented us from getting MLPerf scores altogether: Distributed runs could not reach the requested accuracy maxing out just below 70%. In addition, accuracies were very oscillatory after about 50 epochs. This is in contrast to single node runs where accuracy increases monotonically until the criterion is reached. The low accuracies in distributed runs have been noticed by other users and has been reported as issues on script's GitHub page [7]. There is no current resolution to these and maintainers' response was that the script is currently only targeting single node performance. With that, we have given up on obtaining MLPerf scores.

However, next Tensorflow release, 1.13, significantly improved distributed training accuracy and while oscillatory behavior continued, we were able to reach the required threshold. However, other issues remained; specifically the benchmarking script was not terminating after meeting the threshold and accuracy tests were perform after each step wasting computational time. However, because these MLPerf runs were for internal purposes only we decided to work around these by (i) running calculation longer and then pro-rate computation time relative to the point where the criterion was first reached and (ii) accepting the performance hit of extra accuracy checks.

Our MLPerf Image Classification benchmarks were run on up to 4 Lenovo SR670 servers each equipped with 4 Nvidia 32 GB V100 GPU cards. Each server contained 2 Intel Xeon Gold 6142 CPUs (16 physical cores) and 384 GB of memory. Intel's OmniPath was used as the fast speed interconnect for the distributed runs. On the software side, CentOS 7.6 with Cuda 10.0 was used with Tensorflow 1.13.1 being run from a singularity container.

During the runs, we noticed the following factors that are crucial for high performance:

1. XLA (Accelerated Linear Algebra), a new option enabled in official 1.12 builds, provides about 50% throughput boost and is crucial for good performance in both single node and distributed runs
2. XLA is experimental and one of downsides is that is cannot be used together with a parameter_server parallelization options, which we used in our previous works [6, 8]. However, distributed_replicated parallelization works and provides similar performance.
3. As observed previously [6], a high-speed network, about 100 GB speed, is necessary for good distributed performance.
4. Parallelization efficiency can be increased substantially by running multiple parameter servers on a single server. One parameter server per V100 GPU provides best performance at the scale investigated at this work.

The results are summarized in Table 2. Please note that while we have followed all the requirements for MLPerf, these data have not been submitted and/or validated by MLPerf and thus cannot be considered official MLPerf results.

Table 2. MLPerf-like scores for distributed runs performed in this work on Lenovo SR 670 equipped with V100 GPUs.

Nodes	GPUs/node	Total GPU	Time-to-train [minutes]	Epochs	Images/sec/GPU
1	1	1	1118	61	1165
1	4	4	283	61	1151
2	4	8	185	72	1039
4	4	16	98	75	1021

The results show:

1. Scale-up parallelization efficiency is very high, about 95%.

2. Distributed Tensorflow runs require more epochs to reach desired accuracy as discussed above.
3. Networking overhead causes about 10% performance loss in distributed runs
4. Time-to-train and throughput do not scale efficiently when going from 1 node to 2, but going from 2 to 4 is highly efficient. This can be interpreted as distributed DL training having a one-time cost associated with it.

We have also run this benchmark on SR670 equipped with 8 T4 GPU cards instead of V100. The results for 1 node are shown in Table 3. As seen in the previous case, Tensorflow scale up is highly efficient.

Table 3. MLPerf-like scores for single node runs on Lenovo SR670 servers equipped with 8 T4 GPUs.

Nodes	GPUs/node	Total GPU	Time-to-train [minutes]	Epochs	Images/sec/GPU
1	1	1	3610	61	360
1	4	4	912	61	357
1	8	8	470	61	346

5 Towards Improving MLPerf

As argued in Introduction, MLPerf scores do not provide information about computational efficiency. One way to remedy this is having additional metrics submitted alongside main MLPerf scores. This would enable IT decision makers to evaluate performance, efficiency, and other factors when making purchasing decisions.

Possible additional metrics include:

1. Throughput per GPU (or other compute unit)
2. Throughput per Watt
3. Total energy consumed during training

These quantities are evaluated in Table 4 for all the runs discussed in this work. To estimate energy consumption, we assume that GPUs draw their listed power during the entire run. Per Nvidia specification, the following power ratings were used: 300 W for SXM2 V100 (Nvidia runs), 250 W for PCIe V100 (this work), and 70 W for T4 (this work).

As intended, the additional metrics complement the main MLPerf score and provide a more complete picture of AI workloads. Throughput per compute device provides a measure of computational intensity and, as discussed previously, it exposes inefficiency of large scale runs.

Throughput per Watt, provides a measure of energy efficiency of the run. Another way to measure this is to use total power used during the run. The latter option is, in

Table 4. Additional metrics proposed in this work to measure computational efficiency.

MLPerf Run	GPU type and count	Time-to-train [minutes]	Throughput/GPU	Throughput/Watt	Estimated total energy [kWatt Hour]
Nvidia #12	8 × V100	135	1229	4.1	5.4
Nvidia #20	16 × V100	70	1201	4.0	5.6
Nvidia #17	640 × V100	6.2	436	1.45	19.8
Nvidia #25	512 × V100	7.4	456	1.52	18.9
This work unofficial	4 × V100	283	1151	4.6	4.76
This work unofficial	16 × V100	98	1021	4.1	6.53
This work unofficial	8 × T4	470	346	4.9	4.7

our opinion, preferable because it fits best with MLPerf's simple and elegant design and provides an easy-to-understand information. The benchmark readers would have a direct information about how much power is being used to accomplish AI tasks and computational system builders would have an incentive to optimize their design for overall power efficiency.

However, there are practical difficulties with obtaining accurate energy consumptions during these runs. Values used in this work have been estimated from listed power consumptions, but those are only reached under full loads. For example, in the highly distributed runs #17 and #25, throughput decreases by 2/3 indicating that GPUs are waiting for data, which likely means that the power consumption is reduced during that time. Therefore, our energy estimates for those runs are almost certainly overestimates.

An accurate energy usage measurement can be complicated and impractical, but even estimated values are useful and thus we propose to handle the power consumption for MLPerf entries the following way:

1. Use estimated power consumption of computing units when no power consumption measurement was made. Label the data "Estimated".
2. When electricity consumption was measured in some way, publish the submitted value with a link to the power measurement protocol submitted by users. Note that there are many possibilities such as Use Nvidia's software tools, out-of-band monitoring, or using power meters at power supplies. Any of these would be acceptable and encouraged because they improve over using listed power consumption data. Over time, the submissions and protocols can be re-evaluated to see if submitters gravitate towards a particular protocol.

An additional possibility is to use a cost-based metric. This is an attractive option, which is being used by DawnBench. The downside is that due to different pricing models, cloud-based and on-prem hardware would have separate scores that cannot be compared interchangeably. Potential inclusion of this metric requires additional discussion in the community.

Overall, at this time we cannot make a clear recommendation for a single metrics to use. Energy-based ones would improve situation but can be difficult to accurately measure. Cost-based ones would not be universal. Throughput, the simplest possible measure, carries useful information but cannot compare across different hardware. One solution may be multiple additional metrics along the score. More discussion in the community is needed to settle this issue.

6   Conclusions and Future Works

Need for a comprehensive and yet usable benchmark is growing. MLPerf suite of benchmarks has offered a way to meet this need. Its scores are easy-to-understand and cover multitudes of AI workloads. However, the scores provide no information about computational efficiency and we find that the best results are actually highly inefficient. We propose to augment the MLPerf score with two additional metrics: throughput per compute unit and total power needed to accomplish individual MLPerf objectives.

This work has focused on Deep Learning part of MLPerf. Our future plan is to continue this work to characterize the proposed metrics for additional use cases including different neural networks and datasets. We will also evaluate the performance on a wider variety of hardware systems and software frameworks.

References

1. MLPerf. https://www.mlperf.org/
2. Bench Research: Deep Bench. https://github.com/baidu-research/DeepBench
3. Coleman, C.A., et al.: DAWNBench: an end-to-end deep learning benchmark and competition. In: Proceedings of the 31st Conference on Neural Information Processing Systems (NIPS 2017) (2017)
4. Bourrasset, C., et al.: Requirements for an enterprise AI benchmark. In: Nambiar, R., Poess, M. (eds.) TPCTC 2018. LNCS, vol. 11135, pp. 71–81. Springer, Cham (2019). https://doi.org/10.1007/978-3-030-11404-6_6
5. TensorFlow. https://tensorflow.org
6. Hodak, M., Dholakia, A.: Towards evaluation of tensorflow performance in a distributed compute environment. In: Nambiar, R., Poess, M. (eds.) TPCTC 2018. LNCS, vol. 11135, pp. 82–93. Springer, Cham (2019). https://doi.org/10.1007/978-3-030-11404-6_7
7. Tensorflow Benchmarks Issue # 247. https://github.com/tensorflow/benchmarks/issues/247
8. Hodak, M., Ellison, D., Seidel, P., Dholakia, A.: Performance implications of big data in scalable deep learning: on the importance on bandwidth and caching. In: 2018 IEEE International Conference on Big Data, pp. 1945–1950 (2018)

ADABench - Towards an Industry Standard Benchmark for Advanced Analytics

Tilmann Rabl[1,2(✉)], Christoph Brücke[2], Philipp Härtling[2], Stella Stars[2],
Rodrigo Escobar Palacios[3], Hamesh Patel[3], Satyam Srivastava[3],
Christoph Boden[4], Jens Meiners[5], and Sebastian Schelter[6]

[1] HPI, University of Potsdam, Potsdam, Germany
tilmann.rabl@hpi.de
[2] bankmark, Passau, Germany
{christoph.bruecke,philipp.haertling,
stella.stars}@bankmark.de
[3] Intel, Hillsboro, USA
{rodrigo.d.escobar.palacios,hamesh.s.patel,
satyam.srivastava}@intel.com
[4] Mercedes Benz.io, Berlin, Germany
christoph.boden@mercedes-benz.io
[5] EWE, Oldenburg, Germany
j.meiners@ewe.de
[6] NYU, New York City, USA
sebastian.schelter@nyu.edu

Abstract. The digital revolution, rapidly decreasing storage cost, and remarkable results achieved by state of the art machine learning (ML) methods are driving widespread adoption of ML approaches. While notable recent efforts to benchmark ML methods for canonical tasks exist, none of them address the challenges arising with the increasing pervasiveness of end-to-end ML deployments. The challenges involved in successfully applying ML methods in diverse enterprise settings extend far beyond efficient model training.

In this paper, we present our work in benchmarking advanced data analytics systems and lay the foundation towards an industry standard machine learning benchmark. Unlike previous approaches, we aim to cover the complete end-to-end ML pipeline for diverse, industry-relevant application domains rather than evaluating only training performance. To this end, we present reference implementations of complete ML pipelines including corresponding metrics and run rules, and evaluate them at different scales in terms of hardware, software, and problem size.

1 Introduction

Enterprises apply machine learning (ML) to automate increasing amounts of decision making. This trend, fueled by advancements in hardware and software,

© Springer Nature Switzerland AG 2020
R. Nambiar and M. Poess (Eds.): TPCTC 2019, LNCS 12257, pp. 47–63, 2020.
https://doi.org/10.1007/978-3-030-55024-0_4

has spurred huge interest in both academia and industry [36]. Today, the market for ML technology and services is growing and this trend will even increase in the coming years [13]. This has lead to the development of a huge variety of ML tools and systems, which are providing ML functionality at different levels of abstraction and in different deployment infrastructures. Examples include recently popularized deep learning systems such as TensorFlow [2], PyTorch [25], and MXNet [10], which greatly benefit from specialized hardware such as GPUs; well established Python-based libraries such as scikit-learn [26]; and solutions on the Java Virtual Machine such as SparkML [23] and Mahout Samsara [33], which are based on general-purpose data flow systems and integrate well with common cloud infrastructures. Additionally, there are many specialized cloud ML services, which typically address only certain verticals such as machine translation, object detection, or forecasting.

This diversity makes it increasingly difficult for users to choose between the options for real-world use cases and has led to one-dimensional methods of comparison, which either measure the best accuracy achievable or the speed of the model training in isolation. While both metrics are important, they do not address the fundamental challenges of ML in practice. In practice, one has to not only train ML models, but execute end-to-end ML pipelines, which include multiple phases such as data integration, data cleaning, feature extraction, as well as model serving. Many of these phases have hyperparameters (e.g., the vector dimensionality if feature hashing is used), which need to be tuned analogously to model hyperparameters. All hyperparameters of an ML pipeline will impact both accuracy and speed of a model, and successfully deploying an ML system requires to trade-off the two. The artificial restriction on only measuring model training has led to a narrow focus on a few well researched data sets, such as Netflix [5], MNIST [20], or ImageNet [19]. While these data sets are highly relevant to the specific tasks at hand, they are not necessarily representative for end-to-end real-world ML pipelines "in the wild", which often include data integration, data cleaning, and feature extraction as the most tedious tasks.

We discuss some of the neglected challenges in these tedious tasks in the following: The input data may dramatically vary in size across the pipeline, it could reside in relational tables that need to be joined, and numerical representations may be sparse or dense. The emphasis of workloads may vary between exploration and continuous improvement of model quality and model serving. Furthermore, the requirements encountered in industrial settings extend beyond model accuracy as solutions have to scale, be reasonably easy to maintain and adapt, and experimentation has to adhere to strict budgets. These notable differences between real-world requirements and offline evaluations on static, pre-processed data sets also led Netflix to discard the wining solutions the Netflix Prize contest, as *"the additional accuracy gains [...] measured did not seem to justify the engineering effort needed to bring them into a production environment."* [3]. An industry standard benchmark for advanced analytics should reflect these trade-offs and requirements. It should cover complex end-to-end ML pipelines and include a broad range of use cases beyond well established data sets.

In this paper, we outline ADABench, an end-to-end ML benchmark addressing these challenges. Unlike previous benchmarks [1,5,19], we cover the complete ML lifecycle, from data preparation all the way to inference. The benchmark is built to cover real business requirements and includes different scale ranges, which are mapped to problem sizes typically found in industry. As a basis, we use an up-to-date market potential analysis [13], which we intend to convert into 16 use cases, out of which we present six in this paper. These use cases are designed to cover various dimensions of analytics in the retail business vertical. Our benchmark model draws from industry standards as specified from the Transaction Processing Performance Council[1] (TPC) and the Standard Performance Evaluation Corporation[2] (SPEC). Our core contributions are:

- We propose a novel end-to-end ML benchmark that covers different business scale factors, and industry relevant metrics (Sect. 2).
- We specify the first four out of 16 planned use cases that cover a wide range of industry-relevant ML applications (Sect. 2.1).
- We detail our reference implementations of the proposed use cases, and report first performance evaluations for different scale factors (Sect. 3).

In the following, we will give an overview of the implemented use cases, outline the benchmark specification, and present first results running our use cases along several dimensions of scalability, namely software (Python-environment vs. Spark-environment), hardware (single-node vs. scale-up cluster), and size (MBs vs. GBs).

2   Machine Learning Benchmark

ADABench covers the complete end-to-end pipeline of ML workloads as described by Polyzotis et al. [28], which contains several additional steps besides model training, such as data integration, data cleaning, feature extraction, and model serving. From a business perspective, it is relevant to consider that people conducting advanced data analytics usually spend most of their time in tasks like data preparation [15]. Given this widely agreed-on fact, an ML benchmark should also consider these phases. In general, each of the phases can be a one-time action, as in a single prediction; an iterative process, e.g., a daily forecast; or a continuous process, as in an online recommendation scenario. In the following, we describe the first four use cases in detail and give details about the core aspects of the benchmark specification.

2.1   Use Cases

To account for the diversity of real-world scenarios, the ADABench workload is comprised of multiple ML use cases, each covering a whole pipeline. Our use

---

[1] http://www.tpc.org.

[2] http://www.spec.org.

cases are derived from retail business applications and analysis tasks common in online businesses according to their market potential identified by McKinsey [13]. We select the first two cases out of the two highest impact business problem areas: customer service management and predictive maintenance. The second two use cases cover prediction and hyper-personalization in form of customer segmentation. The final benchmark aims to not only provide a specification and a data generator but also reference implementations for each use case. The current version includes two such reference implementations for each use case: (a) an implementation based on Apache Spark [39], and (b) an implementation based on Python libraries such as scikit-learn [26] and pandas [22]. We adapt the Parallel Data Generation Framework (PDGF) for data generation [31].

Use Case 1: 'Trip-Type Classification'. The first use case (UC1) is a classification task that falls into the category of customer service management. The goal is to identify the type of shopping a customer wants to do, i.e., if a customer is on a large weekly grocery trip, wants to buy ingredients for a dinner, or is shopping for clothing. Based on the classification, the shopping experience of customers can be improved. UC1 is inspired by a Kaggle competition[3]. However, the data set and implementation are completely independent. The use case employs structured data from a transaction database as input. These transactions include the amount of items bought or returned, the department from which they originate, a line number, the day of the week, an order ID to distinguish different sessions, and a trip type. The task is to train a classifier to predict the trip type based on the transactional data. Our reference implementation is based on XGBoost [9] for model training, and pandas/scikit-learn and Apache Spark for general data handling and pre-processing. The pipeline first loads the data into memory and filters all samples that contain NULL values. Then the features are extracted. There are three types of features: (a) aggregates, i.e., sum and absolute sum of items bought or returned per order, (b) a one-hot encoding of the weekday of the order, and (c) a pivotization of the different departments occurring in the order, i.e., sum of items bought or returned per department per order. The basic task is to unstack the data, such that a single order is expressed as a single vector instead of a set of records. After pre-processing, XGBoost is trained using *soft-prob* as objective function. The key performance metric for training and serving is throughput while a threshold on the weighted F1-measure has to be met.

Use Case 2: 'Predictive Maintenance'. The second use case (UC2) is a classification task in the category of predictive maintenance. It is inspired by an approach to predict failures published by Chigurupati et al. [11]. The goal is to predict hardware failures in advance based on sensor data measured in periodical time intervals. The key idea is to separate the log data into categories depending on the timely distance to failure. A proxy for this generic use case is to predict imminent hard-drive failures based on daily S.M.A.R.T.[4] measurements [35]. We provide semi-structured data from log files as input. As part of the preprocessing

---

[3] https://www.kaggle.com/c/walmart-recruiting-trip-type-classification.
[4] Self-Monitoring, Analysis and Reporting Technology.

stage, this data needs to be parsed and filtered to be further used for training or serving. The main challenge is a highly imbalanced data set, i.e., non-failures are much more common than failures. The characteristics and distributions of the synthetic data set are inspired by hard drive statistics published by Backblaze[5]. The data set contains log entries with a time stamp, an ID (model and serial number), a series of S.M.A.R.T. attribute values, and a binary label indicating whether a complete failure occurred. Analogous to the first use case, the reference implementations for this use case are also based on pandas, scikit-learn, and Spark. The main tasks of the preprocessing stage are (a) labeling of the training samples and (b) up-sampling of the minority (failure) class. For that, we split the training samples into failures, log entries that occurred on the day or one day before the actual failure, and non-failures, log entries that occurred two or more days before a failure or log entries of disks that never failed anyway. Then the samples of the failure class are sampled with replacement until there are equal amounts of samples for each class, the up-sampled data set is used to train a support vector machine (SVM). Since imminent failures are predicted to enable pro-active measures (such as replacing faulty drives before they crash), the key quality metric here is a low false positive rate at a high true positive rate. We measure this using area under the receiver operating curve (AUC). The key performance metric is throughput again in this case.

Use Case 3: 'Sales Prediction'. The third use case (UC3) is a regression task in the category of forecasting. The aim is to predict store and/or department sales from historical sales data, i.e., weekly sales numbers from previous years are used to find seasonal and regional patterns and forecast future sales. Based on these predictions stores can optimize their expenditure for sales promotion and personnel planning. UC3 is borrowing the idea from a Kaggle competition[6] but the data generation and implementation are independently built. The data consists of sales numbers aggregated by stores, departments, and weeks over several years. Every store has sales data for every department over every week of the years. Sales peaks are sampled from a normal distribution. Sales curves between departments follow a similar seasonal pattern. No other additional information, e.g., product group or amount of sale, is provided. Our data is generated and then exported into a CSV file. As in the other use cases our reference implementation uses pandas, scikit-learn, and Spark. In the first step of our pipeline, the sales numbers are loaded from that CSV. A preprocessing step is not necessary in this use case, since we already generate aggregated data. In the training phase, we build a seasonal model for each store and each department using a Holt-Winters exponential smoothing approach. This model is then used to predict forecasts for all stores and departments and exported into a CSV file. The key performance metric is processing time of each step, we measure the mean squared error as a quality metric.

---

[5] https://www.backblaze.com/b2/hard-drive-test-data.html.

[6] https://www.kaggle.com/c/walmart-recruiting-store-sales-forecasting.

Use Case 4: 'Customer Segmentation'. The forth use case (UC4) is a clustering task. Clustering is an unsupervised machine learning technique. In customer segmentation, customers are divided into groups based on similar characteristics. By segmenting users, campaigns can be more efficient, because they can be directed to the correct target audiences. UC4 performs behavioral segmentation, as the problem to be solved is finding clusters based on aggregate features that group customers based on their spending and returning behavior. The input in this use case consists of order and return transactions. We use k-means clustering to calculate user clusters based on the data provided. The patterns in the data are used to identify and group similar observations. First, we load the data into memory and clean it (we remove unnecessary elements, e.g., duplicates, transactions not assigned to a customer, or cancel orders without counterpart). The features extracted after that are (a) return ratio, i.e., total value of the returns divided by the total value of the orders and (b) number of purchases per customer. The scaled feature vector and the number of clusters are input for the k-means algorithm used in training. The key performance metric for training and serving is throughput. The quality metric measures the mean of the distances of the predicted clusters to the clusters of the reference implementation.

Use Case 5: 'Spam Detection'. The fifth use case (UC5) is a supervised classification task in the category of discovering new trends/anomalies. Spam detection means to find comments, reviews, or descriptions with spam content. The input in this use case consists of reviews or comments in a retail business. The problem to be solved is to identify those reviews that are spam. The analysis uses Naive Bayes. Naive Bayes methods are a set of supervised learning algorithms based on Bayes' theorem. The data loaded into memory for training is text labeled as spam or ham, for serving unlabeled text. After cleaning (e.g., removing duplicates), the pipeline performs preprocessing to convert the text into a numerical feature vector (like tokenization of the text, removing stopwords, building n-grams, and computing the term frequency–inverse document frequency). This feature vector is fed to the multinomial Naive Bayes algorithm. The output after serving is an array of label predictions. The performance metric is throughput, the time that is needed to run through all the steps of reading the data, data transformation, training and serving. To evaluate the quality of the classification, the quality metric is *F1 Score*, since it takes both precision and recall of the classifications into consideration.

Use Case 6: 'Product Recommendation'. Use Case 6 (UC6) is a recommendation task in the category of personalization. The aim is to recommend items to a user based on their and other users previous similar ratings, i.e., find next-to-buy recommendations. Proof of concept has been done with the MovieLens dataset[7] that consists of user-item-rating triplets for various movies. Our data generation and implementation creates similar triplets. Each user is given a main user category for which the bulk of product ratings are generated.

---

[7] https://grouplens.org/datasets/movielens/.

The rest is filled with ratings from other user categories. Ratings for products in their main category have a normal distribution around a high mean, ratings in the other categories have a normal distribution around a low mean. Our data is generated and exported into a CSV file. We use pandas, scikit-learn, and Spark for our reference implementation. The actual recommendation is done by SurPRISE[8] in Python and by the collaborative filtering module of Spark[9]. As the first step of our pipeline the pre-generated ratings are loaded. In a preprocessing step in Python we transform the pandas DataFrame in a dataset that SurPRISE can utilize. The Spark implementation does not need a preprocessing step. The training phase consists of a matrix factorization done with a singular value decomposition algorithm in python and an alternating least squares algorithm in Spark. The resulting model is then used to predict the rating for every user-item pair and lastly to return the top 10 recommendations for every user. The key performance metric is throughput. As a quality metric we use mean-squared-error and mean-absolute-error.

For the remaining 10 use cases (which are out of the scope of this paper), we aim for diversity along several dimensions: the structure of the data (structured vs. unstructured), type of data (numerical, audio, visual, textual, etc.), business case (predictive maintenance, customer service management, etc.), and ML methods and algorithms (classification, regression, recommendation, clustering, deep neural networks, etc.).

2.2   Benchmark Details

Data Model, Scale Factor, and Execution. The ADABench data model is structurally related to the BigBench data model [4,17]. Analogous to BigBench, we design a data warehouse model, which is used as a source for many of the ML use cases, especially for analyses related to customer management, sales, and other transactions. Additionally, we add sources such as click logs, text, and sensor readings. We further extended the data set to capture a broader variety of data types and demand more preprocessing. Some of the extensions are taken from the ideas presented in the proposal for BigBench 2.0 [30], i.e., diverse data types (text, multi-media, graph) and different velocities of data (streaming vs. batch).

ADABench incorporates different data set sizes that are used in industry and academia. We identified five different classes that are reflected in five scale factors, XS - XL, which represent data problem sizes of 1 GB to 10 PB respectively, shown in Table 1. These classes are related to the size of the operations found in industry. The smallest class, XS, relates to a very small operation typically done by a single individual at a single location. S represents an operation driven by a small team at a single location with lightly distributed computing capabilities. At Scale Factor M the use of a small cluster of commodity hardware is necessary. To run an L scale, a rather large cluster is required and this kind of

---

[8] http://surpriselib.com/.

[9] https://spark.apache.org/docs/latest/ml-collaborative-filtering.html.

Table 1. Data size and number of cores for each scale.

Scale	Workload	Problem size (GB)	Total cores approx.
Extra Small (XS)	Small data science projects	10^0	4–8
Small (S)	Traditional analytical tasks	10^1	8–32
Medium (M)	Lower tier big data tasks	10^3	32–320
Large (L)	Big data tasks	10^5	320–3200
Extra Large (XL)	Internet company tasks	10^7	3200–32000

setup is typically found in global organizations handling large amounts of data and transactions. Finally, we define the XL boundary, which is a quite rare scale factor only seen at large Internet companies. Data in ADABench is synthetically generated using tools such as PDGF [32]. The data generation process provides three major functionalities. ❶ *High data generation velocity* that achieves the described scale factors XS-XL in a reasonable time frame. ❷ *Data generation that incorporates characteristics and dependencies concerning the respective scale factor.* As a result, a higher data volume contains not more of the same information but new, previously unseen characteristics. Hence the data becomes more complex with an increasing scale factor. For this, we propose an approach that is build on the assumption that rare occurrences become more common, in absolute terms, the more data is generated. For instance in case of UC1 there might be only three different classes at scale factor XS in the synthetic data set, whereas there might be 40 at scale factor M. This approach can be generalized for several supervised learning tasks, by ensuring that certain phenomena have a high probability while others have a low probability. One artifact of this approach is that the different classes become more imbalanced with increasing volume, which in turn also makes the data more realistic. ❸ *Introduction of errors into the data* to simulate a real-world production environment. These errors can be, e.g., missing values, outliers, and wrong data types. While the first functionality eases the utilization of the benchmark, the other two aim to close the gap between laboratory grade experiments and real-world application fuzziness. For *UC 1* and *UC 3* - *UC 6* functionality two is highly important because large scale data should contain previously unseen information. For *UC 2* the third functionality is of higher importance since the false positive rate is the critical measurement and must be robust to erroneous input data.

In order to cover various business setups and challenge machine learning deployments in different ways, we specify two general modes of execution: Sequential execution and parallel execution of the use cases. During sequential execution, every use case has to be run exclusively from start to end, while in the parallel execution mode, all use cases can be run in parallel. In both setups, we allow for a pipelined execution of individual steps within a use case. This is similar to the TPC's benchmark execution model (e.g., TPC-DS [27] or TPCx-BB [4]), with the distinction that we do allow for the parallel execution of different use cases rather than the parallel execution of streams of all queries.

Metrics. In ADABench, we define individual metrics for each use-case, which are aggregated (via geometric mean) into one global metric summarizing the entire benchmark. For each use case, we define individual metrics, which are a combination of measurements of the stages in a use-case. We use the geometric mean to weight the diverse use cases equally in the final metric and equally encourage optimization on all stages. Driven by the industry-oriented scenario we aim to cover with ADABench, we chose *throughput* in *samples per second* as the main performance measure while defining thresholds for prediction quality metrics such as accuracy or AUC and latency that have to be met. This is similar to recent proposals like DAWNBench, which propose a time-to-accuracy metric [14] and reflects industry requirements. Most use cases define a training and a serving stage, which we measure separately (TP_t and TP_s)and summarize in the total throughput for the use case TP_i (see Eq. 1). The formula for the total throughput is shown in Eq. 2.

$$TP_i = \sqrt{TP_{ti} * TP_{si}} \tag{1}$$

$$TP = \sqrt[n]{\Pi_{i=1}^{n} TP_i} \tag{2}$$

The final performance metric, $ADASps@SF$, is the throughput at a scale factor. This means that systems can only be compared at the same scale factor. Besides performance metrics, we also specify price performance and energy performance metrics. These are defined according to TPC standards [37,38]. This means, the price performance is defined as the total cost of the execution by a pay-as-you-go model divided by $ADASps@SF$. Similarly, the energy performance is defined as the total consumed energy per benchmark execution divided by $ADASps@SF$.

3   Evaluation

In this section, we present results of an experimental evaluation of the six use cases UC1 to UC6 introduced in Sect. 2.1. While providing valuable insights about system performance, the experiments also show how the benchmark operates with respect to metrics and measurements. We evaluate the reference implementations of both use cases with a focus on the first four scale factors discussed in Sect. 2.2: XS, S, M, and L. We use two different compute clusters with nodes of the following specs:

- **Small node:** 1 Intel Xeon CPU @ 2.10 GHz, 10 threads (virtualized) and 64 GB RAM
- **Big node:** 2 Intel Xeon CPUs @ 2.30 GHz, 72 threads and 768 GB RAM

As discussed in Sect. 2.1, we have two different reference implementations for each use case: one based on pandas, scikit-learn, named *Python* and one based on Apache Spark. The experiments are deployed on one node for *Python* and on 10 nodes for *Apache Spark* for both *small* and *big* node configurations. Fig. 1, 2, 3, 4, 5 and 6 show the results of these experiments for different scale factors.

For each use case and scale factor, we generate three synthetic data sets: one for training, one for serving, and one for scoring. We use the data sets for training and serving for the throughput tests and the data set for scoring to measure model quality. As discussed in Sect. 2.2, *throughput* in samples per second is the main performance measure evaluated in the experiments. The trained models have to adhere thresholds for model quality: For instance the F-Measure for UC1 was above 0.8 and the AUC for UC2 was higher than 0.95. The other use cases have similar quality thresholds.

We found that for the trip type classification (UC1), Spark had a higher throughput during training, starting at a relatively low scale factor of 1 (see Fig. 1, which approximately corresponds to 100,000 orders with an average of 10 line items per order, that is 1,000,000 line items in total. In case of the implementation based on pandas, scikit-learn, and XGBoost for UC1 approximately half of the time is spent for pre-processing the data and the remaining half is spent for the actual model training. Since the pre-processing includes joins and pivotization, Spark is much better suited for this task and outperforms pandas using more efficient join strategies. Another reason why Spark performs better is XGBoost's parallelization capabilities. Using Spark and hence all 10 nodes of

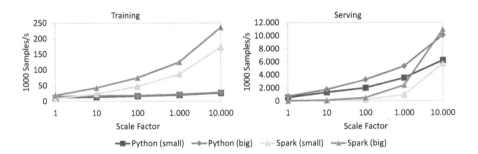

Fig. 1. Throughput measured for the training and serving stage at different scale factors. The Python-based implementation is shown in blue and red when run on a small or big node respectively. Analogous the Spark-based implementations are show in yellow and green. (Color figure online)

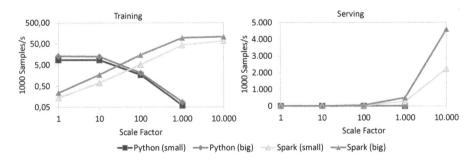

Fig. 2. Throughput measured for UC02 training and serving stage as in Fig. 1.

the cluster also enables XGBoost to leverage the increased computational power, i.e., distribute the training over all the nodes in the cluster. For the serving stage of UC1, we observe similar results, yet the tipping point is at a much higher scale factor. We conclude that serving an XGBoost model does not require much computational power; hence as long as the data fits into memory, the Python based implementation has higher throughput than Spark.

In contrast to UC1 where Spark outperforms a single node solution based on pandas and XGBoost, we see that for UC2 the data size has to be increased significantly before Spark outperforms the Python-based implementation (see Fig. 2). We attribute this to the fact this use case is light on pre-processing. Only when the data becomes too big to fit into memory a Spark cluster performs better. For serving, we see the similar results as in UC1: a Spark cluster is only reasonable for high volume and/or velocity. One interesting finding is that the serving throughput of the Python implementation for UC2 decreases drastically with an increasing model size, i.e., more training samples. This probably is based on the fact that there are more support vectors and it can most likely be compensated using a form of regularization.

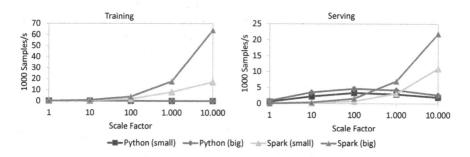

Fig. 3. Throughput measured for UC03 training and serving stage as in Fig. 1.

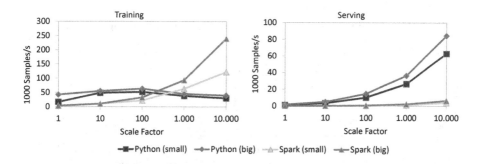

Fig. 4. Throughput measured for UC04 training and serving stage as in Fig. 1.

The experiments for UC3 (see Fig. 3) show a different characteristic. We can see that the Holt-Winters implementation for Spark is performing better for the training as well as for the serving stage. It can observed that with increasing scale factor the serving throughput decreases for the Python-based implementation. This is caused by memory pressure, which means that the more data is processed the lower is the throughput. For UC4, the clustering use-case, illustrated in Fig. 4, we see similar effects as for UC2. As long as the data can be handled in memory on a single node the Python-based implementation is faster than the Spark implementation. But the limit, in terms of throughput, is reached rather fast and the Spark-based implementation is outperforming the Python-based implementation between scale factor 100 and 1000, depending on the available memory. Because the k-Means algorithm is highly parallelizable and the Spark environment has access to ten times as many cores, we see a drastic increase of the Spark implementation at bigger scale factors. Serving on the other hand does not require a lot of compute resource and both implementation have not reached their respective limits for scale factors up to 10000. In spam classification as in UC5 (see Fig. 5) neither implementation is reaching their throughput limit but for the training the Spark-based implementation has much better scaling capabilities than the Python-based one. The inverse is true for serving. The last use-case UC6 is a recommendation use-case (see Fig. 6). It can be observed that with a higher scale factor and hence a bigger user-item-rating matrix performance

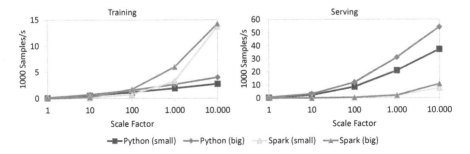

Fig. 5. Throughput measured for UC05 training and serving stage as in Fig. 1.

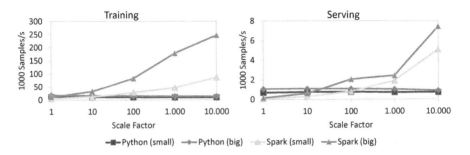

Fig. 6. Throughput measured for UC06 training and serving stage as in Fig. 1.

is suffering for the Python-based implementation during training and constant during serving. Whereas the Spark-based implementation can make use of the additional computational power and has not reached its throughput limit up to scale factor L.

Since the main goal of this benchmark is to compare different ML systems for complete pipelines, we introduce a combined benchmark metric: the *ADABench Metric – ADASps@SF –* as defined in Sect. 2.2. This metric is given by the geometric mean of all use case metrics, where each use case's metric is the geometric mean across the training and serving throughput. Using the geometric mean weights the use cases and their phases equally and, therefore, is more stable for diverse workloads. Figure 7 illustrates the ADABench Metric for our reference implementation and test systems at the different scale factors.

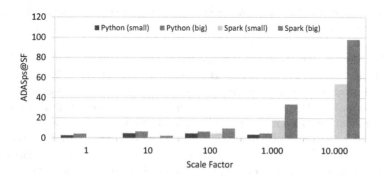

Fig. 7. ADABench Metric - combined metric of all stages and use case per systems and scale factor (higher is better)

Given this metric, we see that a Spark-based implementation outperforms the Python-based implementation at high scale factors, while the Python-based implementation clearly dominates at smaller scale factors, with scale factor 100 being the tipping point.

In summary, we can see that our initial set of use cases already captures a variety of performance characteristics. Some use cases rely heavily on pre-processing the data before training a model, while others employ algorithms that are computational more expensive. We can also see that our implementations in Python and Spark behave differently in scaling. In general, Python is more efficient for smaller scale factors, while Spark outperforms Python when data sets do not fit in memory. It has to be noted that in all experiments, Spark has 10 times more hardware resources than Python.

4   Related Work

In this section, we give an overview on benchmarking in the ML space in the past and previous approaches in benchmarking ML systems. We discuss popular benchmarks, their focus and metrics, and identify strengths and weaknesses.

In general, the current benchmarking landscape can be divided into three distinct types of benchmarks [18]: *Component-level benchmarks* test and compare only a single component of a system or application. They could, for example, run a specific operation of an application on different processors. Component benchmarks are interesting to the developers of the *component under study* (CUS) or to select the best instance of the CUS. We found that most of the current component-level benchmarks are hardware benchmarks in essence, which compare different hardware components in terms of training or inference performance. A typical component-level benchmark is *DeepBench* [24]. *System-level benchmarks* tests and compares complete ML systems. Typically, they cover set of different use cases in their workload and the metrics measure performance over a set of executions. *Algorithmic competitions* such as the Netflix Prize [5] or the ImageNet competition [19] compare different algorithms or models on a constrained problem. Recent work acknowledges that data preparation time is a major bottleneck for many ML applications and discusses a repository of related tasks to foster research in this area [34].

BigDataBench [16] is a benchmark with 13 representative real-world data sets and more than 40 workloads that can be characterized in five different domains: search engines, social networks, e-commerce, multimedia processing and bioinformatics. Moreover, the workloads have a varied data sources and cover diverse applications scenarios, including search engines, e-commerce, relational data queries, basic datastore operations (OLTP), and artificial intelligence (AI). It also uses two types of metrics: user-perceivable metrics, which are simple and easy to understand by non-expert users, and architectural metrics, which provide details targeted for architecture research. It can be categorized as a system-level benchmark. Unlike ADABench, BigDataBench does not include dedicated end-to-end scenarios.

AdBench [6] is a proposal system-level end-to-end benchmark with workloads that are representative of web and mobile advertising. The patterns exhibited by workloads are often seen in workloads from other sectors, such as financial services, retail, and healthcare. The benchmark combines workloads for ad-serving, streaming analytics, streaming ingestion, ML for ad targeting, and other big data analytics tasks. In addition, AdBench introduces a set of metrics to be measured for each stage of the data pipeline and scale factors of the benchmark. Unfortunately, there is no official implementation or complete specification of AdBench available.

BigBench [12,17,29] was developed can be seen as a basis for ADABench. Its strengths are that it is inspired by real-world use cases as well as its ease to use. A major drawback as far as a ML-specific benchmarking is concerned is its focus on traditional data analytics. BigBench only contains a small number of machine learning-related queries and features no metrics to compare different ML implementations.

DawnBench [14] as well as its industry-backed successor MLPerf [1] are benchmarking deep learning systems in terms of training time. The main contribution of DawnBench, and MLPerf consequently, is the novel time-to-accuracy metric. They are a hybrid between a system-level benchmark and an algorithmic competition. Both consists of a set of different and well-studied ML challenges, such as image classification, machine translation, sentiment analysis. There are many more benchmarks or benchmark attempts that are leveraging already existing competitions or challenges, e.g., convnet-benchmarks[10] or MLBench[21], but to the best of our knowledge, ADABench is the only end-to-end ML benchmark proposal.

Several studies have researched the performance characteristics of ML algorithms and workloads on specific systems. In contrast to these, we study end-to-end performance. However, we benefit from the insights of these studies and, for example, provide single- and multi-node implementations as proposed by Boden et al. [7,8].

5   Conclusion

In this paper, we present our vision towards an industry standard benchmark for end-to-end machine learning. Our benchmark, ADABench, is comprised of complete machine learning use cases, which include data preparation and pre-processing, model training and tuning, as well as model serving. We use up-to-date market research to identify most relevant scenarios, and create novel machine learning pipelines for those. As an initial step, we have implemented four use cases in a Python (pandas, scikit-learn) and a Spark environment. Our evaluations show the different trade-offs in terms of performance based on data size, choice of environment, and complexity. We are currently implementing further use cases, also using deep neural networks. We will continue with the development of our benchmark with the goal of a wide coverage of machine learning technology and use cases along the dimensions identified by market research as most relevant, and aim to establish this proposal as a standard.

References

1. MLPerf (2018). https://mlperf.org/, https://mlperf.org/
2. Abadi, M., Barham, P., Chen, J., et al.: Tensorflow: a system for large-scale machine learning. In: OSDI, pp. 265–283 (2016)
3. Amatriain, X.: Building industrial-scale real-world recommender systems. In: RecSys, pp. 7–8 (2012)
4. Baru, C., et al.: Discussion of BigBench: a proposed industry standard performance benchmark for big data. In: Nambiar, R., Poess, M. (eds.) TPCTC 2014. LNCS, vol. 8904, pp. 44–63. Springer, Cham (2015). https://doi.org/10.1007/978-3-319-15350-6_4
5. Bennett, J., Lanning, S., et al.: The netflix prize. In: Proceedings of KDD Cup and Workshop, p. 35 (2007)
6. Bhandarkar, M.: AdBench: a complete data pipeline benchmark for modern data pipelines. In: TPCTC, pp. 107–120 (2016)

---

[10] https://github.com/soumith/convnet-benchmarks.

7. Boden, C., Rabl, T., Markl, V.: Distributed machine learning-but at what cost. In: Machine Learning Systems Workshop at Conference on Neural Information Processing Systems (2017)

8. Boden, C., Spina, A., Rabl, T., Markl, V.: Benchmarking data flow systems for scalable machine learning. In: SIGMOD Workshop on Algorithms and Systems for MapReduce and Beyond, pp. 5:1–5:10. BeyondMR (2017)

9. Chen, T., Guestrin, C.: Xgboost: a scalable tree boosting system. In: ACM SigKDD, pp. 785–794 (2016)

10. Chen, T., Li, M., Li, Y., et al.: Mxnet: a flexible and efficient machine learning library for heterogeneous distributed systems. arXiv preprint arXiv:1512.01274 (2015)

11. Chigurupati, A., Thibaux, R., Lassar, N.: Predicting hardware failure using machine learning. In: Reliability and Maintainability Symposium (RAMS), pp. 1–6 (2016)

12. Chowdhury, B., Rabl, T., Saadatpanah, P., Du, J., Jacobsen, H.-A.: A BigBench implementation in the hadoop ecosystem. In: Rabl, T., Jacobsen, H.-A., Raghunath, N., Poess, M., Bhandarkar, M., Baru, C. (eds.) WBDB 2013. LNCS, vol. 8585, pp. 3–18. Springer, Cham (2014). https://doi.org/10.1007/978-3-319-10596-3_1

13. Chui, M., et al.: Notes from the AI Frontier - insights from hundreds of use cases. Technical report, McKinsey Global Institute (2018)

14. Coleman, C., et al.: Analysis of DAWNBench, a time-to-accuracy machine learning performance benchmark. CoRR abs/1806.01427 (2018)

15. Deng, D., Fernandez, R.C., Abedjan, Z., et al.: The data civilizer system. In: CIDR (2017)

16. Gao, W., Zhan, J., Wang, L., et al.: BigDataBench: a dwarf-based big data and AI benchmark suite. CoRR abs/1802.0 (2018)

17. Ghazal, A., et al.: BigBench: towards an industry standard benchmark for big data analytics. In: SIGMOD (2013)

18. Jain, R.: The Art of Computer Systems Performance Analysis - Techniques for Experimental Design, Measurement, Simulation, and Modeling. Wiley Professional Computing. Wiley, Hoboken (1991)

19. Krizhevsky, A., Sutskever, I., Hinton, G.E.: ImageNet classification with deep convolutional neural networks. In: Advances in Neural Information Processing Systems, pp. 1097–1105 (2012)

20. LeCun, Y.: The mnist database of handwritten digits (1998). http://yann.lecun.com/exdb/mnist/

21. Liu, Y., Zhang, H., Zeng, L., Wu, W., Zhang, C.: Mlbench: benchmarking machine learning services against human experts. PVLDB **11**(10), 1220–1232 (2018)

22. McKinney, W., et al.: Data structures for statistical computing in Python. In: Proceedings of the 9th Python in Science Conference, pp. 51–56 (2010)

23. Meng, X., Bradley, J., Yavuz, B., et al.: Mllib: machine learning in apache spark. J. Mach. Learn. Res. **17**(1), 1235–1241 (2016)

24. Narang, S.: DeepBench (2016). https://svail.github.io/DeepBench/

25. Paszke, A., Gross, S., Chintala, S., et al.: Automatic differentiation in pytorch. In: NIPS Autodiff Decision Workshop (2017)

26. Pedregosa, F., Varoquaux, G., Gramfort, A., et al.: Scikit-learn: machine learning in Python. J. Mach. Learn. Res. **12**, 2825–2830 (2011)

27. Poess, M., Rabl, T., Jacobsen, H.A.: Analysis of TPC-DS: the first standard benchmark for SQL-based big data systems. In: Proceedings of the 2017 Symposium on Cloud Computing (2017)

28. Polyzotis, N., Roy, S., Whang, S.E., Zinkevich, M.: Data management challenges in production machine learning. In: SIGMOD, pp. 1723–1726 (2017)
29. Rabl, T., Frank, M., Danisch, M., Gowda, B., Jacobsen, H.-A.: Towards a complete BigBench implementation. In: Rabl, T., Sachs, K., Poess, M., Baru, C., Jacobson, H.-A. (eds.) WBDB 2015. LNCS, vol. 8991, pp. 3–11. Springer, Cham (2015). https://doi.org/10.1007/978-3-319-20233-4_1
30. Rabl, T., Frank, M., Danisch, M., Jacobsen, H.A., Gowda, B.: The vision of Big-Bench 2.0. In: Proceedings of the Fourth Workshop on Data Analytics in the Cloud DanaC 2015, pp. 3:1–3:4. ACM, New York (2015)
31. Rabl, T., Frank, M., Sergieh, H.M., Kosch, H.: A data generator for cloud-scale benchmarking. In: Nambiar, R., Poess, M. (eds.) TPCTC 2010. LNCS, vol. 6417, pp. 41–56. Springer, Heidelberg (2011). https://doi.org/10.1007/978-3-642-18206-8_4
32. Rabl, T., Poess, M.: Parallel data generation for performance analysis of large, complex RDBMS. In: DBTest 2011, p. 5 (2011)
33. Schelter, S., Palumbo, A., Quinn, S., Marthi, S., Musselman, A.: Samsara: declarative machine learning on distributed dataflow systems. In: NIPS Workshop MLSystems (2016)
34. Shah, V., Kumar, A.: The ML data prep zoo: towards semi-automatic data preparation for ML. In: DEEM, pp. 11:1–11:4 (2019)
35. Stevens, C.E.: Information TPC-Cechnology - ATA/ATAPI Command Set - 2 (ACS-2). Technical report, ANSI INCITS (2011)
36. Sun, C., Shrivastava, A., Singh, S., Gupta, A.: Revisiting unreasonable effectiveness of data in deep learning era. In: ICCV (2017)
37. Transaction Processing Performance Council: TPC-Energy Specification, version 1.5.0 (2012)
38. Transaction Processing Performance Council: TPC Pricing Specification, version 2.5.0 (2019)
39. Zaharia, M., Chowdhury, M., Franklin, M.J., Shenker, S., Stoica, I.: Spark: cluster computing with working sets. In: HotCloud, p. 10 (2010)

TPCx-BB (Big Bench) in a Single-Node Environment

Dippy Aggarwal[1]([✉]), Shreyas Shekhar[1], Chris Elford[1], Umachandar
Jayachandran[2], Sadashivan Krishnamurthy[2], Jamie Reding[2],
and Brendan Niebruegge[2]

[1] Intel Corporation, Santa Clara, OR, USA
{dippy.aggarwal,shreyas.shekhar,chris.l.elford}@intel.com
[2] Microsoft Corporation, Redmond, USA
{umachandar.jayachandran,skrish,jamie.reding,brnieb}@microsoft.com

Abstract. Big data tends to concentrate on the data volume and variety which requires large cluster capabilities to process diverse and heterogeneous data. Currently, NoSQL/Hadoop-based cluster frameworks are known to excel at handling this form of data by scaling across nodes and distributed query processing. But for certain data sizes, relational databases can also support these workloads. In this paper, we support this claim over a popular relational database engine, Microsoft* SQL Server* 2019 (pre-release candidate) using a big data benchmark, Big-Bench. Our work in this paper is the industry first case study that runs BigBench on a single node environment powered by Intel® Xeon^{TM} processor 8164 product family and enterprise-class Intel® SSDs. We make the following two contributions: (1) present response times of all 30 Big-Bench queries when run sequentially to showcase the advanced analytics and machine learning capabilities integrated within SQL Server 2019, and (2) present results from data scalability experiments over two scale factors (1 TB, 3 TB) to understand the impact of increase in data size on query runtimes. We further characterize a subset of queries to understand their resource consumption requirements (CPU/IO/memory) on a single node system. We will conclude by correlating our initial engineering study to similar research studies on cluster-based configurations providing a further hint to the potential of relational databases to run reasonably scaled big-data workloads.

Keywords: TPCx-BB · Microsoft* SQL Server* 2019 · Big data · BigBench · Machine learning · Natural language processing

1 Introduction

With the popularity of Big Data, organizations are continuously confronted with the challenge of storing, processing and analyzing diverse, complex form of data (structured, semi-structured, and un-structured) with relatively limited storage and computation power of traditional tools and processes when compared

© Springer Nature Switzerland AG 2020
R. Nambiar and M. Poess (Eds.): TPCTC 2019, LNCS 12257, pp. 64–83, 2020.
https://doi.org/10.1007/978-3-030-55024-0_5

to cluster-based configurations. There are currently two alternatives to handle analysis over this form of data: (a) scale-up (adding CPU power, memory to a single machine), (b) scale-out (adding more machines in the system creating a cluster). Several commercial and open-source systems have emerged over the past several years as a scale-out solution to handle this data form [25–30]. Additionally, researchers from different communities including data management, machine learning, systems and computer architecture are also continuously working towards proposing innovative approaches to manage big-data workloads [31–35].

On one hand, having a variety of solutions is an advantage, for the flexibility they offer big data users in making a choice for the solution that best fits their needs; on the other hand, it also presents the challenge of assessing the functionality and performance of different systems and having a comparative view to even arrive at a decision. Benchmarking is a standard process embraced by organizations and researchers for measuring and demonstrating performance of their products. Additionally, it helps to identify the potential areas for performance optimizations, drive engineering efforts, and through this process, provide insights into the requirements for the next version of product/system under test.

Several big data benchmarks have been proposed recently out of which BigBench is considered as the first end-to-end solution designed to evaluate entire systems [5,6,10]. There exists another category of benchmarks called microbenchmarks. They are designed to evaluate specific system components or features of Big Data solutions For example, NNBench [8] tests the performance of NameNode component in HDFS, Terasort [9] is another benchmark used to evaluate performance of MapReduce framework by measuring the amount of time it takes to sort one terabyte of randomly distributed data. Similarly, there are several other active efforts in the benchmarking community that are mainly targeted at evaluating specific components [5,6].

Han et al. [6] present a survey of open-source big data benchmarks. The authors classify the surveyed benchmarks across four different dimensions: (1) types of big data systems they serve (Hadoop-based, DMBSs/NOSQL data stores, and specialized systems which require processing on particular data types such as graphs, streaming data), (2) workload generation techniques, (3) input data generation techniques, and (4) performance metrics. In another literature study, Ivanov et al. [5] provide a summary of big data benchmarks discussing their characteristics and pros and cons. Ghazal et al. [7] highlight three specific areas that make BigBench unique when compared to the other big data benchmarks. Along with those three attributes (technology-agnostic, end-to-end benchmark as opposed to a microbenchmark, coverage of the workload to address variety aspect of big data), one other aspect that distinguishes BigBench from other big data benchmarks is that it has been endorsed and adopted by a standardized benchmark committee, TPC* (Transaction Processing Performance Council).

---

*Other names and brands may be claimed as property of others

In the database world, TPC is the organization that is responsible for defining, publishing, auditing, and maintaining database benchmarks. TPCx-BB* was originally created in 2016 to showcase Hadoop style big-data analytics cluster Scale Out scenarios. It is based on a scientific proposal, BigBench, which was later adopted by TPC as an industry-standard benchmark [42]. The mostly read query mix and data consistency guidelines make it very friendly to scale-out Hadoop style implementations. It is unique compared to other influential database benchmarks defined by TPC in two ways. First, the other benchmarks such as TPC-H*, TPC-DS* are pure SQL benchmarks while TPCx-BB includes additional processing paradigms (machine learning and natural language processing) and data formats (unstructured and semi-structured) which emulates the text of user product reviews and web clickstream logs for an e-commerce site. BigBench uses this data for a number of machine learning and natural language processing queries to mine the reviews for interesting artifacts, data classification and clustering. Second, TPCxBB is an express benchmark which means that it not only comes with a specification document listing functional requirements, but also offers a ready to use executable kit that can be quickly deployed and used for benchmarking [24]. The original implementation of BigBench uses Hadoop and Hive [15].

Since its adoption by TPC, several organizations have published results of their studies using this benchmark to demonstrate competitiveness of their products in the big data market [10–13,19]. However, all of these contributions address a cluster-based configuration with data processing split across multiple nodes. The original TPCx-BB implementation provided on the TPC site also uses Hadoop-based framework and processing engine, Hive that requires a cluster setup. Rabl et al. [43] provide a proof of concept of running 30 BigBench queries on a Teradata Aster Database which executes queries using SQL-MR (Map Reduce) interface. The tests were conducted on a 8 node cluster.

Certain database use cases such as those emulated by TPCx-BB/BigBench with limited data sharing dependencies are amenable to scale-out and achieve performance benefits by parallelizing over a cluster of [typically cheaper] servers working together to process "large" to "enormous" databases. This is in contrast to traditional OLAP benchmarks like TPC-H which feature more data sharing dependencies and showcase the scale up potential of a single [typically more expensive] server being able efficiently process "medium" to "large" databases. The definition of "medium", "large", and "enormous" datasets is quite subjective and changes over time leaving a fair amount of overlap between use cases designed for scale-out via Hadoop type design and scale-up via traditional database design. With the advancements in hardware technologies and how the database performance is heavily influenced by the underlying resources available to it, we investigate the potential of running BigBench on a single node platform as opposed to a cluster-based configuration.

We present our preliminary results from running BigBench on a system powered by Intel technologies and a relational database engine, Microsoft* SQL Server* 2019 (pre-release). The goal is to demonstrate advanced analytics capabilities and performance of SQL Server* 2019 and reinforce the position that scale-up remains an option for an important subset of database sizes. We make the following two contributions:

1. We present the results of running all 30 BigBench queries over a relational database engine and a single node configuration powered by Intel technologies. It serves to illustrate the functional capabilities of Microsoft* SQL Server* engine for processing queries that go beyond pure relational, SQL paradigm.
2. We present our preliminary results from experiments designed to understand the impact of increase in input dataset size on query runtime. We analyze the results across 1 TB and 3 TB. We further analyze the runtime behavior of a subset of queries over 3 TB to understand their resource consumption requirements (CPU/IO/memory) on a single node system.

It is important to note that we do not reference any official TPCx-BB benchmark metrics and our results only include query execution times since official metrics reporting is only permitted in TPC-audited results.

The remainder of this paper is organized as follows. Section 2 covers the necessary background concepts including Microsoft* SQL Server* 2019 advanced features that make it amenable to big data workloads such as BigBench and an overview of BigBench data model and queries. We discuss our single node based experimental setup in Sect. 3 with our results in Sect. 4. Section 5 presents the work related to big data benchmarking and compares our initial results with existing academic studies that have all been over cluster-based environment. Finally, Sect. 6 summarizes the paper with ideas for future work.

2   Background Concepts

In this section, we first present concepts that are important to understand the terms referenced later in the paper. These include (1) Microsoft SQL Server 2019 Extensibility Framework which enables execution of machine learning and natural language processing algorithms from within SQL Server, and (2) an overview of TPCxBB data model and queries.

Microsoft SQL Server Extensibility Framework. Using machine learning libraries to build prediction and forecasting models and perform statistical operations is a common scenario these days and R and Python are the two most popular languages used for machine learning. However, there are two inherent challenges while processing data using R/Python libraries: (1) complete data needs to be loaded in memory before any computation can be performed, (2) data needs to be available/moved to the server where R/Python runtimes are installed. Microsoft alleviates these issues for the data resident in SQL Server by introducing external, machine learning execution engines (R/Python) and libraries as a part of SQL Server offering. This feature is called machine learning extensibility framework and gives user the ability to execute code in an external runtime engine without leaving SQL Server environment.

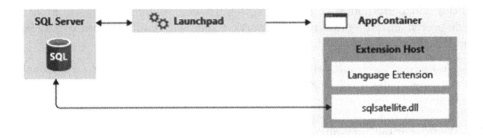

Fig. 1. Architecture Diagram for Microsoft* SQL Server* Third Party (Java) Extensibility Framework [38]

Starting with SQL Server* 2016, Microsoft introduced extensibility framework as an add-on to the core database engine thus allowing execution of machine learning algorithms implemented in R from within SQL Server*. Microsoft's implementations of machine learning algorithms (RevoScaleR library) allows processing of datasets that may not completely fit in memory [39]. BigBench includes five machine learning queries (5, 20, 25, 26, 28) covering clustering, logistic regression, and classification. SQL Server* 2019 added support for yet another external runtime engine, Java, to the extensibility framework that now allows the user to run pre-compiled Java code fully integrated within core database query execution [40]. BigBench workload includes four queries (10, 18, 19, 27) which require the use of open-source java libraries. Having built-in support for java extensions and machine learning algorithms within SQL Server allows efficient execution and use of those libraries for benchmarking SQL Server database system using the bigbench workload.

Figure 1 shows the architecture for extensibility framework (specifically Java). Machine learning algorithms in R or Python also uses similar framework with a few differences explained as follows. There are essentially three major components that are involved in execution of R, Python, or Java code from within SQL Server. These include Launchpad, external runtime process, and SqlSatellite. The data exchange between SQL Server and external runtime is managed by SqlSatellite. A call to an external runtime process from SQL Server is initiated using a built-in stored procedure sp_execute_external_script provided by SQL Server. It initiates Launchpad which is a service that comes in packaged within SQL Server when we choose to include Machine Learning services with it. The launchpad service further starts a launcher dll which is either RLauncher.dll, PythonLauncher.dll, commonlauncher.dll depending on the external runtime user wishes to invoke. Microsoft allows only trusted launchers which are either published or certified by Microsoft. This constraint serves two purposes. First, the trusted launchers are guaranteed to meet performance and resource management requirements established by SQL Server. Second, the policy ensures security of the data residing in SQL Server. Although the external runtime executes in a separate process from SQL Server, but it is a part of the SQL server framework which facilitates data access and operations on the server. In case of external code based on Java, commonlauncher.dll initiates and manages a process ExtHost which performs two functions: (1) uses sqlsatellite for communication and providing data/scripts to the extension code from SQL Server, (2) hosts another module, Language Extension which loads and communicates with JVM/Java-based user code.

A query in SQL Server that uses this extensibility framework and parallel execution mode may result in a large number of concurrent external processes being provisioned to facilitate parallelism and satisfy the query plan. We present two BigBench queries in appendix to highlight SQL Server* capabilities around both machine learning and natural language processing queries.

BigBench Workload. BigBench is the scientific research proposal which was later adopted by TPC to define an end-to-end, express benchmark, TPCx-BB. It is end-to-end because it is designed to evaluate performance of complete system as opposed to specific components or features of system under test. The benchmark models a fictitious retailer company selling products to customers via both physical and online stores. Twenty queries out of thirty in the workload address big data uses cases defined in McKinsey report [16] and the remaining ten queries are based on another decision-support benchmark defined by TPC, known as TPC-DS [10,14].

In our experiments, we demonstrate results of 30 BigBench queries when run sequentially with a single query running at any given point in time. This portion of the benchmark is called "power run". We capture data across two scale factors: 1000 and 3000 (1 TB and 3 TB). We collect each query's start, end, and execution times, and data on the resource utilization for the complete run of thirty queries using Microsoft Windows Performance Tool, perfmon [17]. These two datasets (perfmon and query runtime information) when analyzed together allows us to identify performance of each query over the complete duration of the run.

3   Experimental Setup

In this section, we describe the system setup that we used for running our experiments.

Hardware: We use a single node system running Windows Server 2016 Datacenter with a pre-release candidate of Microsoft SQL Server 2019 (CTP 2.4) installed as the database engine. The system is equipped with a 4-socket Intel® Xeon™ Platinum 8164 processor (2 GHz), each with 26 physical cores (total 104 cores), 3 TB main memory (48 DIMMs of 64 GB each, Frequency: 2400 MHz), and up to 40 TB of storage powered by Intel® SSDs. We believe that the current setup can be further tuned and there is potential for additional performance gains even with the current experiments. This paper focuses on presenting our initial results with the goal of showcasing the potential of scale-up configurations for big data workloads.

Our storage configuration is as follows. We have two storage bays with each bay populated with 24 Intel® SSD drives. The configuration is shown in Table 1. For each bay, we created RAID0 across 7 × 800 GB Intel® SSD drives for storing database files (10 TB total storage for database data files) and followed same configuration for tempdb drives (10 TB total storage for tempdb files). TempDB is configured and placed on separate drives from the database files (mdf) to isolate any the impact of any spills that may occur during query execution and RAID0 ensures good performance. At query runtime, data is read in parallel from the two data drives. Logical drives for storing raw data (flat files)were created using 6 × 800 GB Intel® SSD drives resulting in 4.36 TB storage on each storage bay. The remaining 4 SSDs of 1.5TB each were used to storage backup files. Lastly, for SQL log files, we included a single 800 GB Intel® SSD.

Table 1. Storage configuration details per storage bay

File type	SSD details	# of files per file type
Datafiles/Tempdb files/Flat files/Log	Intel® SSD DC S3700 (800 GB)	7/7/6/1
Backup files	Intel® SSD DC S3500 (1.6 TB)	4

Software. We enabled following two features for SQL Server: *lock pages in memory* and *large pages* (-T834 flag). Using large pages allows SQL Server to allocate allowed memory capacity at the time of startup and leverage CPU support for large virtual memory pages. The amount of memory allocated by SQL Server is equal to the minimum of 'max server memory' and physical memory available on the system. We set the max server memory to 2.4 TB for our experiments leaving ˜600 GB for other processes running on the system and execution of machine learning services from within SQL Server [41]. This practice improves query runtime since any memory required by a SQL query at runtime is not dynamically allocated from OS and initialized at the time of execution, but is readily available for use.

In terms of the available memory for query execution, we configured memory grant % in resource governor settings in SQL Server, setting it to 75% [22]. This ensures that each individual query can get maximum of 75% of the available memory to SQL Server instance.

4   Results

In this section, we present our results from running TPCxBB workload over two different scale factors: 1000, 3000. The experiments were conducted using the schema and query implementations that were specifically developed to run Big-Bench on SQL Server. Since the original implementation of BigBench supports Hive on MapReduce, queries had to be translated to enable running them on a relational engine, SQL Server in our case. We first present our data scalability experiments to understand the trends in query response times with increase in dataset size. Next, we discuss hardware resource utilization for a subset of queries which stresses different categories of resources. The methodology we followed for collecting data for each scale factor is a restart of SQL server in order to clear the buffer pool, followed by running all 30 queries sequentially in ascending order. Table 2 shows contribution of each query group (Pure SQL, ML, NLP) to the total runtime for 30 queries.

In terms of the total elapsed time for the complete run, 1 TB took 11,712 s ($\tilde{1}$95 min) while it took 44,376 s($\tilde{7}$39 min) with a 3 TB scale factor. Baru et al. [10] present results from running Big-Bench on a 6-node Cloudera cluster (20 cores and 128 GB main memory per node) with Hive/MapReduce framework. The 30 queries run in sequential order on their configuration took more than 1200 min. They also conducted similar study on a larger cluster with 544 nodes (12 cores and 48 GB main memory per node) and it took more than 200 min to run all 30 queries. Our experiments were run on a single node with lesser number of cores compared to

Table 2. Query runtimes % per query group vs. scale factor (ML and NLP queries scale better than SQL)

Group	1TB	3TB
NLP	63.89	41.90
ML	6.16	3.08
SQL	29.95	55.02

each of these cluster setups, yet finishes in less time. One of the reasons for this performance gain can be attributed to the foundational schema-based nature of relational databases. In Hadoop based systems, data is directly loaded onto HDFS in raw format without assigning any particular structure to it. While this often results in faster data load times, eventually the cost manifests at the query runtime since the data needs to be parsed to be able to pull only the required information.

In another study conducted in Frankfurt Big Data Lab [18], researchers used BigBench on a 4 node cluster with a total of 30 cores/60 threads and 128 GB total memory and using Hive/MapReduce as the execution framework. Absolute runtimes of all 30 queries were reported showing how a single query (query 4) by itself took more than 900 min. While our results can not be directly compared to the 4-node cluster setup because of the difference in hardware configurations, it still points to the potential of scale up configurations to run reasonably sized big data workloads.

The other important point to note in Table 2 is how SQL queries dominate the overall query runtime with increase in scale factor. We elaborate on this behavior in the discussion around scalability experiments for specific query groups.

Data Scalability for ML Queries. While Table 2 presents a high-level picture, next we focus on specific queries and organize our results per query group. Figure 2 shows the scaling behavior of all 30 queries over scale factors: 1000 and 3000. In this section, we focus on five machine learning queries (5, 20, 25, 26, 28). These queries cover clustering (20, 25, 26), regression and classification (5, 28). All the five queries scale well (up to 2x) with overall 3x increase in data size. While additional data from higher scale factors such as 10 and

30 TB are required to validate the trend further, the current performance we are observing can be attributed to following two areas within SQL Server: (1) the distributed and parallel computation of machine learning algorithms based on Microsoft implementations of these algorithms (RevoScaleR library) and the data exchange model used between SQL Server and Machine Learning engine. (2) multi-threaded execution of SQL queries which read and join data from the database tables to prepare input data for ML algorithms used later in the query.

Data Scalability for NLP Queries. In this section, we focus on the scaling behavior of natural language processing queries (10, 18, 19, 27) over scale factors: 1000 and 3000 in Fig. 2. Except query 18, rest three queries all scale linearly or even better with increase in scale factor. This seems to be an artifact of the amount of data that is actually passed to the java extensions framework for running the underlying pre-compiled Java code for negative sentiment analysis required in this query. Query 18 uses a set of SQL operators including joins, scans, and filters to prepare the data for sentiment analysis using Java and that input data shows 6× increase (4,013,405 vs. 24,634,495 rows) between scale factors 1000 and 3000. In this context, the query did scale well ($\tilde{4}$× for $\tilde{6}$× increase in data size). In our current set of experiments for NLP queries, we restricted parallelism and used lesser number of cores than available on the system and we plan to investigate this further to seek further optimizations.

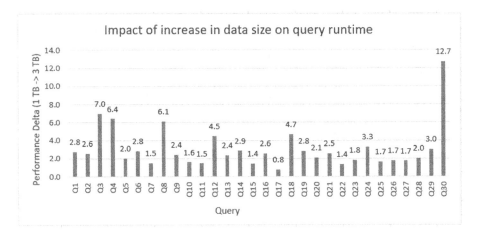

Fig. 2. Scalability of BigBench queries with increase in scale factor

Data Scalability for Pure SQL Queries. Having discussed NLP and ML queries, we now discuss scalability trends for SQL queries. Queries 3, 4, 8, 12, and 30 appear as the worst scaling queries among the 21 SQL queries. For query 8, even though the runtime increased by 6× from 1 TB to 3 TB, the absolute runtimes are relatively small (11.89 s for 1 TB and 77.87 s for 3 TB). Similarly query 12 takes 4× time to finish with 3x increase in data size. But again, the absolute run times are quite short (4.95/22.27 s). We will elaborate on the remaining three queries (3, 4, 30) and query 2 which seems to be scaling well. Figure 5 offers an insight into query characteristics for 3, 4 and 30.

Query 3 shows a 7× increase in runtime with only 3x increase in data size. This query reads data from one of the largest tables, web_clickstreams. On analyzing resource utilization pattern from performance monitor, the query consistently shows high CPU utilization (95%) over both scale factors with minimal disk activity. This points to the fact that running it on a system with even higher number of cores would potentially yield performance gains unless it is busy waiting, i.e. spinning. We plan to investigate this behavior further.

Query 4 is memory bound with spills to tempdb at both 1 TB and 3 TB scale factors. The memory grant information from query plans also shows the memory pressure observed during this query. The maximum available memory for any query based on our current settings is 1.3 TB where as query 4 desires 7 TB memory for 1 TB scale factor and it needs 22 TB for 3 TB. The CPU utilization for this query decreased from 37% on average on 1 TB to 21% on 3 TB, and Figures 3 and 4 show the reason behind this drop in utilization. It is either during the time period where query was writing to Tempdb or during a phase where there is no Tempdb activity but utilization is still low. This is coming from few single-threaded operations including stream aggregate. The high memory capacity requirement highlighted here captures the characteristic of the query as opposed to bottlenecks in underlying hardware or SQL Server processing model.

Query 30 shows similar resource utilization behavior as query 4. There is a drop in CPU utilization because of the increased I/O activity with Tempdb at 3 TB.

CPU Utilization over time

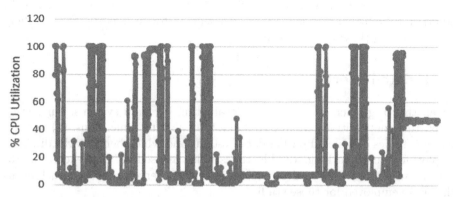

Fig. 3. CPU Utilization for query 4 on 3 TB scale factor (Low average utilization: 21%)

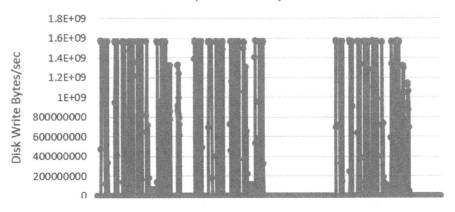

Fig. 4. TempDB write activity over 3 TB for query 4 - Disk Write Bytes/sec (overlaps with few areas of low CPU utilization from Figure 3)

While queries 3, 4, and 30 offer scope for further tuning for performance optimizations, there are also queries which showed positive scaling behavior (queries 2, 11, 15, 22). Queries 11, 15, 22 do not show much variation in their run times with the increase in data size. The runtime for query 2 is increased by 2.5× (101 vs. 259 s) while the input datasize went up three times. Analyzing the resource consumption for this query, we observe that the CPU utilization increased from 21% on average on 1 TB to 34% on average on 3 TB, highlighting the performance benefit gained from a system with high number of cores. However, there is also disk activity coming from spills to Tempdb (16 GB on 1 TB vs. 82 GB on 3 TB) that is impacting query runtime. But overall, query 2 does scale well.

This concludes our discussion on query behavior and performance over two different scale factors. While most of the queries scale well, we do identify few queries (3, 4, 30) that may have additional opportunities for optimization. In addition, running experiments over higher scale factor such as 10 TB might help in highlighting those areas as well.

5   Related Work

Given that BigBench is designed for evaluating big data systems, our survey of existing contributions is directed along the following dimensions: (1) identify related studies conducted on big data systems and which benchmarks did they employ for benchmarking, (2) identify studies focused on BigBench, and (3) performance studies focused on single node SQL Server and the benchmarks that were employed for those studies.

For the first case, there exists several contributions that focus on evaluating and comparing various SQL-on-Hadoop systems and many of them use either TPC-H, TPC-DS inspired benchmarks [1–3,36], or microbenchmarks as

Query		CPU Utilization	DataDB		TempDB	
			Data read (GB)	Data written (GB)	Data Read (GB)	Data Written (GB)
3	1 TB	95%	3.03	0.00	1.74	1.15
4		37%	2.58	0.00	703.00	702.00
30		91%	0.32	0.00	0.00	0.00
3	3 TB	97%	9.44	0.00	5.50	2.48
4		21%	8.28	0.00	9512.00	9521.00
30		34%	0.00	0.00	3920.00	3924.00

Fig. 5. Processor/Disk Characteristics of worst scaling SQL queries - 3, 4, 30

described in Sect. 1 [5,6,8,9]. Floratou et al. [1] study the performance differences of two SQL engines - Hive and Impala against data stored in Hadoop using TPC-H and TPC-DS based workloads. Chen et al. [3] present a performance evaluation of five SQL-on-Hadoop solutions using a subset of TPC-DS queries. Similarly, Poggi et al. [2] present results of a performance study characterizing SQL-on-Hadoop solutions provided by four major cloud providers using TPC-H.

All of these contributions study big data systems but none of them uses BigBench which includes a broader set of processing paradigms (machine learning, natural language processing) and variety of data formats including semi-structured (web-clickstreams) and unstructured data (product reviews) data. Also, BigBench has support for up to petabyte scale databases while TPC-H or TPC-DS are limited to 100 TB. The current publications of TPC-H/DS concentrate primarily on 10 TB databases while for BigBench we have a result with 30 TB of data as well [19,37].

Next, we summarize few research studies that have used BigBench over different frameworks to evaluate performance of hardware and software components of their systems. In a recent study in 2017, Poggi et al. [11] complemented their prior work by looking at BigBench to characterize Spark and Hive performance across different PaaS (Platform-as-a-Service) offerings. There have been few studies and official submissions at TPC that employ BigBench to analyze and compare performance of Big Data offerings [18,19]. But all of these evaluations are over cluster-based environments. We are not aware of any studies that have explored BigBench on a single node configuration and a relational database engine such as Microsoft* SQL Server*. Wang et al. [12] share results on running BigBench on a 9-node Cloudera cluster. Their experiments are designed to understand the impact of core and disk scaling and tuning CPU frequency on query response time. While we are yet to do similar studies, our preliminary results show how queries 2, 4, and 30 are impacted by disk bandwith since we observe spills to Tempdb for each of these queries (primarily queries 4 and 30). Cao et al. [13] present results over a cluster-based configuration (two cluster setups - 9 node, 60 node) running

BigBench for Hive over MapReduce. Complete run of 30 queries on their 9-node cluster (total of 216 cores and 2.2 TB memory) takes 34,076 s while 3 TB run on our system takes 44,376 s. Now, we do observe optimization opportunities which if implemented can improve the total runtime and the core count on the cluster setup is almost double of what we have on our system. The paper does not show individual query times which would have enabled us to compare each query's performance. CPU intensive queries siuch as query 3 would significantly benefit from higher number of cores. Baru et al. [10] looked at 1 TB scale factor over a 6-node cluster configuration with a total of 120 cores and 768 GB main memory but their total runtime is still much higher than our system. Authors have mentioned that it is raw, out-of-the-box performance and the runtimes could potentially improve with tuning. The study done by Ivanov et al. [18] presents detailed analysis and results on running BigBench over a 4-node cluster using Hive and Spark frameworks and across multiple scale factors. Given that the configuration had a total of 128 GB memory for the 1 TB BigBench scale factor, it is not practical to compare their runtimes with our results. The authors also present resource utilization of a subset of queries and it would be worthwhile to study it and identify if there are any insights that can be gained about the core characteristics of the workload from it.

On our third survey dimension identifying contributions which have looked at benchmarking single node SQL Server*, the evaluations have been based on TPC-H or TPC-DS [4,20,21,37]. Our work is the first attempt to measure and demonstrate performance of Microsoft* SQL Server* 2019 (pre release) on the Intel® Xeon^{TM} processor 8164 product family using BigBench as the workload.

6   Conclusions and Future Work

This paper presents our experiences and initial experiments using BigBench on a single node configuration powered by Intel technologies and a relational database system, Microsoft* SQL Server*. Our initial results on 1 and 3 TB data sizes demonstrate advanced capabilities of Microsoft SQL Server 2019 (pre-release candidate) to handle heterogeneous and volume aspects of big data and how even a single-node, relational database configuration can scale up to big data workloads.

Given that this paper is an early study, there exists several avenues for future research. Firstly, collecting and analyzing performance over higher scale factors which are even more representative of the data volume aspect in big data is an ongoing study. Secondly, profiling the benchmark to assess sensitivities of BigBench queries to the number of cores, core frequency, memory, and storage in a single node environment is another promising direction. There are similar studies done over cluster-based environments. Combined with the existing studies on cluster-based configurations, these results can be used by practitioners to compare the query resource requirements and processing methodology in a single vs. multi-node configuration, and thus understand the impact of these different architectures on the performance of big data workloads. Also, it would be important to identify optimal platform configuration settings since the current configuration may have been overconfigured for the scale factors considered in this study. Another interesting direction would be to expand analysis to address multiple concurrent streams. Richins et al. [23] have done a comprehensive analysis using BigBench on a cluster-based configuration. The authors have identified thread level parallelism as a major bottleneck. It would be worthwhile to investigate if similar behaviour shows up on single-node setup as well and drive further analysis based on the results.

Acknowledgements. We thank Harish Sukhwani, Mahmut Aktasoglu, Hamesh Patel from Intel, and Jasraj Dange and Tri Tran from Microsoft Corporation for their constructive feedback that helped to improve the paper. We are immensely grateful to Nellie Gustafsson from Microsoft for her help in revising machine learning queries to match the benchmark specification. We thank Arun Gurunathan, Sumit Kumar, Nellie Gustafsson, and Gary Ericson for their inputs on revising the section on extensibility framework. The authors would also like to acknowledge Vaishali Paliwal and Charles Winstead from Intel Corporation for their overall support and project guidance, Sridharan Sakthivelu for the technical discussions, and Ketki Haridas for her early contributions to the work.

Appendix

In this section we present two BigBench queries (10, 20) to highlight SQL Server capabilities towards implementing queries that use machine learning algorithms and third-party libraries such as Java. Query 10 is a sentiment analysis query that uses java libraries and query 20 employs a k-means clustering algorithm in machine learning. While we used SQL Server* CTP 2.4 version for our experiments, the code shown here is based on the latest CTP 3.0 version to highlight the latest feature implementations supported by Microsoft at the time of writing of this paper [40].

Query 10 - Using Java based libraries and user code

```
/*
Query description
For all products, extract sentences from its product reviews that
    contain positive or negative sentiment and display for each item the
    sentiment polarity of the extracted sentences (POS OR NEG) and the
    sentence and word in sentence leading to this classification*/

CREATE OR ALTER PROCEDURE [dbo].[query10] @param1 nvarchar(20), @param2
    nvarchar(15) , @param3 bigint, @param4 nvarchar(50), @param5
    nvarchar(20), @query nvarchar(400)
AS
BEGIN
-- Saving query results in a table
drop table if exists Q10Results;
Create table Q10Results
```

```
(
itemid bigint
,sentence varchar(4000)
,sentiment varchar(3)
,token varchar(20)
)
--The method invoked in the Java code is always the "execute" method
EXEC sp_execute_external_script
  @language = N'Java'
, @script = N'Query10.SentimentAnalysis'
, @input_data_1 = @query
, @params = N'@tablename nvarchar(20), @serverInstanceName nvarchar(15)
    , @port bigint, @modelsParentFolder nvarchar(50), @databaseName
    nvarchar(20)'
, @tablename = @param1
, @serverInstanceName = @param2
, @port= @param3
, @modelsParentFolder= @param4
, @databaseName= @param5
with result sets ((itemsk bigint, sentence varchar(4000), sentiment
    varchar(3), word varchar(20)));
END
GO

--Now execute the above stored procedure and provide the input
    parameters and an input query
EXECUTE [dbo].[query10] N'Q10Results', N'SQL2019CTP3', 11212,
    N'C:\NLPSQLCTP25', N'TPCxBB_1GB_2019', N'SELECT pr_item_sk,
    pr_review_content FROM product_reviews option(maxdop 20)'
GO
END
```

Query 20 - Using machine learning k-means algorithm

```
DROP PROCEDURE IF EXISTS [q20_create_customer_return_clusters]
GO
CREATE PROCEDURE [dbo].[q20_create_customer_return_clusters]
AS
/*
```
This procedure uses R to classify customers into different groups based
    on their purchase & return history.

Query description
Customer segmentation for return analysis: Customers are separated along
    the following dimensions: return frequency, return order ratio
    (total number of orders partially or fully returned versus the total
    number of orders), return item ratio (total number of items returned
    versus the number of items purchased), return amount ration (total
    monetary amount of items returned versus the amount purchased),

```
    return order ratio. Consider the store returns during a given year
    for the computation. */
BEGIN

DECLARE @model_generation_duration float
  , @predict_duration float
  , @instance_name nvarchar(100) = @@SERVERNAME
  , @database_name nvarchar(128) = DB_NAME()

-- Input query to geenerate the purchase history & return metrics
  , @input_query nvarchar(max) = N'
SELECT
  ss_customer_sk AS customer,
  ROUND(COALESCE(returns_count / NULLIF(1.0*orders_count, 0), 0), 7) AS
      orderRatio,
  ROUND(COALESCE(returns_items / NULLIF(1.0*orders_items, 0), 0), 7) AS
      itemsRatio,
  ROUND(COALESCE(returns_money / NULLIF(1.0*orders_money, 0), 0), 7) AS
      monetaryRatio,
  COALESCE(returns_count, 0) AS frequency
FROM
  (
    SELECT
      ss_customer_sk,
      -- return order ratio
      COUNT_BIG(DISTINCT ss_ticket_number) AS orders_count,
      -- return ss_item_sk ratio
      COUNT_BIG(ss_item_sk) AS orders_items,
      -- return monetary amount ratio
      SUM( ss_net_paid ) AS orders_money
    FROM store_sales s
    GROUP BY ss_customer_sk
  ) orders
  LEFT OUTER JOIN
  (
    SELECT
      sr_customer_sk,
      -- return order ratio
      COUNT_BIG(DISTINCT sr_ticket_number) as returns_count,
      -- return ss_item_sk ratio
      COUNT_BIG(sr_item_sk) as returns_items,
      -- return monetary amount ratio
      SUM( sr_return_amt ) AS returns_money
    FROM store_returns
    GROUP BY sr_customer_sk
  ) returned ON ss_customer_sk=sr_customer_sk
'

EXECUTE sp_execute_external_script
        @language = N'R'
```

```
            , @script = N'
# Define the connection string
connStr <- paste("Driver=SQL Server;Server=", instance_name,
    ";Database=", database_name, ";Trusted_Connection=true;", sep="");
cc <- RxInSqlServer(connectionString=connStr)
rxSetComputeContext(cc)

customer_returns <- RxSqlServerData(sqlQuery = input_query, colClasses =
    c(customer = "numeric", orderRatio = "numeric",
                            itemsRatio = "numeric", monetaryRatio =
                                "numeric", frequency =
                                "numeric"),connectionString =
                                connStr);

# Output table to hold the customer group mappings
return_cluster = RxSqlServerData(table = "customer_return_clusters",
    connectionString = connStr);

# set.seed for random number generator for predictability
set.seed(10);

# generate clusters using rxKmeans and output key / cluster to a table
model_generation_duration <- system.time(clust <- rxKmeans( ~ orderRatio
    + itemsRatio + monetaryRatio + frequency, customer_returns,
    numClusters = 10
                , outFile = return_cluster, outColName = "cluster",
                    extraVarsToWrite = c("customer"), overwrite =
                    TRUE))[3];
'
    , @input_data_1 = N''
    , @params = N'@instance_name nvarchar(100), @database_name
        nvarchar(128),@input_query nvarchar(max),
        @model_generation_duration float OUTPUT'
    , @instance_name = @instance_name
    , @database_name = @database_name
    , @input_query=@input_query
    , @model_generation_duration = @model_generation_duration OUTPUT;

    PRINT CONCAT(N'Model generation time: ', @model_generation_duration,
        ' seconds.');

END
GO
exec [dbo].[q20_create_customer_return_clusters]
```

References

1. Floratou, A., Minhas, U.F., Özcan, F.: SQL-on-Hadoop: full circle back to shared-nothing database architectures. Proc. VLDB Endowment **7**(12), 1295–1306 (2014)
2. Poggi, N., et al.: The state of SQL-on-Hadoop in the Cloud. In: 2016 IEEE International Conference on Big Data (Big Data), pp. 1432–1443. IEEE, December 2016
3. Chen, Y., et al.: A study of SQL-on-hadoop systems. In: Zhan, J., Han, R., Weng, C. (eds.) BPOE 2014. LNCS, vol. 8807, pp. 154–166. Springer, Cham (2014). https://doi.org/10.1007/978-3-319-13021-7_12
4. Larson, P.A., et al.: Enhancements to SQL server column stores. In: Proceedings of the 2013 ACM SIGMOD International Conference on Management of Data, pp. 1159–1168. ACM, June 2013
5. Ivanov, T., et al.: Big data benchmark compendium. In: Nambiar, R., Poess, M. (eds.) TPCTC 2015. LNCS, vol. 9508, pp. 135–155. Springer, Cham (2016). https://doi.org/10.1007/978-3-319-31409-9_9
6. Han, R., John, L.K., Zhan, J.: Benchmarking big data systems: a review. In: IEEE Transactions on Services Computing, pp. 580–597 (2017)
7. Ghazal, A., et al.: Bigbench V2: the new and improved bigbench. In: 2017 IEEE 33rd International Conference on Data Engineering (ICDE), pp. 1225–1236. IEEE, April 2017
8. https://github.com/c9n/hadoop/blob/master/hadoop-mapreduce-project/hadoop-mapreduce-client/hadoop-mapreduce-client-jobclient/src/test/java/org/apache/hadoop/hdfs/NNBench.java . Accessed 29 May 2019
9. https://www.ibm.com/support/knowledgecenter/en/SSGSMK_7.1.1/mapreduce_integration/map_reduce_terasort_example.html . Accessed 29 May 2019
10. Baru, C., et al.: Discussion of bigbench: a proposed industry standard performance benchmark for big data. In: Nambiar, R., Poess, M. (eds.) TPCTC 2014. LNCS, vol. 8904, pp. 44–63. Springer, Cham (2015). https://doi.org/10.1007/978-3-319-15350-6_4
11. Poggi, N., Montero, A., Carrera, D.: Characterizing bigbench queries, hive, and spark in multi-cloud environments. In: Nambiar, R., Poess, M. (eds.) TPCTC 2017. LNCS, vol. 10661, pp. 55–74. Springer, Cham (2018). https://doi.org/10.1007/978-3-319-72401-0_5
12. Wang K., Bian B., Cao P., Riess M. https://www.intel.com/content/dam/www/public/.../cofluent-tpcx-bb-express-paper.pdf. Accessed 1 June 2019
13. Cao, P., et al.: From BigBench to TPCx-BB: standardization of a big data benchmark. In: Nambiar, R., Poess, M. (eds.) TPCTC 2016. LNCS, vol. 10080, pp. 24–44. Springer, Cham (2017). https://doi.org/10.1007/978-3-319-54334-5_3
14. TPC-DS, http://www.tpc.org/tpcds/. Accessed 29 May 2019
15. Big Data Benchmark for BigBench. https://github.com/intel-hadoop/Big-Data-Benchmark-for-Big-Bench. Accessed 29 May 2019
16. Big data: The next frontier for innovation, competition, and productivity. https://www.mckinsey.com/business-functions/digital-mckinsey/our-insights/big-data-the-next-frontier-for-innovation. Accessed 29 May 2019
17. Windows Performance Monitor Overview. https://techcommunity.microsoft.com/t5/Ask-The-Performance-Team/Windows-Performance-Monitor-Overview/ba-p/375481. Accessed 29 May 2019
18. Ivanov, T., Beer, M.G.: Evaluating hive and spark SQL with BigBench. arXiv preprint arXiv:1512.08417 (2015)

19. TPCx-BB - Top Ten Performance Results. http://www.tpc.org/tpcx-bb/results/tpcxbb_perf_results.asp. Accessed 29 May 2019
20. TPC-DS Top Performance Results. http://www.tpc.org/tpcds/results/tpcds_perf_results.asp. Accessed 29 May 2019
21. Sen, R., Ramachandra, K.: Characterizing resource sensitivity of database workloads. In: 2018 IEEE International Symposium on High Performance Computer Architecture (HPCA), pp. 657–669. IEEE, February 2018
22. View Resource Governor Properties. https://docs.microsoft.com/en-us/sql/relational-databases/resource-governor/view-resource-governor-properties?view=sql-server-2017. Accessed 29 May 2019
23. Richins, D., Ahmed, T., Clapp, R., Reddi, V.J.: Amdahl's law in big data analytics: alive and kicking in TPCx-BB (BigBench). In: 2018 IEEE International Symposium on High Performance Computer Architecture (HPCA), pp. 630–642. IEEE, February 2018
24. Huppler, K., Johnson, D.: TPC express – a new path for TPC benchmarks. In: Nambiar, R., Poess, M. (eds.) TPCTC 2013. LNCS, vol. 8391, pp. 48–60. Springer, Cham (2014). https://doi.org/10.1007/978-3-319-04936-6_4
25. Apache Hadoop. https://hadoop.apache.org/. Accessed 30 May 2019
26. Apache Spark. https://spark.apache.org/. Accessed 30 May 2019
27. Apache Cassandra. http://cassandra.apache.org/. Accessed 30 May 2019
28. Apache Hive. https://hive.apache.org/. Accessed 30 May 2019
29. Microsoft Azure HDInsight. https://azure.microsoft.com/en-us/services/hdinsight/. Accessed 30 May 2019
30. Teradata Aster. https://downloads.teradata.com/aster. Accessed 30 May 2019
31. Bakshi, K.: Considerations for big data: architecture and approach. In: 2012 IEEE Aerospace Conference (2012)
32. Jia, Z., et al.: Characterizing and subsetting big data workloads. In: 2014 IEEE International Symposium on Workload Characterization (IISWC), pp. 191–201. IEEE, October 2014
33. Malik, M., Rafatirad, S., Homayoun, H.: System and architecture level characterization of big data applications on big and little core server architectures. ACM Trans. Model. Performance Eval. Comput. Syst. (TOMPECS) 3(3), 14 (2018)
34. Madden, S.: From databases to big data. IEEE Internet Comput. 16(3), 4–6 (2012)
35. Chen, J., et al.: Big data challenge: a data management perspective. Front. Comput. Sci. 7(2), 157–164 (2013)
36. Santos, M.Y., et al.: Evaluating SQL-on-Hadoop for big data warehousing on not-so-good hardware. In: Proceedings of the 21st International Database Engineering & Applications Symposium, pp. 242–252. ACM, July 2017
37. TPC-H Top Performance Results. http://www.tpc.org/tpch/results/tpch_perf_results.asp. Accessed 30 May 2019
38. Extensibility architecture in SQL Server Language Extensions. https://docs.microsoft.com/en-us/sql/language-extensions/concepts/extensibility-framework?view=sqlallproducts-allversions. Accessed 29 July 29 2019
39. RevoScaleR package. https://docs.microsoft.com/en-us/machine-learning-server/r-reference/revoscaler/revoscaler. Accessed 11 June 2019
40. What new in SQL Server Language Extensions?. https://docs.microsoft.com/en-us/sql/language-extensions/language-extensions-whats-new?view=sqlallproducts-allversions. Accessed 11 June 2019
41. Resource governance for machine learning in SQL Server. https://docs.microsoft.com/en-us/sql/advanced-analytics/administration/resource-governance?view=sql-server-2017. Accessed 13 June 2019

42. Ghazal, A., et al.: BigBench: towards an industry standard benchmark for big data analytics. In: Proceedings of the 2013 ACM SIGMOD International Conference on Management of Data, pp. 1197–1208. ACM, June 2013
43. Rabl, T., et al.: BigBench specification V0.1. In: Rabl, T., Poess, M., Baru, C., Jacobsen, H.-A. (eds.) WBDB -2012. LNCS, vol. 8163, pp. 164–201. Springer, Heidelberg (2014). https://doi.org/10.1007/978-3-642-53974-9_14

CBench-Dynamo: A Consistency Benchmark for NoSQL Database Systems

Miguel Diogo[1]([✉]) [iD], Bruno Cabral[2] [iD], and Jorge Bernardino[2,3] [iD]

[1] Department of Informatics Engineering, Universidade de Coimbra, Coimbra, Portugal
mdiogo@student.dei.uc.pt
[2] Centre of Informatics and Engineering, University of Coimbra – CISUC, Coimbra, Portugal
bcabral@dei.uc.pt
[3] Polytechnic of Coimbra – ISEC, Coimbra, Portugal
jorge@isec.pt

Abstract. Nowadays software architects face new challenges because Internet has grown to a point where popular websites are accessed by hundreds of millions of people on a daily basis. One powerful machine is no longer economically viable and resilient in order to handle such outstanding traffic and architectures have since been migrated to horizontal scaling. However, traditional databases, usually associated with a relational design, were not ready for horizontal scaling. Therefore, NoSQL databases have proposed to fill the gap left by their predecessors. This new paradigm is proposed to better serve currently massive scaled-up Internet usage when consistency is no longer a top priority and a high available service is preferable. Cassandra is a NoSQL database based on the Amazon Dynamo design. Dynamo-based databases are designed to run in a cluster while offering high availability and eventual consistency to clients when subject to network partition events. Therefore, the main goal of this work is to propose CBench-Dynamo, the first consistency benchmark for NoSQL databases. Our proposed benchmark correlates properties, such as performance, consistency, and availability, in different consistency configurations while subjecting the System Under Test to network partition events.

Keywords: Consistency · Availability · Network fault tolerance · NoSQL databases · Benchmark · Dynamo · Cassandra

1 Introduction

The Internet has grown to a point where billions of people have access to it, not only from a desktop but also from smartphones, smartwatches, and even other servers and services. Nowadays systems need to scale. The monolithic database architecture, based on a powerful server, does not guarantee the high availability and network partition required by today's web-scale systems, as demonstrated by the CAP (Consistency, Availability, and Network Partition Tolerance) theorem [1]. Strong consistency is a property that has been relaxed to achieve a more scalable database system. Relational databases foundations were designed to support strong consistency, where each transaction must be immediately

© Springer Nature Switzerland AG 2020
R. Nambiar and M. Poess (Eds.): TPCTC 2019, LNCS 12257, pp. 84–98, 2020.
https://doi.org/10.1007/978-3-030-55024-0_6

committed, and all clients will operate over consistent data states. Also, reads from the same object will present the same value to all client requests. Although strong consistency is the ideal requirement for a database, it deeply compromises horizontal-scalability. Horizontal scalability is a more affordable approach when compared to vertical scalability. It enables higher throughput and data distribution across multiple database nodes. On the other hand, vertical scalability relies on a single powerful database server to store data and answer all requests. Although horizontal scaling may seem preferable, CAP theorem presents that when network partitions occur, one has to opt between availability and consistency [2]. Horizontal scaling has inspired a new category of databases called NoSQL. These systems have been created with a common requirement in mind, scalability. Several NoSQL designs prioritize high-availability over a more relaxed consistency strategy, an approach known as BASE (Basically Available, Soft-state and Eventually consistent) [3].

Although performance frameworks, such as YCSB [4], have been developed for benchmarking NoSQL databases, they lack a consistency tier to fully compare the tradeoffs annunciated by the CAP theorem.

In this work, we propose CBench-Dynamo, a benchmark for testing consistency and availability on a horizontal-scaled system. We also define how to address the main quality attributes of a benchmark, i.e. Relevance, Reproducibility, Fairness, Verifiability, and Usability [5]. Our goal is to extract different measurements on performance, consistency, and availability with different consistency configurations of the System Under Test (SUT) while subjecting this system to network partition events.

Finally, we will run the proposed benchmark on a Cassandra cluster and discuss the resulting measurements.

2 Related Work

Cooper et al. [6] propose the YCSB (Yahoo! Cloud Serving Benchmark), a benchmarking framework for cloud serving systems. It comes to fill the need for performance comparisons between NoSQL databases and keep tracking of their tradeoffs such as read performance versus write performance, latency versus durability, and synchronous versus asynchronous replication. Although benchmark tiers such as performance and scaling are included in YCSB, it lacks other tiers such as availability and consistency.

Bailis et al. [7] suggest an approach that predicts the expected consistency of an eventually consistent Dynamo data store using models the authors developed called Probabilistically Bounded Staleness (PBS). This approach lacks a benchmark framework.

The work of Bermbach and Tai [8] propose a benchmark methodology on Amazon's cloud database AWS S3. This is the closest work of what we aim to do in this paper. Bermbach and Tai project a long-term monitor system on AWS S3 to evaluate how this service changes its consistency ability over time and the benchmark approach used can be easily extended for other usages and databases as we aim to demonstrate in our paper.

Patil et al. [9] propose a benchmark architecture that evaluates time to consistency. The authors extend the YCSB framework and add support to distributed architectures by using ZooKeeper for coordination. However, since 2011, development of the YCSB++

framework has been discontinued, and Cassandra support is still in progress. Only HBase and Acumulo support are available, but they are outdated as major releases of both databases have been released. YCSB++ also does not fully evaluate consistency trade-offs based on the CAP theorem as YCSB++ does not support network partition events.

Our work differentiates from the rest by proposing the first NoSQL consistency benchmarking framework and testing it on Cassandra. To the best of our knowledge, no such framework compares consistency levels to other quality attributes such as availability and performance while subjecting the target system to network partition events.

3 Dynamo

Dynamo design and implementation were first introduced by Amazon as a highly available key-value storage system [10]. Since then, Amazon has built many cloud services emerged around this design, e.g. Amazon DynamoDB and Amazon S3.

Dynamo prioritizes eventual consistency, targeted to applications that need an "always writeable" database where no updates are rejected due to failures or concurrent writes.

Dynamo was designed to scale incrementally, hence it was designed with a partition mechanism in mind. Dynamo's partition mechanism is based on a consistent hashing to distribute the load across multiple data nodes. The output of this hashing function can be illustrated as a ring as seen in Fig. 1, in which the highest output wraps around the smallest one. Each node is assigned a random value within the range of the hashing function. To know which node will store a given data value, the correspondent key of this value is hashed. Then, we walk the ring clockwise, from the smallest to the largest number, to find the first node with a position larger than the hashing result.

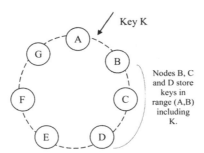

Fig. 1. Partitioning and replication of keys in Dynamo ring [10].

4 Consistency in Dynamo-Based Databases

Amazon's Dynamo based databases such as Cassandra, all use the same variant of quorum-style replication [11]. Quorum-style replication is associated with a replication factor N, i.e. the number of replicas that some data eventual will be in. Read and write consistency can be configured as follows, *ONE*, *QUORUM*, or *ALL*.

The following configurations describe the differences between the three *write consistency* levels for Dynamo-based database systems [12]:

- *ALL*: data is written on all replica nodes in the cluster before the coordinator node acknowledges the client. Therefore, this configuration has: *Strong Consistency* and *High latency*.
- *QUORUM*: data is written on a given number of replica nodes in the cluster before the coordinator node acknowledges the client, where this number is called the quorum. This configuration has: *Eventual Consistency* and *Low latency*.
- *ONE*: data is written in at least one replica node. This configuration has: *Eventual Consistency* and *Low latency*.

Analogous to the write consistency levels, the following configuration constants describe the differences between the three *read consistency* levels for Dynamo-based database systems [12]:

- *ALL*. The coordinator node returns the requested data to the client only after all replicas have responded. This configuration has: *Strong consistency* and *Less availability*.
- *QUORUM*. The coordinator node returns the requested data to the client only after a quorum of replicas has responded. This configuration has: *Eventual consistency* and *High-availability*.
- *ONE*. The coordinator node returns the requested data to the client from the closest replica node. This configuration has: *Eventual consistency* and *High availability*.

Under normal operation, i.e. without network partition events, given the number of replicas required for a read operation as R, the number of replicas required for a write operation as W, and the replication factor as N, Dynamo-based databases guarantee consistency when [11]:

$$R + W > N \tag{1}$$

Given R_{Quorum} and W_{Quorum}, as Read Consistency and Write Consistency set to *QUORUM*, respectively, and the *floor* function that takes as input a real number and round it down to the closest integer. The conversion from the *QUORUM* notation to the R, W notation is as follows:

$$R_{QUORUM}, W_{QUORUM} = R, W = floor\left(\frac{N}{2} + 1\right) \tag{2}$$

Under abnormal operations where a network partition event had occurred, if consistency is set to strong, i.e. *ALL*, availability is compromised as the Fig. 2 illustrates. The scenario illustrated by Fig. 2 describes a situation where a read operation needs to involve the total number of replicas N in order to retrieve the data to the client. In case of a network partition, e.g. *node C* crashes, the coordinator of the request, *node A*, was not able to serve data, hence the total number of replicas had been involved in the operation, and the coordinator had no other option than announcing a lack of service availability to the client, resulting in a *TIMEOUT* response.

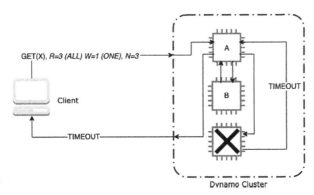

Fig. 2. Data request on abnormal operation where a node fails, and strong read consistency is set (i.e. *ALL*).

Under abnormal operations where a network partition event had occurred, if consistency is set to eventual configuration *(ONE)*, we achieve service availability even in the presence of a node crash as the Fig. 3 illustrates. The scenario illustrated by Fig. 3 describes a situation where a read operation only needs to involve one replica in order to retrieve the requested data to the client. Because only one replica had been involved, the response may not contain the latest data as this example suggests. Although consistent responses are not ensured, this configuration results in a high-available service.

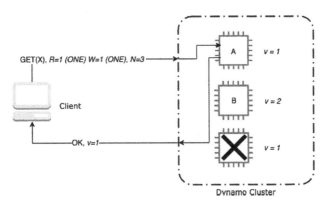

Fig. 3. Data request on abnormal operation where a node fails, and eventual read consistency is set (i.e. *ONE*).

For Dynamo-based databases, high availability does not necessarily ensures write persistence. When addressing the concept of availability, in terms of service availability and not data availability, i.e. when a request is made, a successful response is given even if such key does not exist anymore. The response is successful, even if the response refers to the inexistent of such resource. There may be the case when, for instance, a configuration of $W = 1$ *(ONE)* is set and the same node crashes right afterward, the data is lost and there is no acknowledgment to the client that such abnormality had happened. To avoid such events, W *values* greater than 1 increase data redundancy and, consequently, the probability of all replicas that contain the data fail is reduced.

5 CBench-Dynamo

A benchmark is a standardized tool to evaluate and compare competing systems or components according to specific characteristics. These characteristics can be performance, dependability, among others.

According to [5] the benchmarks can be categorized into three types: specification-based benchmarks, kit-based benchmarks, and a hybrid based on the latest two. Specification-based benchmarks are simulated based on a specific business problem by imposing certain functions that must be achieved, such as required input parameters and expected outcomes. This type of benchmark imposes a big development investment on presenting multiple implementations for the same problem and proceed with an evaluation of that set of development. While for specification-based benchmark, the specification is a set of rules implemented by the third party to load and run the benchmark. The Kit-based benchmarks use the specification as a guide for implementing the benchmark kit. A hybrid category can be provided mostly as a kit but allows some functions to be implemented depending on each individual benchmark run.

In this section, we propose CBench-Dynamo, a consistency benchmark that is a standard procedure to evaluate and compare consistency in the System Under Test (SUT). The specification we aim to present proposes a benchmark approach to test consistency and availability in Dynamo-based NoSQL databases while subjecting these systems to network partition events. Therefore, we aim to contribute towards standardizing consistency benchmarking and lead vendors to better understand which system better suits their requirements.

5.1 CBench-Dynamo Properties

Benchmark researching and industry participants describe a benchmark into the following properties [5]: Relevance, Reproducibility, Fairness, Verifiability, and Usability.

Although the proposed benchmark, CBench-Dynamo can be adapted to run in dedicated instances it has only been tested with Amazon EC2 instances. Some orchestration playbooks, such as easy instance setup, must be adapted to work on dedicated machines. However, we aim to make the system more generic and versatile in future work. For the present paper, our goal is to define the workload approach and present preliminary empirical results from the benchmark tests using this workload.

Relevance. Relevance is the most important property when defining a benchmark [5]. The relevance of a benchmark splits up into two dimensions, the spectrum of its applicability and the degree of relevance in the given area.

The CBench-Dynamo is designed to target all Dynamo-based databases and the area of relevance is the study of the properties consistency, availability and network partition tolerance, of a horizontal-distributed database system. This benchmark aims to be a framework to facilitate the decision process of choosing the most appropriate NoSQL database depending on the degree of performance, availability, consistency, and network fault tolerance required for running a given application.

Reproducibility. Reproducibility will be attained as CBench-Dynamo exports the instances' hardware and software facts via Ansible. In addition, the workload specifications will be also exported at the end of the associated run.

The goal of this extensive and detailed description is for other people to obtain identical results by configuring the whole system as described.

Fairness. Fairness is the ability of the results being supported by the system merit without artificial constraints. To reach fairness a set of artificial constraints must be consent and well defined. CBench-Dynamo defines the following constraints:

- The SUT must be a Dynamo-based NoSQL database system, e.g. Cassandra;
- The SUT must have the same hardware, network and operating system components when comparing benchmark test results targeting similar SUT;
- The Workload Coordinator must support a JVM to run the benchmark test and Python to analyze and translate the data into meaningful measurements;
- The fact that the Workload Coordinator uses Java and Python to coordinate the benchmark and post-process all the data, respectively, makes the system highly portable and therefore fair as JVM and Python based applications can run virtually in any system.

Verifiability. It is important that results are trustworthy. Results must be validated and decrease the possibility of chance or manipulation.

CBench-Dynamo results from academic work, all the workloads presented here were subject to peer-review by other researchers.

Usability. Usability is the degree of how easy a system is to use. The CBench-Dynamo has detailed instructions for making the benchmark easy to use and several layers of abstractions were taken into account so that only a minimum input is needed to start a benchmark test.

All the proposed benchmark modules are hosted on GitHub. There is a repository for each of these modules, modified YCSB [13], analyzer [14], and orchestration playbooks [15].

5.2 Architecture Specification

CBench-Dynamo is composed of a **Workload Coordinator**, a **Load Balancer** and a Dynamo cluster (**SUT**). All these components are orchestrated by the **orchestrator** via Ansible playbooks, as illustrated in Fig. 4.

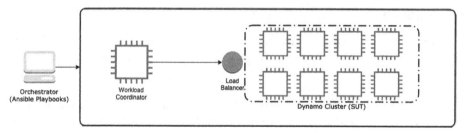

Fig. 4. CBench-Dynamo architecture specification.

Orchestrator. The *orchestrator* via Ansible playbooks allows the vendor to configure and run a benchmark test via the *Workload Coordinator*. The following configurations are needed prior a benchmark testing:

- IP addresses of the instances of the SUT;
- IP address of the load balancer that serves as the external gateway of the SUT;
- YCSB project home directory;
- Analyzer project home directory;
- Analysis results output directory;
- Ansible facts output directory;
- List of workload configurations with the following parameters: {*workload description, YCSB database driver descriptor (e.g. cassandra-cql), write and read consistency levels (i.e. ONE, QUORUM or ALL), number of threads used, number of objects to update, number of updates/versions per object}*.

The *orchestrator* is responsible for the following benchmark testing stages:

- Setup a dynamo cluster composed of *AWS EC2 Ubuntu 16.04 Xenial 64 bits* clean instances (only Cassandra setup was implemented);
- Prepare the data space for running the customized YCSB workload, i.e. a table called *workload* with two string-type fields, *y_id* and *version*;
- Request the Workload Coordinator to run a list of given workload configurations and reboot the SUT in each iteration;
- Request the Workload Coordinator to analyze the test output it has collected at the end of the test;
- Download from the *workload coordinator* the analysis output as a.csv file containing all the measures. Each line is the result of a single workload test.

Workload Coordinator. The workload coordinator is responsible for running CBench-Dynamo workloads.

Load Balancer. The load balancer is responsible for uniformly distribute the query load throughout the SUT.

SUT. The SUT is composed of a dynamo-based cluster.

5.3 Workload

This paper proposes a workload that evaluates how consistency, performance, and availability are affected when consistency is configured either to prefer a high-available system or a high-consistent system while in a distributed system, such as Dynamo-based databases, where network partition events may occur.

The proposed workload is a customized YCSB workload and follows the methodology proposed by Bermback and Tai [8]. Bermback and Tai propose a benchmark methodology to study how Amazon S3 handles consistency over a long time period. This long-term experiment proposes a single writer and a variable number of readers as Fig. 5 suggests. To achieve a uniformly load throughout the cluster's replicas and avoid always hitting the same replica, writer and readers interact with the cluster through a load balancer.

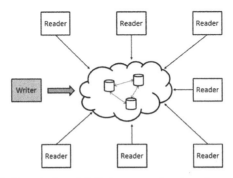

Fig. 5. Bermback and Tai's long-term benchmark approach.

Our benchmark is composed of two stages, the load, and run stages. The load stage is off the record for benchmark purposes. This stage's goal is to load all the objects into the database. These objects are composed only of two fields, *key,* and *version.*

During the benchmark run phase, both update and read operations occur uniformly. When configuring a workload run, the parameters *threads* indicate how much writers and readers will be running, as only one writer is used, the number of readers is calculated as *threads-1.* Each write operation increments a given object's version and each read operation reads the version of a given object.

The writer and the readers each have their task plan pre-generated at the beginning of the test and the benchmark ends when all the objects have been updated and read from until the pre-configured final version. Each operation is registered into a common file and follows the structure represented in Fig. 6.

The generated data is sufficient to infer whether a consistency anomaly had happened. For a given object's key, if a read operation returns a version inferior to a version already written by some write operation in the past, there was a consistency anomaly.

At the same time this occurs, there is a module that is disconnecting from time to time one instance at a time from the cluster to simulate network partition events (see Fig. 7). For every operation that the cluster was not able to retrieve a successful answer, the version assumes the *UNAVAILABLE* value as Fig. 6 suggests.

...

writer_id:0, key:*9345f1bae61442dab3f167c02d19a4a8,*
timestamp:*17309459474301, **version:***1*

...

reader_id:2*, key:9345f1bae61442dab3f167c02d19a4a8,*
timestamp:*17309253174394, **version:***0*
reader_id:1*, key:9345f1bae61442dab3f167c02d19a4a8,*
timestamp:*17309253174398, **version:***UNAVAILABLE*

...

Fig. 6. Proposed benchmark's results data structure.

All consistency anomalies are then processed and translated into the following measurements: *availability probability, consistency probability, write latency,* and *read latency.*

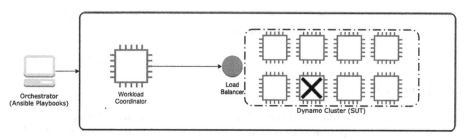

Fig. 7. Network partition event scenario

6   Benchmark Testing

For the first test of the proposed benchmark, we chose Cassandra as the SUT. Cassandra is a database system built with distributed systems in mind, like almost every NoSQL systems. Following the CAP theorem, Cassandra by default is on the AP (Availability and Network Partition Tolerance) side, hence prioritizing high-availability when subject to network partitioning. As we will further see, Cassandra's consistency can be tuned to be a CP (Consistency and Network Partition Tolerance) database system, so it becomes a strong consistent database when subject to network partitioning [12].

6.1   Testing Architecture

CBench-Dynamo requires an architecture composed of an *orchestrator*, a *workload coordinator*, and a *dynamo cluster* as the SUT. The following architecture was defined for our first test (see Fig. 8):

Orchestrator. The orchestrator is a MacBook Pro 13-inch, 2017, 2.3 GHz Intel Core i5 with 8 GB of RAM.

Workload Coordinator. The workload coordinator is an Amazon EC2 C5n.xlarge instance (4 vCPUs, 10.5 GB RAM).

SUT. The System Under Test is a Cassandra cluster composed of eight Amazon EC2 M5d.large instances. Each cluster instance will be rebooted and reloaded between workloads by the Orchestrator and the Workload Coordinator.

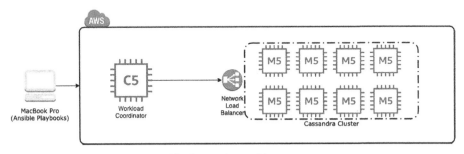

Fig. 8. Testing architecture

6.2 Experiment

In this section, we present the results obtained after running the proposed workload configurations. Our experiment targets an 8-node Cassandra cluster and combines different consistency configurations, i.e. *ONE, QUORUM, ALL*, as described in Table 1. The common input parameters for every configuration are the following:

- Replication Factor: 3;
- Total number of objects: 1.000.000;
- Versions/updates per object: 2;
- Network partition event duration: 2 s;
- Interval between network partition events: random between [1 s, 25 s].

Table 1. Cassandra's benchmark workload configurations.

Configuration	SUT	Write consistency	Read consistency
1	Cassandra	*ALL*	*ALL*
2	Cassandra	*ONE*	*ONE*
3	Cassandra	*QUORUM*	*ONE*
4	Cassandra	*ONE*	*QUORUM*
5	Cassandra	*QUORUM*	*QUORUM*

Consistency and Availability. When in a configuration both read and write consistency is ALL, we achieve results of Strong Consistency while compromising availability. This happens as theorized because all replicas must be involved before returning to the client. If some replica is down, resulting from a network partition event, the request can't fulfill and the response to the client reports an unavailable service. Although this configuration generated an availability of 99.7539%, the industry does not consider this value high. Availability is usually represented by how many nines the availability probability has (see Table 2). The value we attained in the *ALL-ALL* configuration only has 2-nines, which means that this number only falls into the second level of availability, hence translating into 3.65 days of availability when rounding down the number to 99.0000%. Many businesses that require high-availability may fail with such a long unavailable service time.

Table 2. Availability and nines notation [16].

Availability(%)	Downtime per year
90.0000 (one nine availability)	36.53 days
99.0000 (two nines availability)	3.65 days
99.9000 (three nines availability)	8.77 h
99.9900 (four nines availability)	52.60 min
99.9990 (five nines availability)	5.26 min
99.9999 (six nines availability)	31.56 s

In the other hand, when querying Cassandra with no consistency constraints by setting both read and write operations to involve just one replica (write consistency = ONE and read consistency = ONE), we achieved 100% of availability, but we have compromised consistency down to the lowest value achieved in the whole experience.

As of configurations using QUORUM combined with ONE, we achieved a more balanced consistency/availability relation. As we had chosen a replica factor of three, the *QUORUM* involves two replicas when processing a client request. When reading with *ONE* and writing with *QUORUM*, the request may involve the third replica that was not part of the QUORUM for that given data object, hence returning an outdated version. When inverting the order, the *ONE* in the writing and the *QUORUM* in the reading, it seems not to have such a drastic deterioration in consistency, however availability loses a nine.

For a *QUORUM-QUORUM* configuration, we achieved strong-consistency and high-availability. This configuration can tolerate some network partition events unless the number of replicas down compromises the quorum. Because our network partition events had disconnected one replica at a time, the quorum had never been compromised, hence the results we had are represented in Fig. 9.

Performance. Our second analysis is in terms of read and write operation latencies given a consistency setting. As Fig. 10 illustrates, for an *ALL-ALL* configuration we

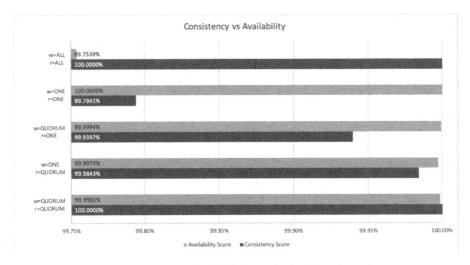

Fig. 9. Consistency and availability results for all configurations.

achieved as expected the highest latencies of all configurations because all replicas had to be involved in read and write operations.

For the *ONE-ONE* configuration, because only one replica needed to be involved in read and write operations, the latencies are the lowest among all configurations tested when combining the two latencies. However, when compared solely on mixed *ONE-QUORUM* configurations, *ONE* latency in these last configurations are better.

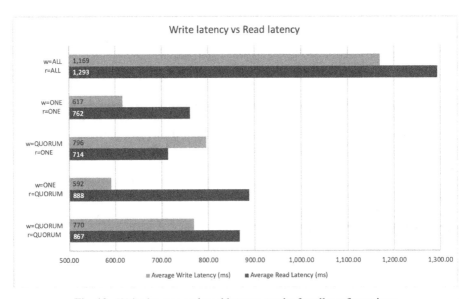

Fig. 10. Write latency and read latency results for all configurations.

Finally, for *QUORUM-QUORUM* configuration we achieved the most balanced configuration between latency, consistency, and availability.

7 Conclusions and Future Work

In this paper, we have proposed CBench-Dynamo as a new benchmark methodology focused on study the three properties of the CAP theorem, consistency, availability, and network partition tolerance. From the best of our knowledge, this benchmark specification for studying performance, consistency, and availability on different consistency configurations while subjecting the SUT to network partition events has never been proposed before.

In this paper, we have conceptualized, defined, and experimented our proposed benchmark resulting in interesting data on how consistency and network partition events influence consistency, availability, and performance. This benchmark is a valuable tool for testing already existing NoSQL databases against the client requirements, but also to test new databases implementations that aim a certain level of performance, consistency, availability, and network partition tolerance. We also made CBench-Dynamo benchmark available on GitHub [14, 15].

For future work, we intend to support more NoSQL databases and evolve the proposed benchmark to be a well industry establish framework to test NoSQL databases, so that the users have a deeper understanding of the tradeoffs of each configuration and what system and system configurations suits better their requirements.

References

1. Brewer, E.: Towards robust distributed systems. Pod. Principles Distrib. Comput. Conf. **1**, 1–12 (2000)
2. Gilbert, S., Lynch, N.: Brewer's conjecture and the feasibility of consistent, available, partition-tolerant web services. SIGACT News **33**, 51–59 (2002)
3. Pritchett, D.: BASE: an acid alternative. Queue **6**, 48–55 (2008)
4. Yahoo! GitHub Repository: YCSB (Yahoo! Cloud Serving Benchmark). https://github.com/brianfrankcooper/YCSB
5. Henning, J.L., Arnold, J.A., Lange, K.-D., et al.: How to Build a Benchmark, pp. 333–336 (2015)
6. Cooper, B.F., Silberstein, A., Tam, E., et al.: Benchmarking cloud serving systems with YCSB. In: Proceedings of the 1st ACM Symposium on Cloud Computing, pp 143–154. ACM, New York (2010)
7. Bailis, P., Venkataraman, S., Franklin, M.J., et al.: Quantifying eventual consistency with PBS. Commun. ACM **57**, 93–102 (2014)
8. Bermbach, D., Tai, S.: Benchmarking eventual consistency: lessons learned from long-term experimental studies. In: Proceedings- 2014 IEEE International Conference Cloud Engineering, IC2E 2014, pp. 47–56 (2014)
9. Patil, S., Polte, M., Ren, K., et al.: YCSB ++: benchmarking and performance debugging advanced features in scalable table stores. In: Proceedings of the 2nd ACM Symposium on Cloud Computing, pp. 9:1–9:14. ACM, New York (2011)
10. DeCandia, G., Hastorun, D., Jampani, M., et al.: Dynamo: Amazon's highly available key-value store. In: Proceedings Symposium Operations System Princ, pp. 205–220 (2007)

11. Bailis, P., Venkataraman, S., Franklin, M.J., et al.: Probabilistically bounded staleness for practical partial quorums. Proc VLDB Endow **5**, 776–787 (2012)
12. Diogo, M., Cabral, B., Bernardino, J.: Consistency models of NoSQL databases. Fut. Internet **11**, 43 (2019)
13. Diogo, M.: GitHub Repository: YCSB-Consistency (2019)
14. Diogo, M.: GitHub Repository: CBench-Analyser (2019). https://github.com/migueldiogo/cbench-analyser
15. Diogo, M.: GitHub Repository: ansible-dynamo-clusters (2019). https://github.com/migueldiogo/ansible-dynamo-clusters
16. Marcus, E.: The myth of the nines. In: Blueprints High Available (2003). https://searchstorage.techtarget.com/tip/The-myth-of-the-nines

Benchmarking Pocket-Scale Databases

Carl Nuessle$^{(\boxtimes)}$ (ID), Oliver Kennedy (ID), and Lukasz Ziarek (ID)

University at Buffalo, Buffalo, NY 14260, USA
{carlnues,okennedy,lziarek}@buffalo.edu

Abstract. Embedded database libraries provide developers with a common and convenient data persistence layer. They are a key component of major mobile operating systems, and are used extensively on interactive devices like smartphones. Database performance affects the response times and resource consumption of millions of smartphone apps and billions of smartphone users. Given their wide use and impact, it is critical that we understand how embedded databases operate in realistic mobile settings, and how they interact with mobile environments. We argue that traditional database benchmarking methods produce misleading results when applied to mobile devices, due to evaluating performance only at saturation. To rectify this, we present POCKETDATA, a new benchmark for mobile device database evaluation that uses typical workloads to produce representative performance results. We explain the performance measurement methodology behind POCKETDATA, and address specific challenges. We analyze the results obtained, and show how different classes of workload interact with database performance. Notably, our study of mobile databases at non-saturated levels uncovers significant latency and energy variation in database workloads resulting from CPU frequency scaling policies called governors—variation that we show is hidden by typical benchmark measurement techniques.

Keywords: PocketData · Mobile · SQLite · Android

1 Introduction

General-purpose, embedded database libraries like SQLite and BerkeleyDB provide mobile app developers with full relational database functionality, contained entirely within an app's namespace. These libraries are used extensively in apps for smartphones, tablets, and other mobile computing devices, for example as the recommended approach for persisting structured data on iOS and Android. However, database libraries can be a bottleneck [39], causing sluggish app performance and unnecessary battery drain. Hence, understanding database library performance and different database library configurations is critical, not just for library developers—but for any developer looking to optimize their app.

Unfortunately existing tools for measuring the performance of data management systems are presently targeted exclusively at server-class database systems [1,9,12,13,24], including distributed databases [3,21] and key value

© Springer Nature Switzerland AG 2020
R. Nambiar and M. Poess (Eds.): TPCTC 2019, LNCS 12257, pp. 99–115, 2020.
https://doi.org/10.1007/978-3-030-55024-0_7

Feature	Server-DB	Mobile-DB
Throughput	Crucial	Less Relevant
Latency	Relevant	Crucial
Startup Cost	Irrelevant	Relevant
Energy	Relevant	Crucial
Simult. Clients	10k+	1
Max Workload	100k+/s	400/s
HW Sharing	None or VM	Shared

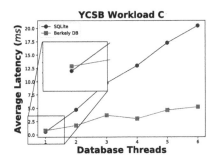

(a) **Differences between server-class and pocket-class database workloads**

(b) **Database performance on YCSB workload A.**

Fig. 1. Measuring mobile database performance using server-class benchmarks produces misleading results.

stores [2,8,35]. Unsurprisingly, server-class database systems optimize for different criteria than do embedded databases like SQLite or BerkeleyDB (Fig. 1a). Thus, existing measurement tools can not be used directly to assess the performance of embedded databases. In this paper, we focus on one specific impedance mismatch: *Server-class database benchmarks use throughput as a proxy for overall database performance.* To determine performance, server-class benchmarks measure throughput at saturation: The maximum query rate a database can sustain.

However, the measurement of throughput is vastly less important on phones. While there are many tasks, both interactive and background, phone databases are per-app. Our prior study [18] found that smartphone database instances need to cope with bursts of at most a few hundred queries, well below the throughput potential of a single thread, and well below saturation.

To understand why measurement at saturation is a problem, consider Fig. 1b, which illustrates the results of one server-class benchmark (YCSB Workload C) applied to SQLite and BerkeleyDB, each using their default settings. Each point represents another thread worth of load being offered to the database. As more concurrent load is added, latency increases as contention overheads compound. The result is seemingly a clear victory for BerkeleyDB. However, this graph is not representative of actual smartphone usage. In the low throughput area that is representative (the zoomed-in portion of the graph), the systems are competitive, with SQLite actually being the faster of the two on most workloads.

More generally, by measuring performance at lower throughputs, results are more affected by noise from OS and hardware optimizations, background activity, and other sources endemic to phones. Although this noise significantly impacts embedded database performance, existing performance measurement techniques do not accurately capture it. In this paper, we identify several sources of measurement error arising from measuring performance at low throughputs, and show how they can produce misleading results. We introduce POCKETDATA, a mobile benchmarking toolkit, designed to work around these error sources. To build POCKETDATA, we extend the Android Operating System Platform (AOSP) [14] with new logging capabilities, control over relevant system properties, and a benchmark-runner app. These extended capabilities help expose the precise causes of performance differences between systems or experimental trials. The result is a *toolkit for obtaining reliable, reproducible results when evaluating data management technologies on mobile platforms* like smartphones[1].

In our recent study of mobile database workloads [18], we made two key observations: (1) mobile workloads are dominated by key-value style queries, and (2) mobile database workloads are bursty. Following the first observation, we build on the Yahoo Cloud Services Benchmark (YCSB) [8], a popular key-value workload generator. To account for the latter observation, we extend the YCSB workload generator to operate at lower throughputs. We use the resulting workload generator to evaluate both performance and power consumption of SQLite on Android. One key finding of this evaluation was that for specific classes of workload, Android's default power management heuristics cause queries to take longer and/or consume more power. For example, we observe that *the default heuristics are often significantly worse than far simpler naive heuristics.* On nearly all workloads we tested, *running the CPU at half-speed significantly reduces power consumption, with minimal impact on performance.* Android's heuristics introduce higher latency and increase energy consumption due to excessive micromanagement of CPU frequencies.

The specific contributions of this paper include: 1. We identify sources of error in database performance measurement at low-throughputs (Sect. 2). 2. We propose a database benchmarking framework called POCKETDATA that makes it possible to mitigate these sources of error (Sect. 3). 3. We present results from an extensive benchmarking study of SQLite on mobile devices (Sect. 4). We cover related work and conclude in Sect. 5 and Sect. 6, respectively.

2   The Need for Mobile Benchmarking

Understanding the performance of data management systems is critical for tuning and system design. As a result, numerous benchmarks have emerged for *server-class data management systems* [1–3,8,9,12,13,21,24,35]. In contrast, mobile data management [23,28,30] is a very different environment (Fig. 1a). Here, we focus on one key difference: *mobile workloads operate significantly below saturation.* Measuring at saturation makes sense for typically multi-client server-class databases, which aim to maximize throughput. However, typical mobile data management happens at much lower rates [18], and on resource- and power-constrained hardware. As a result, metrics like latency and power consumption are far more important, while measuring performance at saturation hides meaningful performance quirks that can arise in practice.

The Performance Impact of Frequency Scaling Is Hidden at Saturation. The most direct effect of measuring at below saturation is related to a

---

[1] Available for download at http://pocketdata.info.

feature called frequency scaling, which allows the operating system to adjust CPU performance in response to changing load. As load drops, lower CPU frequencies can significantly extend battery life. While frequency scaling does exist on server-class database hardware, battery-powered mobile devices remain perpetually concerned with conserving energy. As such, they are far more aggressive with frequency scaling. During periods of low load, the OS can vary CPU frequencies to dozens of settings, or disable CPU cores altogether.

The particular policy heuristics to implement this adjustment are termed *governors*, such as the Ondemand governor used in most Linux distributions as well as earlier Android phones, or the Interactive governor used in more recent Android phones. Though their specific policies differ, both governors rely on only a single input datum: how busy the CPU is. By measuring the database at saturation, the CPU is kept completely, continuously busy, and virtually all governors react identically to this input: by running the CPU at maximum speed.

Figure 2a illustrates the impact of running below saturation. To simulate operation at lower throughputs, we injected periodic thread sleeps into YCSB [8] Workload C. The left bar cluster shows the results of three throughputs: At saturation (0ms delay), constant throughput below saturation (1ms delay), and bursty throughput below saturation (lognormal delay)². Adding delays increases the time spent off-core (dark-blue), as expected. However, the time spent doing useful work on the CPU (light-red) also increases. To confirm this is a result of frequency scaling, we re-ran the experiment, but with the CPU pinned to maximum frequency (right bar cluster). Here, on-core time is almost constant.

Making matters worse, the frequency scaling operation is expensive: No activity can be scheduled for several milliseconds while the core is scaled up or down. Hence, when the CPU is running at a low frequency, a database with a burst of work takes a double performance hit: first from having an initially slower CPU and second from waiting while the core scales up. Ironically, this means that a database running on a non-saturated CPU could significantly improve latencies by simply busy-waiting to keep the CPU pinned at a high frequency.

I/O Performance Is Different at Saturation. I/O on mobile devices is quite distinct from I/O on server-class devices. Most notably, mobile devices use exclusively flash media for persistent storage. Writes to flash-based storage are bursty, as the flash media's internal garbage collection identifies and reclaims overwritten data blocks. On write-heavy workloads, this effect is far less pronounced below saturation, as the disk has a chance to "catch up".

CPU frequency scaling also plays a significant role in embedded database I/O behavior as well. Repeated idling, such as from lower loads or I/O-blocked operations are interpreted by the OS as a lack of work to be done and a signal to scale down cores to save power.

Governors Are Indistinguishable at Saturation. Running benchmarks at full saturation, as a server-class study would do, obscures a broader performance factor. Consider Fig. 2b, which shows the effect of frequency scaling on total

---

² Here, we follow [18], which observes lognormal delay with a 6ms mean in typical use.

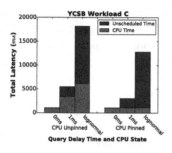
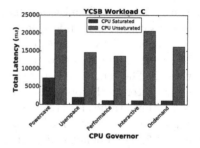

(a) **Saturated v. Unsaturated**   (b) **Latency by governor.**

Fig. 2. Performance on for Workload C (read-only) (Color figure online)

latency when run with different CPU governor policies. The dark (blue) bars show database performance when the CPU is saturated; the lighter (red) bars show performance when the CPU is unsaturated. Each cluster shows the total latency for a workload when run under a particular CPU governor policy.

When running Workload C queries at saturation (dark-blue), database performance latency is nearly identical across all governor choices, excepting the Powersave governor which deliberately runs the CPU at lowest speed. Only when the workload is run below saturation (light-red) do significant differences between the governors begin to emerge. These differences can have a significant impact on real-world database performance and need to be addressed.

3   PocketData

Traditional database benchmarks [8,29,36] are designed to run on server-class databases, and rank databases by either the maximum number of queries processed per second (i.e., throughput) or equivalently the minimum time taken to process a batch of queries. In both cases, database performance is measured at saturation, which can produce misleading results when run on the mobile platform. In this section, we first propose adjusting classical database benchmarks to run below saturation and then outline the POCKETDATA workflow and runtime.

3.1   Benchmark Overview

The initial input to POCKETDATA is a database and query workload, such as one generated by an existing server class benchmark. Specifically, we require an initial database configuration (e.g., as generated by TPC-H's dbgen utility), as well as a pre-generated workload: a sequence of queries (e.g., as generated by TPC-H's qgen utility). POCKETDATA operates in three stages: First, a pre-processing stage prepares the query workload for later stages. Second, the benchmark database configuration is installed on the test device, and finally the prepared workload is evaluated.

Inter-query Delays. The POCKETDATA test harness simulates performance at levels below saturation by injecting delays in between queries. These delays are randomly generated by POCKETDATA's workload preprocessor, which extends the pre-generated query workload with explicit instructions to sleep the benchmark thread. The length and regularity of the inter-query delays is provided to as a parameter to the preprocessor. Throughout the remainder of the paper, we consider three values for this parameter: 1. A **log**normally distributed delay, mirroring typical app behavior [18]. 2. A fixed **1 ms** inter-query delay, for comparison, and 3. **Zero** delay, or performance at saturation.

3.2   Benchmark Harness

The second and third stages are run by the benchmark harness, whicc a driver application and a rooted version of the standard Android platform with customized performance parameters. The application part of the benchmark connects to an embedded database through a modular driver. We developed drivers for: 1. Android OS's native SQLite integration, 2. BerkeleyDB through JDBC, and 3. H2 through JDBC. As it is used almost exclusively on the two major mobile platforms, our focus in this paper is on evaluating SQLite[3].

The benchmark harness takes three parameters: A CPU governor, a database configuration, and a workload annotated with delays. The selected governor is enabled by the benchmark as the phone boots up. After boot, the benchmark next initializes the database to the selected configuration, creating database files (if needed), creating tables, and pre-loading initial data. Once the database is initialized, the benchmark app exits and restarts.

After the benchmark app restarts it loads the pre-defined workload into memory. The choice to use a pre-defined, pre-loaded trace was made for two reasons. First, this ensures that overheads from workload generation remain constant across experiments; there is no cost for assembling the SQL query string representation. Second, having the same exact sequence of queries allows for completely repeatable experiments across different experimental configurations.

Metrics Collected. Log data was collected through ftrace. We instrumented the Android kernel, SQLite database engine, and driver application to log and timestamp the following events: 1. I/O operations like FSync, Read, and Write; 2. Context switches to and from the app's namespace; 3. Changes in CPU voltage scaling; and 4. Trace start and end times.

Logging context switches allows us to track points where the app was scheduled on-core, track background application use, and see when cores are idling. This is crucial, as unlike in server-class database measurement, we are intentionally operating the embedded database at well below saturation. The overhead of native-code platform events (1) and kernel-level events (2–3) are minimal. Trace start and end times, while injected from the app, are only 2 events and have minimal total impact.

---

[3] Complete benchmark results are available at http://www.pocketdata.info/.

3.3   The PocketData Benchmark

We base the PocketData measurement workload on insights drawn from our prior study [18], which found that smartphone queries typically follow key-value-style access and update patterns. Queries or updates operate on individual rows, or (rarely) the entire table. A quarter of apps observed by the study used exclusively key-value-style queries. Even the median app's workload was over 80% key-value style queries. Accordingly, we build PocketData by adapting the workloads from YCSB [8], an industry standard benchmark for key-value stores. We used an initial database of 500 records, approximately the median size of databases in our prior study [18] and a workload of 1800 operations per trial.

4   Benchmark Results

We organize this section by first discussing our application of the Pocket-Data benchmark to our test environment. We then overview the results obtained from our study, and highlight areas identified for potential system performance improvement. Finally, we discuss measurement variance trends we observed, and identify two sources of this variance.

Reference Platforms. Our database benchmarking results were obtained from two Android Nexus 6 devices, running Android OS 6.0.1, with 2 GB RAM and a Quad-core 2.3 GHz CPU (quality bin 2 for both devices). One of the Nexus 6 devices was modified to permit energy measurements, which we collected using a Monsoon LVPM Power Meter[4]. To ensure measurement consistency, we modded the AOSP on the device to disable a feature that turns the screen on when it is plugged in or unplugged—the screen remained off throughout the benchmark. For one set of experiments, in order to analyze the source of variance in database latencies, we additionally modded the SQLite engine in AOSP to monitor time spent performing I/O operations.

4.1   Results Obtained and Analysis Method

Our key findings for the Nexus 6 are as follows:

- Below saturation, Android's default governors keep the CPU at approximately half-speed, even on CPU-intensive workloads, reducing performance.
- A governor that pins the CPU to half-speed outperforms both default governors on virtually all workloads below saturation.
- Below saturation and on a fixed workload, both of Android's default governors also under-perform with respect to power consumption.

S Using the Monsoon meter, we measured the total energy consumed by the system, from launch to completion of the benchmark runner app while running a single workload. To account for a spike in power consumption as the runner

---

[4] http://www.msoon.com/LabEquipment/.

app launches and exits, we count net energy use relative to a null workload that simply launches and exits the benchmark without running any queries.

Results by Workload. The multiple workloads within the POCKETDATA benchmark yield finer insight into performance under different types of conditions. For conciseness, we focus our discussion on a workload subset that explores these differences (A, B, C, E). As shown in Fig. 3 this results in a gradient of read-heavy to write-heavy (C, B, A, respectively), as well as a more CPU-intensive scan-heavy workload. We specifically divide our discussion into three categories of workload: Read-heavy (B,C), Write-heavy (A), and Scan-heavy (E).

Workload	Description
YCSB-A	50% write, 50% read zipfian
YCSB-B	5% write, 95% read zipfian
YCSB-C	100% read zipfian
YCSB-E	5% append, 95% scan zipfian

Fig. 3. The four YCSB workloads.

A second dimension of analysis is CPU load. As we discussed in the introduction, system performance can change dramatically when the CPU operates below saturation. Thus, we present results for two different CPU conditions: saturated (0 ms delay) and unsaturated (lognormal delay).

Next, we ran each workload under each of 5 different CPU governor policies. 3 of them are non-default choices: **Performance** (run at the highest possible speed, 2.65 GHz), **Fixed-50** (The customizable Userspace governor set to run at a fixed midpoint frequency of 1.26 GHz), and **Powersave** (run the CPU at the lowest possible speed, 300 MHz). The last 2 choices, **Interactive** and **Ondemand**, are the current and previous Android defaults as discussed in Sect. 2.

The 4 workloads (A, B, C, and E), 2 CPU saturation settings, and 5 governor policies produce 40 measurement combinations. We ran each combination 3 times, and report the average and 90% confidence intervals. As we discuss below, certain workload combinations proved much more consistent in measurement than others. We observed measurement variance resulting from I/O blocking and the phone's power source. To investigate this aspect further, we re-ran several representative workloads, while measuring database file access time at the SQLite-kernel boundary. We re-ran each of these workloads under each of 3 different power source settings, 6 additional times each.

4.2 Read Heavy Workloads

Read-heavy database workloads are particularly important, as reads account for three-quarters of a typical database workload [18]. Energy consumption is also a key issue on mobile. CPU governors, in turn, heavily influence the behavior of both of these factors. We therefore focus on the performance-energy relationship of database operations under different governor settings. Our study results show that *system default governors result in sub-optimal latencies and energy costs for database workloads* in the bulk of representative read-heavy scenarios.

Workloads Are CPU-Bound but Respond Quickly. Latencies from read operations are due nearly entirely to CPU time (plus explicit benchmark delays) as a consequence of pre-caching performed by the SQLite database library. Figure 2a, for read-only workload YCSB-C, illustrates this clearly: there is virtually no unscheduled time beyond the total time spent explicitly waiting (0 s, 2 s, and 12 s, respectively). There was very little I/O activity under C, nearly all of it immediately at the start of the workload as the table is pre-fetched. Because of this pre-fetching, reads are serviced mostly from cache and there is little blocking.

Non-default Governors Offer Better Performance. Mobile platforms must always balance performance against energy. Figures 5 and 6 show the database latency and energy cost for each of the 5 governor choices for 2 read-heavy loads: C is read-only; B adds 5% writes. An ideal governor would be as close to the bottom left of the scatterplot as possible – that is, it should optimize both database latency and energy consumption.

Uninterrupted query timing essentially means the CPU will be running at saturation regardless of governor choice, and latencies tend to flatten. Thus, unsurprisingly, on uninterrupted, read-only workloads (Fig. 5a), both default governors nearly match the performance governor's latency. However, as the vertical scale of 5a shows, running saturated read workloads with the Performance governor also significantly *saves* rather than costs energy versus all other choices. On this workload, there is no benefit to be gained by micro-managing system performance, and so the static governor significantly outperforms the dynamic defaults. The saturated 95% read workload B (Fig. 6a) shows similar characteristics, albeit with an even more significant latency gap between the Performance and the default governors. Here, the limited I/O is interpreted by the system as a reduction in workload, and thus an opportunity to ramp down the CPU. However, the overhead of micromanagement again outweighs the benefits.

Unsaturated read-heavy workloads (Figs. 5b and 6b) model bursty, interactive usage patterns. Here, we observe a performance-energy trade-off between the Performance and Fixed-50 governors. On both read-heavy workloads under the performance governor, the average query is processed approximately 0.5 ms faster, while under the Fixed-50 governor power consumption is reduced by approximately a third. Notably, the Fixed-50 governor outperforms both default governors on both workloads and on both axes: Lower energy and lower latency.

Keeping the CPU Hot Can Reduce Energy Costs. We observe that both default governors perform better on saturated workloads. When such saturation is possible, it can be advantageous, not just from a latency but also an energy standpoint, to keep the CPU busy. This makes batching read queries especially important, as doing so can significantly reduce power consumption.

Alternatively, it may be possible for apps to reduce power consumption by busy-waiting the CPU during I/O operations when such operations are short and infrequent.

Frequency Scaling has a Non-monotone Effect on Energy Consumption. On the read-only workload C (Fig. 7a), energy cost is minimized with the CPU running at half (Fixed-50), rather than minimum speed (Powersave). Energy consumption scales super-linearly with frequency and there is an unavoidable fixed energy cost to simply keeping the core powered on (although recall that we keep the screen off during tests). Thus, the benefit of slowing the processor down is outweighed by the cost of keeping the core powered up longer.

Threads are Very Sensitive to Governor Performance Differences. When running read-heavy workloads, unless the CPU is already at saturation, the CPU often runs well below maximum speed under the Interactive governor. Figure 4 shows that, with the addition of 1ms pauses, the CPU frequency is largely stuck near 500 MHz, well below the 2.65 GHz maximum (the minimum is 300 MHz). As the core is running at a lower frequency when a query arrives, the query takes a performance hit. As the query finishes the Interactive governor ramps up the CPU

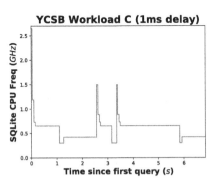

Fig. 4. Benchmark App Thread's CPU Frequency.

unnecessarily, wasting energy. This same effect appears in Fig. 2b, which shows higher latencies for intermittent queries (light-red bars on graph) with either default governor (Interactive or Ondemand) than when the CPU is saturated (Performance).

4.3   Write Heavy Workloads

Write-heavy workloads on the Android platform have higher latencies than their read-heavy counterparts, and latencies of the fixed-speed (non-default) governors scale inversely with energy consumption.

Non-default Governors Again Improve Performance. Fig. 7 shows the latency/energy metrics for Workload A, which is 50% write operations. The results for the saturated workload (Fig. 7a) show that the Fixed-50 governor notably outperforms all others. The Powersave governor has the lowest energy cost, but also has the worst performance. However, for write-heavy threads running on saturated CPUs (which is the case when a series of write operations arrive consecutively), the system default choices again under-perform significantly.

Write-heavy operations that occur intermittently exhibit a similar latency-energy metric to that of intermittent read-heavy threads. As before, Fig. 7b shows the tradeoff: Performance and Powersave offer the opposing extremes of latency and energy, while the Fixed-50 governor compromises between extremes.

4.4 Scan Heavy Workloads

Scan-heavy workloads involve longer-running, CPU-bound queries, which keep the CPU loaded for longer intervals. As a result, we see less variation between saturated and unsaturated workloads.

Table Scans Are CPU-Intensive. In workload E, reads are scan operations. The increase in latency for workload E is mostly due to sharply higher CPU time, with marginally greater non-scheduled non-benchmark delay time.

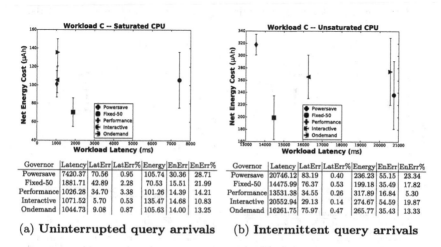

Governor	Latency	LatErr	LatErr%	Energy	EnErr	EnErr%
Powersave	7420.37	70.56	0.95	105.74	30.36	28.71
Fixed-50	1881.71	42.89	2.28	70.53	15.51	21.99
Performance	1026.28	34.70	3.38	101.26	14.39	14.21
Interactive	1071.52	5.70	0.53	135.47	14.68	10.83
Ondemand	1044.73	9.08	0.87	105.63	14.00	13.25

Governor	Latency	LatErr	LatErr%	Energy	EnErr	EnErr%
Powersave	20746.12	83.19	0.40	236.23	55.15	23.34
Fixed-50	14475.99	76.37	0.53	199.18	35.49	17.82
Performance	13531.38	34.55	0.26	317.89	16.84	5.30
Interactive	20552.94	29.13	0.14	274.67	54.59	19.87
Ondemand	16261.75	75.97	0.47	265.77	35.43	13.33

(a) **Uninterrupted query arrivals**   (b) **Intermittent query arrivals**

Fig. 5. Workload C: Latency performance and energy costs.

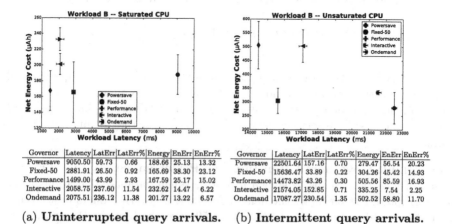

Governor	Latency	LatErr	LatErr%	Energy	EnErr	EnErr%
Powersave	9050.50	59.73	0.66	188.66	25.13	13.32
Fixed-50	2881.91	26.50	0.92	165.69	38.30	23.12
Performance	1499.00	43.99	2.93	167.59	25.17	15.02
Interactive	2058.75	237.60	11.54	232.62	14.47	6.22
Ondemand	2075.51	236.12	11.38	201.27	13.22	6.57

Governor	Latency	LatErr	LatErr%	Energy	EnErr	EnErr%
Powersave	22501.64	157.16	0.70	279.47	56.54	20.23
Fixed-50	15636.47	33.89	0.22	304.26	45.42	14.93
Performance	14473.82	43.26	0.30	505.56	85.59	16.93
Interactive	21574.05	152.85	0.71	335.25	7.54	2.25
Ondemand	17087.27	230.54	1.35	502.52	58.80	11.70

(a) **Uninterrupted query arrivals.**   (b) **Intermittent query arrivals.**

Fig. 6. Workload B: Latency performance and energy costs.

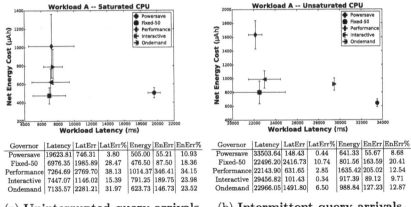

Governor	Latency	LatErr	LatErr%	Energy	EnErr	EnErr%
Powersave	19623.81	746.31	3.80	505.00	55.21	10.93
Fixed-50	6976.35	1985.89	28.47	476.50	87.50	18.36
Performance	7264.69	2769.70	38.13	1014.37	346.41	34.15
Interactive	7447.07	1146.02	15.39	791.25	189.75	23.98
Ondemand	7135.57	2281.21	31.97	623.73	146.73	23.52

Governor	Latency	LatErr	LatErr%	Energy	EnErr	EnErr%
Powersave	33503.64	148.43	0.44	641.33	55.67	8.68
Fixed-50	22496.20	2416.73	10.74	801.56	163.59	20.41
Performance	22143.90	631.65	2.85	1635.42	205.02	12.54
Interactive	29456.82	101.43	0.34	917.39	89.12	9.71
Ondemand	22966.05	1491.80	6.50	988.84	127.23	12.87

(a) **Uninterrupted query arrivals.**   (b) **Intermittent query arrivals.**

Fig. 7. Workload A: Latency performance and energy costs.

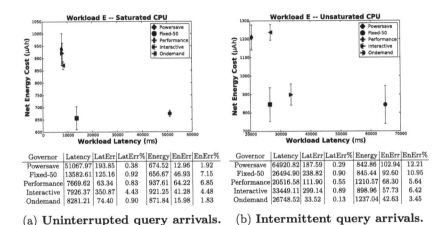

Governor	Latency	LatErr	LatErr%	Energy	EnErr	EnErr%
Powersave	51067.97	193.85	0.38	674.52	12.96	1.92
Fixed-50	13582.61	125.16	0.92	656.67	46.93	7.15
Performance	7669.62	63.34	0.83	937.61	64.22	6.85
Interactive	7926.37	350.87	4.43	921.25	41.28	4.48
Ondemand	8281.21	74.40	0.90	871.84	15.98	1.83

Governor	Latency	LatErr	LatErr%	Energy	EnErr	EnErr%
Powersave	64920.82	187.59	0.29	842.86	102.94	12.21
Fixed-50	26494.90	238.82	0.90	845.44	92.60	10.95
Performance	20516.58	111.90	0.55	1210.57	68.30	5.64
Interactive	33449.11	299.14	0.89	898.96	57.73	6.42
Ondemand	26748.52	33.52	0.13	1237.04	42.63	3.45

(a) **Uninterrupted query arrivals.**   (b) **Intermittent query arrivals.**

Fig. 8. Workload E: Latency performance and energy costs.

This penalty is due to additional actual computation rather than frequency scaling: Unlike with previous workloads, CPU time for E remains relatively unaffected by increased benchmark delay settings. For E, DB usages involving significant scans can still be serviced largely from cache, but they incur computation costs.

Non-default Governors Often Improve Performance. Workload E, comprised of 95% table scans, is shown in Fig. 8. When database operations arrive uninterrupted, Fig. 8a shows the default Interactive governor offers best latency. As in the read-heavy workloads, the Fixed-50 governor (not the Powersave governor) offers the lowest energy cost, with only a slight latency penalty.

Unsaturated scan-heavy threads generally follow the latency-energy trade-off pattern of previous workloads as well. Figure 8b shows that, as before, Performance and Powersave offer opposing extremes of latency and energy metrics. However, both are only negligibly better than the Fixed-50 governor, which also outperforms the default governors on both metrics.

4.5   Sources of Measurement Variance

Energy usage measurements showed significant but constant variation (reflected in the vertical error bars in graphs 5, 6, 7, 8) across all test configurations. Overall energy usage is low, exposing measurement to noise from small variations in background system behavior. Note that the *energy* noise level stays constant, even as overall load increases as in workload E. Conversely, *latency* variance (horizon-

Load	Reads	Writes	Syncs
A	4073	4986	2234
B	3675	572	244
C	3625	0	0
E	3719	1037	464

Fig. 9. Number of SQLite I/O Operations

tal error bars) is low for 3 of 4 workloads. Loads B, C and E, for both saturated and unsaturated CPUs, all had relatively small margins: 11% at most. However, measurement error for load A, particularly for a saturated CPU, was anomalously high: from 15%–38% for all CPU policies except Powersave.

Workload A is write-heavy, involving a relatively large number of I/O operations compared to other loads (see Fig. 9). To confirm that fluctuation in I/O time was indeed the source of the large latency error measurement for A, we instrumented SQLite to measure the time spent blocked on read, write, and fsync operations. We re-ran A with a saturated CPU 20 additional times. Figure 10 compares, for workload A under the default Interactive governor, the latencies of these runs. Total latency varies significantly, exhibiting a bimodal distribution, with one mode

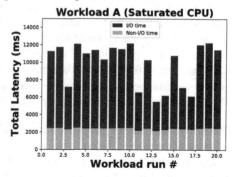

Fig. 10. Effect of I/O operations on workload latency variance (Color figure online)

around 6 s and a second mode at 11 s. Looking deeper, the latency of each run is composed of I/O time (dark blue) and non-I/O time (light orange). While non-I/O time for each of the runs is quite consistent, I/O time also varies bimodally. Likely, this is due to flash storage overhead having to prepare for block erases and writes. The saturated CPUs particularly expose this: unsaturated CPUs allow flash erasure to take place during quiescent periods, rather than forcing the benchmark to block. Workloads B, C and E exhibit much less latency variance, as they lack significant write activity and do not need to erase flash. Workload A is dominated by write costs and thus suffers increased variance.

5   Related Work

Lightweight DBMSes. MySQL [40] got its start as a lightweight DBMS, while libraries like SQLite [30] and BerkeleyDB [28] both provide server-less database functionality within an application's memory space. TinyDB [23] is a lightweight DBMS intended for use in distributed IoT settings. In addition to aiming for a low memory footprint, it allows queries to be scheduled for distributed execution over a cluster of wireless sensor motes. While these approaches target application developers, other efforts like GestureDB [26] target users of mobile devices and optimize for different types of interaction modalities.

Benchmarking. A range of benchmarks exist for server-class databases [4,29,36] and other data management platforms [8,15,20]. However, as we point out, assumptions typically made by these benchmarks produce invalid results when evaluating pocket-scale data management systems. There is however overlap on some non-traditional metrics like energy use in data management platforms [27,31–33]. Notably, configuration parameters optimized for these benchmarks typically involve significant changes to the hardware itself. Through features like frequency scaling on the CPU and RAM, mobile devices are capable of far more fine-grained control on the fly, markedly changing the evaluation landscape.

Conversely, A number of other benchmarks target embedded devices. AndroStep [22] evaluates phone performance in general terms of CPU and energy usage. Energy is also a common specific area of study – Wilke et al. compare consumption by applications [38]. AndroBench [19] studies the performance of file systems, but uses SQLite as a representative workload for benchmarking filesystem performance. While these benchmarks use SQLite as a load generator, it is the filesystem being evaluated and not the database itself.

Profiling Studies. One profiling study by Wang and Rountev [37] explored sources of perceived latency in mobile interfaces. They found databases to be a common limiting factor. A study by Prasad et al. [34] looked at hardware performance profiles relative to CPU quality ratings assigned by the chip manufacturer. They found a wide distribution of thermal profiles and CPU performance for devices ostensibly marketed as being identical. Our previous study [18] used a user-study to explore characteristics of mobile database workloads, and forms the basis for POCKETDATA as described in this paper.

There have a been a number of performance studies focusing on mobile platforms and governors for managing their runtime performance characteristics [6,7,10,11,25]. Most of these studies focus on managing the performance and energy tradeoff and none look at the effect of the governor on embedded database performance. A few make the argument that for more effective over all system utilization considerations of the whole program stack must be made [17] and instead of managing applications individually, system wide services should be created for more wholistic management [16]. More recently, there has been interest in specialized studies focusing on performance and energy consumption of specific subsystems, like mobile web [5]. These studies do not, however, document the competing performance metric tradeoffs between governors. Nor do they explore the effect of system load on performance rankings of governor choices. We view our study and performance debugging methodology for embedded databases on mobile devices to be a first step at understanding the performance effect of the mobile platform on mobile databases.

6 Conclusions

The mobile platform presents unique characteristics for database benchmarking. The systems themselves are resource-limited, and the typical workloads differ markedly from those experienced by traditional server-class databases. Furthermore, mobile systems are structured differently, with power management and flash memory I/O contributing a significant amount of noise to measurement efforts. Measurement systems that fail to account for these differences will miss critical performance information. While we focused our study on SQLite, the system default database, we designed our benchmark to be database-agnostic, and results from POCKETDATA on other configurations can be found on our website http://pocketdata.info.

For a given database and workload, different governors yield different database performance and energy consumption metrics. A non-default governor selection can often improve markedly on either latency or energy performance – sometimes in both. While the database is aware of the information necessary to make this choice, the kernel is not, suggesting opportunities for future improvement. In future work, we will explore how the kernel can be adapted to solicit this information and then incorporate it into a wiser governor selection.

Acknowledgments. This work is supported by NSF Awards IIS-1617586, CNS-1629791 and CCF 1749539.

References

1. Ahmed, M., Uddin, M.M., Azad, M.S., Haseeb, S.: Mysql performance analysis on a limited resource server: fedora vs. ubuntu linux. In: SpringSim (2010)
2. Atikoglu, B., Xu, Y., Frachtenberg, E., Jiang, S., Paleczny, M.: Workload analysis of a large-scale key-value store. SIGMETRICS Perform. Eval. Rev. **40**(1), 53–64 (2012)
3. Baumgärtel, P., Endler, G., Lenz, R.: A benchmark for multidimensional statistical data. In: ADBIS (2013)
4. Bitton, D., DeWitt, D.J., Turbyfill, C.: Benchmarking database systems a systematic approach. In: VLDB, pp. 8–19. Morgan Kaufmann (1983)
5. Cao, Y., Nejati, J., Wajahat, M., Balasubramanian, A., Gandhi, A.: Deconstructingthe energy consumption of the mobile page load. PMACS **1**(1), 6:1–6:25 (2017)
6. Carroll, A., Heiser, G.: An analysis of power consumption in a smartphone. In: USENIXATC, p. 21 (2010)

7. Chen, X., Chen, Y., Dong, M., Zhang, C.: Demystifying energy usage in smartphones. In: DAC (2014)

8. Cooper, B.F., Silberstein, A., Tam, E., Ramakrishnan, R., Sears, R.: Benchmarking cloud serving systems with YCSB. In: SOCC (2010)

9. Curino, C.A., Difallah, D.E., Pavlo, A., Cudre-Mauroux, P.: Benchmarking OLTP/web databases in the cloud: the OLTP-bench framework. In: CloudDB (2012)

10. Dietrich, B., Chakraborty, S.: Power management using game state detection on android smartphones. In: MobiSys, pp. 493–494 (2013)

11. Egilmez, B., Memik, G., Ogrenci-Memik, S., Ergin, O.: User-specific skin temperature-aware dvfs for smartphones. In: DATE, pp. 1217–1220 (2015)

12. Erling, O., et al.: The LDBC social network benchmark: interactive workload. In: SIGMOD (2015)

13. Frank, M., Poess, M., Rabl, T.: Efficient update data generation for DBMS benchmarks. In: ICPE (2012)

14. Google: Android open source project (2018). https://source.android.com/

15. Gupta, A., Davis, K.C., Grommon-Litton, J.: Performance comparison of property map and bitmap indexing. In: DOLAP, pp. 65–71. ACM (2002)

16. Hussein, A., Payer, M., Hosking, A., Vick, C.A.: Impact of GC design on power and performance for android. In: SYSTOR. pp, 13:1–13:12 (2015)

17. Kambadur, M., Kim, M.A.: An experimental survey of energy management across the stack. In: OOPSLA, pp. 329–344 (2014)

18. Kennedy, O., Ajay, J.A., Challen, G., Ziarek, L.: Pocket data: the need for TPC-MOBILE. In: TPC-TC (2015)

19. Kim, J., Kim, J.: Androbench: Benchmarking the storage performance of android-based mobile devices. In: Sambath, S., Zhu, E. (eds.) Advances in Intelligent and Soft Computing, ICFCE, vol. 133, pp. 667–674. Springer, Heidelberg (2011). https://doi.org/10.1007/978-3-642-27552-4_89

20. Klein, J., Gorton, I., Ernst, N.A., Donohoe, P., Pham, K., Matser, C.: Performance evaluation of NoSql databases: a case study. In: PABS@ICPE, pp. 5–10. ACM (2015)

21. Kuhlenkamp, J., Klems, M., Röss, O.: Benchmarking scalability and elasticity of distributed database systems. PVLDB 7(12), 1219–1230 (2014)

22. Lee, K.: Mobile benchmark tool (mobibench)

23. Madden, S.R., Franklin, M.J., Hellerstein, J.M., Hong, W.: TinyDB: an acquisitional query processing system for sensor networks. ACM TODS 30(1), 122–173 (2005)

24. Malkowski, S., Jayasinghe, D., Hedwig, M., Park, J., Kanemasa, Y., Pu, C.: Empirical analysis of database server scalability using an n-tier benchmark with read-intensive workload. In: SAC (2010)

25. Mercati, P., Bartolini, A., Paterna, F., Rosing, T.S., Benini, L.: A linux-governor based dynamic reliability manager for android mobile devices. In: DATE, pp. 104:1–104:4 (2014)

26. Nandi, A., Jiang, L., Mandel, M.: Gestural query specification. PVLDB 7(4), 289–300 (2013)

27. Niemann, R.: Towards the prediction of the performance and energy efficiency of distributed data management systems. In: ICPE Companion, pp. 23–28 (2016)

28. Olson, M.A., Bostic, K., Seltzer, M.I.: Berkeley DB. In: USENIX Annual Technical Conference, FREENIX Track, pp. 183–191. USENIX (1999)

29. O'Neil, P.E., O'Neil, E.J., Chen, X.: The star schema benchmark (SSB) (2007)

30. Owens, M., Allen, G.: SQLite. Springer, Cham (2010). https://doi.org/10.1007/978-1-4302-0136-6_22
31. Poess, M., Nambiar, R.O.: Energy cost, the key challenge of today's data centers: a power consumption analysis of TPC-C results. PVLDB 1(2), 1229–1240 (2008)
32. Poess, M., Nambiar, R.O., Vaid, K.: Optimizing benchmark configurations for energy efficiency. In: ICPE, pp. 217–226. ACM (2011)
33. Poess, M., Nambiar, R.O., Vaid, K., Stephens, J.M., Huppler, K., Haines, E.: Energy benchmarks: a detailed analysis. In: e-Energy, pp. 131–140. ACM (2010)
34. Srinivasa, G.P., Begum, R., Haseley, S., Hempstead, M., Challen, G.: Separated by birth: hidden differences between seemingly-identical smartphone Cpus. In: HotMobile, pp. 103–108. ACM (2017)
35. Tomás, G., et al.: Fmke: a real-world benchmark for key-value data stores. In: PaPoC (2017)
36. Transaction Processing Performance Council: TPC-H, TPC-C, and TPC-DS specifications. http://www.tpc.org/
37. Wang, Y., Rountev, A.: Profiling the responsiveness of android applications via automated resource amplification. In: MOBILESoft, pp. 48–58. ACM (2016)
38. Wilke, C., Piechnick, C., Richly, S., Püschel, G., Götz, S., Aßmann, U.: Comparing mobile applications' energy consumption. In: SAC, pp. 1177–1179. ACM (2013)
39. Yang, S., Yan, D., Rountev, A.: Testing for poor responsiveness in Android applications. In: Workshop on Engineering Mobile-Enabled Systems, pp. 1–6 (2013)
40. Yarger, R.J., Reese, G., King, T.: MySQL and mSQL - databases formoderate-sized organizations and websites. O'Reilly (1999)

End-to-End Benchmarking of Deep Learning Platforms

Vincent Deuschle[1,2]([⊠]), Alexander Alexandrov[1,2], Tim Januschowski[1],
and Volker Markl[2]

[1] Amazon Web Services, Inc., Berlin, Germany
deuscv@amazon.com
[2] Technische Universität Berlin, Berlin, Germany

Abstract. With their capability to recognise complex patterns in data, deep learning models are rapidly becoming the most prominent set of tools for a broad range of data science tasks from image classification to natural language processing. This trend is supplemented by the availability of deep learning software platforms and modern hardware environments. We propose a declarative benchmarking framework to evaluate the performance of different software and hardware systems. We further use our framework to analyse the performance of three different software frameworks on different hardware setups for a representative set of deep learning workloads and corresponding neural network architectures (Our framework is publicly available at https://github.com/vdeuschle/rysia.).

Keywords: Deep learning · Declarative benchmarking · Cloud computing

1 Introduction

Driven by the digitization of ever more aspects of life, the increase of available data as well as computing capacities has given rise to the application of complex predictive models across a wide range of sectors in research and industry. Most notably deep learning, used as an umbrella term for neural network based computational models, continues to capture academic as well as public attention. With their capacity to model complex structures and dependencies within data, neural networks are playing a rapidly increasing role as pattern recognition techniques with powerful means for regression and classification objectives.

The impact of these models and algorithms was fueled (and has driven) the development of a spectrum of publicly available software platforms that implement fundamental deep learning concepts such as auto-differentiation [17] and in particular backpropagation [22]. Build around accessible APIs, these platforms enable researchers to easily specify, train and deploy a broad range of neural network architectures. Simultaneously, advances in modern hardware have made efficient processing of large amounts of data, which are often required to train neural networks possible. Most notably, graphics processing units (GPUs) and

© Springer Nature Switzerland AG 2020
R. Nambiar and M. Poess (Eds.): TPCTC 2019, LNCS 12257, pp. 116–132, 2020.
https://doi.org/10.1007/978-3-030-55024-0_8

GPU-related hardware units have proven to be efficient devices to perform the linear algebra operations that deep learning principles are build on.

This vast spectrum of soft- and hardware choices constitutes a challenge for researchers who are trying to settle on the optimal system combination for a given task, e.g. natural language processing or image classification. With this paper we introduce a novel benchmarking framework as an easy to use tool to compare the performance of various deep learning software platforms and hardware configurations. Utilizing our framework, we have conducted a number of performance experiments with representative deep learning workloads for popular software platforms on CPU-restricted and GPU-accelerated hardware. Specifically, we make the following contributions with this paper:

- We propose a declarative benchmarking framework for deep learning platforms and hardware environments that guarantees comparability and reproducibility with a flexible interface to formulate and represent benchmarking workloads.
- We formulate three different workloads which represent popular subjects in the broader field of deep learning to benchmark feed forward networks [29], convolutional networks [25] and LSTM networks [23].
- We utilize our framework to conduct a number of training and inference experiments, executing the aforementioned workloads, to compare the performance of three different software platforms, namely Tensorflow [16], Apache MXNet [19] and Pytorch [21], in different hardware environments.

The key insights of our work are the following:

- The benefits of GPU-accelerated hardware during training depend on various factors, such as the neural network architecture and corresponding operators (e.g. matrix multiplication or convolution).
- MXNet outperforms both other platforms in most GPU-accelerated hardware environments during training. No platform outperforms any other under all circumstances.
- Pytorch outperforms both other platforms during inference in all tested hardware environments.

In the remainder of this paper we give brief introduction into the background of our work (Sect. 2), introduce our benchmarking framework (Sect. 3), describe our experiments and results (Sect. 4 and Sect. 5) and put our work in the context of other contemporary deep learning benchmarking efforts (Sect. 6).

2   Background

In this section we provide an overview over the background that is required to understand the context of our work. In Sect. 2.1 we introduce the three software platforms that are subject of our analysis. In Sect. 2.2 we describe the hardware environments that we used for our work. Most importantly, we distinguish between *CPU-restricted* and *GPU-accelerated* setups.

2.1   Software Platforms

In this section we introduce the three software platforms that are subject of our analysis. We give a brief overview over each platform and specify which APIs and engines we are analyzing in particular. In Table 1 we provide a concrete listing of all software versions and APIs that are subject of our work.

Table 1. Platform versions, datatypes and operators that we use for our benchmark.

Version	MXNet	Tensorflow	Pytorch
CPU	1.4.1	1.12.2	1.1
GPU	1.4.1	1.12.2	1.1
Datatype	MXNet	Tensorflow	Pytorch
Feed forward, Convolution LSTM CudnnCompatibleLSTMCell	Variable LSTMCell LSTMCell	Variable LSTMBlock-Cell	Variable
Operator	MXNet	Tensorflow	Pytorch
Matrix-Multiplication Convolution (2D) Bias Addition Max Pooling (2D)	linalg_gemm2 Convolution broadcast_add Pooling	matmul conv2d + max_pool	@ conv2d + max_pool2d

Tensorflow. [16] is an open source deep learning platform developed by Google Brain [9]. In it's *symbolic* runtime, which is subject of our analysis, Tensorflow builds, compiles and optimizes a computational graph, that represents a neural network architecture before execution. We have chosen Tensorflow's most low-level *Variable* API as subject of our analysis for feed forward and convolutional neural networks and two different LSTM cells for recurrent models.

Apache MXNet. [19] is an open source deep learning platform that is currently part of the Apache Incubator project [2]. Symbolic as well as imperative programming is supported on CPU-restricted and GPU-accelerated hardware. For a purely symbolic execution, MXNet offers the "Symbol API" and "Module API" to the user, the latter one serving as a wrapper for the Symbol API, providing high level concepts such as in-build optimizer (e.g. gradient descent) to the user. Similar to Tensorflow, we choose the symbolic *Variable* API for feed forward and convolutional networks and prebuild LSTM cells for recurrent models.

PyTorch. [21] is an open source deep learning platform developed by Facebook AI Research [8]. Imperative programming and eager execution are the central design principles with symbolic computation not supported[1]. Computational

---

[1] As of Version 1.0 Pytorch features a just-in-time compiler that will enable user to precompile static models before runtime without the need of symbolic operators.

graphs are not precompiled and may be modified during runtime. To enable backpropagation and the computation of gradients, all operations that are performed during a forward pass through the computational graph are recorded when they occur during runtime. Subject of our analysis is PyTorch's *Tensor* API with prebuild LSTM cells being used for recurrent models.

2.2 Hardware Environments

In this section we describe the hardware setups that are subject of our analysis. We execute our experiments within the Amazon Web Services (AWS) cloud environment [1], utilizing various CPU-restricted and GPU-accelerated EC2 instances [6]. We provide a detailed overview over the specifics of all used hardware environments in Table 2. All experiments are executed in containerized virtual machines, using Docker [5].

Table 2. Hardware configurations of all EC2 instances that we use for training and inference experiments.

EC2 instance	Cores	CPU type	Main memory	GPU
c4.2xlarge	8	2.9 GHz, Intel Xeon E5-2666 v3	15 GiB	n/a
c5.xlarge	4	3.0 GHz, Intel Xeon Platinum	8 GiB	n/a
c5.2xlarge	8	3.0 GHz, Intel Xeon Platinum	16 GiB	n/a
c5.4xlarge	16	3.0 GHz, Intel Xeon Platinum	32 GiB	n/a
c5.9xlarge	36	3.0 GHz, Intel Xeon Platinum	72 GiB	n/a
p2.xlarge	8	2.3 GHz, Intel Xeon E5-2686 v4	61 GiB	NVIDIA Tesla K80
p3.2xlarge	8	2.3 GHz, Intel Xeon E5-2686 v4	61 GiB	NVIDIA Tesla V100

CPU-Restricted Runtime: Deep learning platforms utilize a variety of libraries for efficient linear algebra computation which enable multithreaded parallelism. Regarding the software platforms which are subject to this paper, MXNet and Pytorch both employ OpenBlas [14] by default, while Tensorflow uses the Eigen library [7]. In general, CPU-restricted computation constitutes a performance limitation for deep learning workloads. The degree of parallelism is limited to the number of available CPU threads, which is restricted by the number of available CPU cores. Linear algebra operations however (and consequently deep learning), often benefit from a considerably higher degree of parallelism.

GPU-Accelerated Runtime: The software library most commonly utilized by deep learning platforms to allow GPU-accelerated computations is the NVIDIA CUDA Toolkit [13]. The three platforms that are subject to this paper all utilize CUDA for GPU-accelerated computations. Operators such as matrix multiplication are formalized as *kernels*, which are routines written within the CUDA framework, to be executed on a GPU. Most commonly, deep learning platforms provide CUDA implementations for all operators that may define a computational graph. The performance gain of GPU-accelerated computations depends on a variety of factors. For instance, a frequent data exchange between main memory and GPU may cause a runtime performance overhead.

3   The Rysia Benchmarking Framework

In this section we introduce the Rysia benchmarking framework that we implemented for our experiments. We designed a declarative interface that enables users to specify and execute benchmarking workloads without any coding required. In Sect. 3.1 we describe the guiding design principles of our work. In Sect. 3.2 we describe the architecture of our framework and the corresponding workflow of any benchmarking experiments.

3.1   Design Principles

We propose a new benchmarking approach that aims to preserve the core principles of other approaches while ensuring a higher degree of comparability between software platforms. We follow three guiding principles that define the core concept of our benchmarking framework:

- **Comparability** We ensure *functional equivalence* between platforms for our experiments, meaning that equivalent operations (e.g. matrix multiplication, convolution) are used and the same data (e.g. same mini-batches in each iteration of stochastic gradient descent) is being processed at each step of the computation.
- **Reproducibility** We provide a way to formalize benchmarking workloads in a declarative fashion that enables users to easily store, rerun and modify experiment setups and workload specifications.
- **Flexibility** We implement an easy to use *domain specific language* to enable users to easily specify deep learning models of different architectures for various workloads. Our framework automatically compiles these specifications into platform specific implementations.

By ensuring functional equivalence between platforms, we make sure that for training workloads, each platform reaches the same accuracy after the same amount of training iterations and that the same mathematical operations (e.g. matrix multiplication, convolution) are being performed on the same batches of data in each iteration[2]. We measure the *runtime in seconds* that is required to perform a predefined amount of training iterations.

For inference workloads, we measure the throughput rate for a platform on a given model. This means that we count the number of forward passes that each platform accomplishes in a time window of one minute on a fix sized mini-batch

---

[2] Under ideal conditions, our approach should indeed result in exactly the same accuracy curves between platforms. In reality however, even ensuring that the same operations are performed on exactly the same data in each step, does not result in perfectly aligning accuracy rates.

of samples that are randomly selected from a dataset for each forward pass. Dividing the throughput rate with 60, we measure *mini-batches per second*.

While other benchmarking approaches rely on hardcoded scripts that correspond to a specific workload (e.g. image recognition), we offer a more flexible approach, that lets users easily specify new model architectures, data sets and hyperparameter in a unified, declarative fashion, without having to worry about platform specific implementations. This clear separation of benchmark specification and execution makes it easy to reproduce and compare a large variety of experiments. Our framework ensures that for each workload the concept of functional equivalence holds.

To ensure comparability between platforms it is crucial that identical workloads are executed under the same conditions. This especially includes the hardware environments which we utilize to run our experiments. We believe that the most reliable way to achieve this is a cloud-based runtime. We therefore natively integrate cloud functionality in our framework, enabling the user to choose between local execution and a variety of cloud-based hardware environments that will stay consistent over the course of any batch of experiments.

3.2   Architecture

In this section we describe the architecture of our benchmarking framework. Following the design principles described in the previous section, we have implemented a framework with which we aim to overcome some of the blind spots of other benchmarking approaches. In the remainder of this section, we will give a detailed introduction to the key components of our framework and how they relate to the three principles that we have formulated in the previous section.

As we stated before, comparability, reproducibility and flexibility are the guiding principles of our framework. We believe that the best way to materialize these concepts is to provide the user with an accessible way to formalize benchmarking workloads in a declarative fashion. To achieve that, we introduce the idea of *blueprint* configuration files, in which the user can specify all relevant parameters that define a benchmarking workload. Specifically, these blueprints include:

- A **domain specific language** to formalize deep learning model architectures
- **Hyperparameter** Number of epochs, choice of optimizer, loss function, etc.
- **Metaparameter** Software platform to benchmark, hardware metrics to monitor and number of runs
- **Cloud Parameter** EC2 instance type, Docker image location
- **Data Paths** Path to datasets, result folder path or model parameter path

All blueprints are implemented as Python modules, which are dynamically imported at the beginning of our runtime. The most notable point of these declarative specifications is that they provide a generalized formalization for the user, whereas any platform specific implementation is automatized by our framework. The concept of a generalized domain specific language (DSL) to formalize deep learning models independently from the platform they will be executed on has been popularized first and foremost by the Keras API specification [10]. Users can specify deep learning models that consist of layers, which define the mathematical operation that is performed at the corresponding layer of the model (e.g. feed forward layer correspond to matrix multiplication). The key advantage of this approach is to separate the model architecture from any platform specific implementation, which are generated automatically.

For our benchmarking framework we follow a similar principle, with the focus shifted to build models for benchmarking workloads. Through our DSL, users may specify model architectures that consist of feed forward, convolutional and LSTM layers (with Max Pooling and Flattening as additional operators) since it is commonly assumed that these three operators make up the vast majority of computations in deep learning workloads. Within blueprint files, model architectures are specified as sequences of layers. During runtime, these sequences are converted to models which implement these layers for the platform that has been specified. For feed forward and convolutional layers, this means storing platform specific variables, which represent weight and bias matrices. LSTM layers hold a platform specific LSTM cell. All other layer types correspond to stateless operations. Implementing our own DSL (and not utilizing publicly available Keras implementations), enables us to maintain control over the operators and APIs that we select for each software platform. To ensure comparability across platforms, we have implemented our DSL with functionally equivalent low-level operators (e.g. matrix multiplication or convolution) for each platform.

4   Experiment Setup

In this section we describe the experiments that we conducted within the scope of this paper. Utilizing our framework described in Sect. 3, we analyze and address subjects regarding *training runtime* and *inference throughput* performance. For each subject we specify the questions that we will answer, as well as the corresponding experiment setup, which includes workloads, corresponding model architectures, datasets, and hardware specifications. In the remainder of this chapter we provide a detailed description of all experiments, subjects and corresponding workloads. In Sect. 4.1 we describe the three workloads and corresponding model architectures that we use to analyze the three subjects listed above. In Table 3 we specify the runtime environment of our experiments. In the subsequent two sections, we provide further details for each subject such as individual hyperparameter and utilized hardware setups.

Table 3. Runtime environment that we use for our benchmark.

Version	Docker base image	OS
CPU	ubuntu:16.04	Ubuntu 16.04
GPU	nvidia/cuda:9.0-cudnn7-devel	Ubuntu 16.04
Version	CUDA/CUDNN	Python
CPU	n/a	3.6
GPU	9.0/7.3	3.6

4.1 Workloads and Deep Learning Model Architectures

In this section we specify the workloads and corresponding model architectures that we use for our experiments. Workloads and models will remain consistent across all subjects, meaning that the same three model architectures will be used to benchmark and analyze training and inference performance. We have chosen the following tasks as workloads for this paper, which are canonical and widely applied in the field of deep learning:

- Handwritten digits classification with feed forward networks (MNIST)
- Image classification with convolutional networks (CIFAR-10)
- Sentiment analysis with LSTM Networks (IMDB)

The MNIST dataset [12] consists of greyscale images of handwritten digits. Each image of size 28×28 pixels is being flattened to a one-dimensional vector with 784 features. For this relatively simple classification objective we have chosen a conventional feed forward neural network architecture of three layers with 128, 64 and 10 neurons per layer.

The CIFAR-10 dataset [3] consists of RGB images of ten different objects. Each image is of size $32 \times 32 \times 3$ pixels and each label corresponds to an index for one of ten different objects. To solve this classification problem we chose a convolutional VGG16 neural network architecture [28] with 10 convolutional network layers, followed by three feed forward layers.

The IMDB dataset [26] consists of movie reviews in text form. Each review is treated as a sequence of words and each word is mapped to a word-vector of 50 features, as described by [27]. Each sequence is truncated at 250 words and each sequence that is smaller than 250 words is padded with an according amount of zero-vectors, thus creating samples of size 250×50 each. Since we are performing sentiment analysis, each label marks a review as either "positive" or "negative". To solve this binary sequence classification task, we chose a LSTM network with one layer and 128 cells. The data representation follows [15].

4.2 Training Runtime Performance

For this subject, we compare the runtime performance and hardware utilization profiles of MXNet, Tensorflow and Pytorch for the three different training workloads described in the previous section. Within this context, we will address the following two questions:

Table 4. Hyperparameter for training performance experiments.

	MNIST	CIFAR-10	IMDB
Epochs	200	100	100
Optimizer	SGD	Adam	Adam
Batch size	128		
Learning rate	0.01		
Loss function	Cross-entropy		

- How do different software platforms perform with different training workloads?
- How do different hardware environments perform with different training workloads?

The hyperparameter configurations that we use for our training experiments are listed in Table 4. For each task we use a batch-size of 128 and a learning-rate of 0.01. The number of training epochs varies between tasks. We further chose the cross-entropy loss function for each workload. While the feed forward model for our MNIST job is trained with the vanilla gradient descent optimizer of each framework, we chose the more advanced Adam optimizer [24] for the other two training jobs.

In order to maximize comparability across platforms, we run all experiments on the same types of EC2 instances, thus ensuring consistent hardware configurations across each experiment setup. Table 2 shows the EC2 instances that have been used for each experiment. We compare instances with powerful CPU types (older C4.2xlarge and newer C5.2xlarge) and instances that provide GPU devices (older P2.xlarge and newer P3.2xlarge) in our training experiments.

4.3   Inference Throughput Performance

For this subject we compare the inference throughput performance of MXNet, Tensorflow and Pytorch for multiple different inference workloads. Specifically, we will address the following question:

- How well do different software platforms utilize different numbers of available CPU cores during inference?

We utilize again the three datasets and corresponding model architectures described in Sect. 4.1. We further take the pretrained models from Sect. 4.2 as initial model parameters. For each forward pass we chose mini-batches of 128 samples that are randomly selected from the whole dataset. We measure how many complete forward passes each platform is able to perform for each model within a time window of one minute. As opposed to our training experiments, where we were measuring runtime for a fixed amount of iterations, we measure the number of iterations for a fixed amount of time in our inference setup.

As with our training experiments, we run all throughput experiments on the same types of EC2 instances, in order to maximize comparability. A key difference for our inference subject is, that all experiments are executed on CPU-restricted hardware, since this setup is more commonly used for inference tasks. Table 2 shows the hardware specifications of each instance. We select C5 instances of different sizes with 4, 8, 16 and 36 CPU cores respectively.

5   Experiment Results

In this chapter we analyze the results and findings of the experiments that we conducted in our work as described in Sect. 4. We show all relevant result metrics such as median runtime for training and median throughput for inference experiments.

5.1   Training Performance

In this section we analyze the results and findings of our training performance experiments, described in Sect. 4.2. For each experiment we report the median runtime over seven runs.

Handwritten Digits Classification with Feed Forward Networks: In Fig. 1a we show the observed median runtime for each combination of platform and EC2 instance for the MNIST workload with feed forward networks. On CPU-restricted C4 and C5 instances, we measured the fastest runtime performance for Tensorflow, outperforming both other platforms with a median runtime of 155 s on C4 instances and 132 s on C5 instances. On the newer C5 instance generation we measured the most noticeable speedup for Pytorch and minor speedups for Tensorflow and MXNet.

On GPU-accelerated P2 and P3 instances, MXNet outperforms both Pytorch and Tensorflow by a small margin with a median runtime of 137 s on P2 instances and 120 s on P3 instances. On the newer P3 instance, we measured minor speedups across all platforms, compared to the older P2 instance.

Comparing the runtime on CPU-restricted and GPU-accelerated instances, we measured noticeable speedups for MXNet and Pytorch on the latter. For Tensorflow we did not measure any significant speedup, compared to its already fast CPU-bound performance. In general, performance differences across platforms proved much smaller on GPU-accelerated than on CPU-restricted hardware. Averaging over all platforms and both types of CPU and GPU hardware environments respectively, we have measured a speedup of 1.84 on the latter. We conclude, that for relatively small feed forward neural networks, the speedup of GPU-accelerated hardware needs to be leveraged against the significant cost increase that comes with these types of hardware environments.

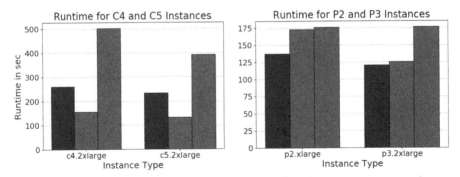

(a) Runtime comparison (training) for the MNIST workload with feed forward networks on different C (left) and P (right) instances.

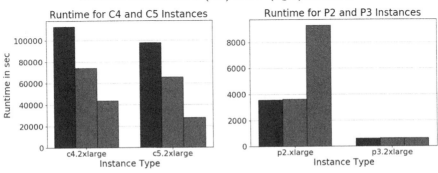

(b) Runtime comparison (training) of the CIFAR-10 workload with convolutional networks on different C (left) and P (right) instances.

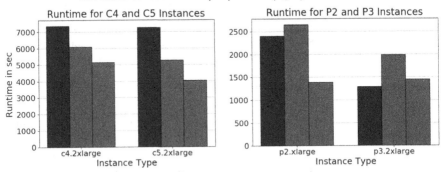

(c) Runtime comparison (training) for the IMDB workload with LSTM networks on different C (left) and P (right) instances.

___ MXNet ___ Tensorflow ___ Pytorch

Fig. 1. Results of our runtime experiments. Each bar shows the median runtime performance of one software platform over seven runs.

Image Classification with Convolutional Networks: In Fig. 1b we show the observed median runtimes for each combination of platform and EC2 instance for the CIFAR-10 workload with a convolutional VGG16 network. On C4 and C5 instances, Pytorch outperforms both other platforms with a median runtime of 43474 s on C4 instances and 27837 s on C5 instances. Each platform shows a minor speedup on the newer C5 instance, compared to the older C4 instance.

On P2 instances we measured virtually identical runtime performance for Tensorflow and MXNet, both outperforming Pytorch with a slightly faster median runtime of 3556 s for MXNet. On P3 instances, we measured the fasted median runtime for MXNet with 600 s, albeit all three platforms perform almost identical.

Across all platforms, we have measured a tremendous performance increase, when training convolutional neural networks in GPU-accelerated hardware environments. Figure 1b shows that all frameworks perform multiple times faster on P2 instances compared to CPU-restricted hardware and again multiple times faster on P3 instances. Comparing the two newer generations of CPU and GPU instances (C5 and P3), MXNet runs roughly 163 times faster on the latter, Tensorflow 109 times faster and Pytorch 44 times. Averaging over all platforms and both types of CPU and GPU hardware environments respectively, we have measured a speedup of 23.05 on the latter.

Sentiment Analysis with LSTM Networks: In Fig. 1c we show the observed median runtimes of seven runs for each combination of platform and EC2 instance for the IMDB workload with LSTM networks. On C4 and C5 instances, Pytorch outperforms both other platforms with median runtimes of 5138 and 4033 s respectively. Each platform shows a minor speedup on the newer C5 instance, compared to the older C4 generation.

On GPU-accelerated instances we measured significant speedups for all three platforms, compared to CPU-restricted hardware environments. On P2 instances, Pytorch outperforms both other platforms by a significant margin with a median runtime of 1386 s. On P3 instances, MXNet runs fastest with a median runtime of 1281 s. We further measured a significant performance increase on the newer P3 generation across all platforms, compared to the older P2 generation.

Overall, we observed that all three platforms are capable of utilizing GPU-accelerated hardware reasonably well, training LSTM networks. Averaging over all platforms and both types of CPU and GPU hardware environments respectively, we have measured a speedup of 3.15 on the latter.

5.2 Inference Throughput Performance

In this section we analyze the results and findings of our inference performance experiments, described in Sect. 4.3. For each experiment we report the median throughput over seven runs.

Handwritten Digits Classification with Feed Forward Networks: In Fig. 2a we show the observed median throughput for each combination of platform and

EC2 instance for the MNIST workload. For all CPU sizes we recorded the highest throughput rate for Pytorch and the lowest for Tensorflow. For Pytorch we observed a constant performance increase up until 16 cores with no further increase beyond that. For MXNet and Tensorflow we measured consistent performance increases up until the maximum of 36 CPU cores, albeit without ever coming close to the throughput rate of Pytorch. Across all platforms and instance types we recorded the highest throughput rate for Pytorch on c5.4xlarge (16 cores) instances with 3077.48 mini-batches per second.

Image Recognition with Convolutional Networks: In Fig. 2b we show the observed median throughput for each combination of platform and EC2 instance for the CIFAR-10 workload. We recorded the highest throughput rate for Pytorch for all CPU sizes, with a continuous performance increase up to the maximum of 36 available cores. While Tensorflow showed a continuous raise in mini-batch throughput with more available cores too, the platform never reached the performance of Pytorch. We measured the lowest throughput rate for MXNet with no performance increase beyond 8 CPU cores. Across all platforms and instance types we recorded the highest throughput rate for Pytorch on c5.9xlarge (36 cores) instances with 12.55 mini-batches per second.

Sentiment Analysis with LSTM Networks: In Fig. 2c we show the observed median throughput for each combination of platform and EC2 instance for the IMDB workload. We observed the highest throughput rate for Pytorch across all CPU sizes with a performance increase up to 16 available CPU cores and a drop in performance afterwards. For Tensorflow we recorded constant increases in performance up until 16 cores. For MXNet we recorded the lowest throughput rate and only observed an increase in performance between four and eight available cores with no further increase afterwards. Across all platforms and instance types we recorded the highest throughput rate for Pytorch on c5.4xlarge (16 cores) instances with 13.25 mini-batches per second.

6   Related Work

In this section we briefly introduce three other benchmarking approaches for deep learning platforms. While similar end-to-end benchmarking concepts have been applied and implemented before, we distinguish our work by offering an end-to-end benchmark that lets users declaratively formulate deep learning workloads in blueprint files.

C. Bourrasset et al. [18] define a set of principle requirements for deep learning training and inference benchmarks in enterprise environments. For end-to-end benchmarks which are subject of our work, the authors identify several relevant metrics such as computation time and efficiency or energy and hardware resource consumption (amongst others). Principal requirements that are stated for benchmarking approaches are reproducibility, portability and comparability. These concepts align with the design principles that we have selected for our work.

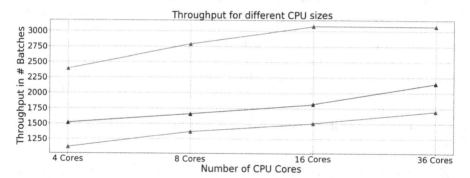

(a) Inference throughput comparison of the MNIST workload with feed forward networks on C5 instances of different sizes.

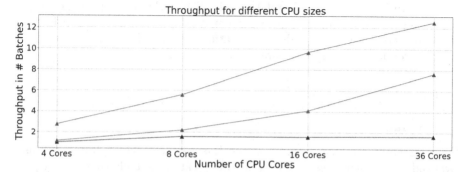

(b) Inference throughput comparison of the CIFAR-10 workload with convolutional networks on C5 instances of different sizes.

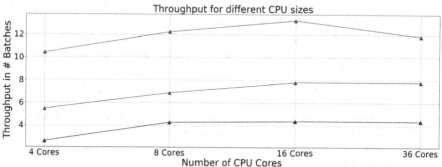

(c) Inference throughput comparison of the IMDB workload with LSTM networks on C5 instances of different sizes.

— MXNet — Tensorflow — Pytorch

Fig. 2. Results of our inference experiments. Each plot shows the median runtime performance of one software platform over seven runs.

MLPerf. [11] is a benchmarking initiative that originated from the DAWNBench project [20] by the Stanford University and is now supported by a variety of academic and industrial actors. MLPerf aims to compare deep learning platforms on a workload level. The primary performance evaluation metric is defined as the wall clock time to train a deep learning model to a target quality. Participators can submit results for a predefined workload in a deep learning platform and a hardware setup of their own choosing. MLPerf strives for *mathematical equivalence*, which is asserted by explicitly predefining a model architecture, hyperparameter as well as initial model parameter that all submissions must follow.

I. Karmanov et al. [4] propose a "Rosetta Stone approach" for benchmarking deep learning platforms. The initiative was originated by data scientists at Microsoft, with contributions by various teams working on different deep learning platforms such as CNTK and Pytorch. The authors describe the project as an attempt to provide reference implementations for various deep learning workloads across a variety of different platforms. The authors predefine model architecture, dataset and hyperparameter for each given workload.

7 Conclusion

7.1 Summary

With this paper we have introduced the Rysia benchmarking framework as a novel end-to-end benchmark for deep learning platforms. Following the key principles of *comparability*, *reproducibility* and *flexibility* we have designed a framework that enables users to specify benchmarking workloads without the need of implementing any underlying functionality. To that purpose we introduced the concept of *blueprint files* in which users may specify any relevant parameters that define a benchmark, such as the model architecture, hyperparameter, datasets and cloud resource specifications. With this clear separation of workload specification and implementation, we guarantee reproducibility as well as flexibility. We further guarantee comparability by ensuring that the platform-specific execution of blueprints are functionally equivalent across platforms. In each computational step our framework utilizes equivalent data structures and operators of each platform. Over the course of this paper we have shown that the aforementioned paradigms are reasonable guidelines for benchmarking approaches which are not fully realized by related work yet.

Utilizing our framework, we have conducted a broad range of representative benchmarking experiments for deep learning platforms and hardware environments. We have shown that the performance of individual software platforms and hardware environments during training depends on a given workload and its corresponding model architecture. For GPU-accelerated hardware we have measured by far the highest speedup when training convolutional networks on image data. For training workloads we have further measured significant performance differences across platforms, with no platform outperforming any other for each workload. We further noticed that symbolic setups with static computational graphs (MXnet and Tensorflow) do not necessarily guarantee better performance than imperative setups with dynamic graphs (Pytorch).

For inference workloads we observed the best performance for Pytorch in all tested hardware environments. The benefits of higher degrees of parallelism (provided by higher numbers of available CPU cores) largely depend on the workload, corresponding model architecture and software platform in question.

7.2 Future Work

In this paper we have shown the merits of separating a benchmark specification from its implementation and execution. By extending this concept, a far broader range of deep learning workloads could be covered and analyzed. Our domain specific language for formalizing model architectures could for instance be extended with further operators (e.g. attention layer, dropout layer, etc.) to cover a broader spectrum of neural network architectures. The crucial prerequisite for an extension of our own work would be the continued focus on functional equivalence during the transformation of a declarative formalization into a platform-specific implementation. We consider the Keras API specification best suited for expressing more complex model architectures.

We have chosen three different deep learning software platforms to compare and analyze. The landscape of available platforms is however far wider and an obvious extension to our own work would be the support and analysis of other platforms. The design principles that we followed throughout our work are universally applicable and not limited to any specific platform.

While we focused on single-node hardware environments in our work, distributed training is a highly relevant research topic within the deep learning community. A valuable extension of our work would be an implementation and analysis of training workloads on multi-node clusters or single machines with multiple GPUs. Our concept of declarative benchmark specifications could be extended accordingly, given that the analyzed software platforms offer distributed training.

References

1. Amazon Web Services. https://aws.amazon.com/. Accessed 28 May 2019
2. Apache Incubator. https://incubator.apache.org/. Accessed 10 June 2019
3. CIFAR-10 dataset. https://www.cs.toronto.edu/~kriz/cifar.html. Accessed 10 June 2019
4. Comparing deep learning frameworks: a rosetta stone approach. https://blogs.technet.microsoft.com/machinelearning/2018/03/14/comparing-deep-learning-frameworks-a-rosetta-stone-approach/. Accessed 10 June 2019
5. Docker Platform. https://www.docker.com/. Accessed 10 June 2019
6. EC2 Instances. https://aws.amazon.com/ec2/instance-types/. Accessed 10 June 2019

7. Eigen Library. http://eigen.tuxfamily.org/index.php?title=Main_Page. Accessed 10 June 2019
8. Facebook AI Research. https://research.fb.com/category/facebook-ai-research/. Accessed 10 June 2019
9. Google Brain. https://ai.google/research/teams/brain. Accessed 10 June 2019
10. Keras Framework. https://keras.io/. Accessed 10 June 2019
11. MLPerf benchmark suite. https://mlperf.org/. Accessed 10 June 2019
12. MNIST database of handwritten digits. http://yann.lecun.com/exdb/mnist/. Accessed 10 June 2019
13. NVIDIA Cuda. https://developer.nvidia.com/cuda-toolkit. Accessed 10 June 2019
14. OpenBlas Library. https://www.openblas.net/. Accessed 10 June 2019
15. Perform sentiment analysis with LSTMs, using TensorFlow. https://www.oreilly.com/learning/perform-sentiment-analysis-with-lstms-using-tensorflow. Accessed 10 June 2019
16. Abadi, M., et al.: Tensorflow: a system for large-scale machine learning. In: OSDI, vol. 16, pp. 265–283 (2016)
17. Baydin, A.G., Pearlmutter, B.A., Radul, A.A., Siskind, J.M.: Automatic differentiation in machine learning: a survey. J. Mach. Learn. Res. **18**(153), 1–43 (2018). http://jmlr.org/papers/v18/17-468.html
18. Bourrasset, C., et al.: Requirements for an enterprise AI benchmark. In: Nambiar, R., Poess, M. (eds.) TPCTC 2018. LNCS, vol. 11135, pp. 71–81. Springer, Cham (2019). https://doi.org/10.1007/978-3-030-11404-6_6
19. Chen, T., et al.: MXNet: a flexible and efficient machine learning library for heterogeneous distributed systems. arXiv preprint arXiv:1512.01274 (2015)
20. Coleman, C., et al.: DAWNBench: an end-to-end deep learning benchmark and competition. Training **100**(101), 102 (2017)
21. Collobert, R., Kavukcuoglu, K., Farabet, C.: Torch7: A matlab-like environment for machine learning. In: BigLearn, NIPS Workshop. No. EPFL-CONF-192376 (2011)
22. Hecht-Nielsen, R.: Theory of the backpropagation neural network. In: Neural Networks for Perception, pp. 65–93. Elsevier (1992)
23. Hochreiter, S., Schmidhuber, J.: Long short-term memory. Neural Comput. **9**(8), 1735–1780 (1997)
24. Kingma, D.P., Ba, J.: Adam: a method for stochastic optimization. arXiv preprint arXiv:1412.6980 (2014)
25. Krizhevsky, A., Sutskever, I., Hinton, G.E.: ImageNet classification with deep convolutional neural networks. In: Advances in Neural Information Processing Systems, pp. 1097–1105 (2012)
26. Maas, A.L., Daly, R.E., Pham, P.T., Huang, D., Ng, A.Y., Potts, C.: Learning word vectors for sentiment analysis. In: Proceedings of the 49th Annual Meeting of the Association for Computational Linguistics: Human Language Technologies, pp. 142–150. Association for Computational Linguistics, Portland, June 2011. http://www.aclweb.org/anthology/P11-1015
27. Pennington, J., Socher, R., Manning, C.D.: GloVe: global vectors for word representation. In: Empirical Methods in Natural Language Processing (EMNLP), pp. 1532–1543 (2014). http://www.aclweb.org/anthology/D14-1162
28. Simonyan, K., Zisserman, A.: Very deep convolutional networks for large-scale image recognition. arXiv preprint arXiv:1409.1556 (2014)
29. Svozil, D., Kvasnicka, V., Pospichal, J.: Introduction to multi-layer feed-forward neural networks. Chemometr. Intell. Lab. Syst. **39**(1), 43–62 (1997)

Role of the TPC in the Cloud Age

Alain Crolotte[1], Feifei Li[2], Meikel Poess[3], Peter Boncz[4], and Raghunath Nambiar[5(✉)]

[1] Teradata, San Diego, USA
alain.crolotte@teradata.com
[2] Alibaba, Hangzhou, China
lifeifei@alibaba-inc.com
[3] Oracle Corporation, Santa Clara, USA
meikel.poess@oracle.com
[4] Vrije Universiteit Amsterdam, Amsterdam, The Netherlands
p.boncz@cwi.nl
[5] AMD, Inc., Santa Clara, USA
raghu.nambiar@amd.com

Abstract. In recent year the TPC Technology Conference on Performance Evaluation and Benchmarking (TPCTC) series have had significant influence in defining industry standards. The 11th TPC Technology Conference on Performance Evaluation and Benchmarking (TPCTC 2019) organized an industry panel on the "Role of the TPC in the Cloud Age". This paper summaries the panel discussions.

1 Introduction

The panel on the "Role of the TPC in the Cloud Age" at the 11th TPC Technology Conference on Performance Evaluation and Benchmarking (TPCTC 2019) brought together industry experts and researchers from a broad spectrum of interests. The panel consisted of:

- Alain Crolotte: Alian has over 25 years of experience in database technology with Teradata. He participated in all TPC decision-support benchmark projects including TPC-D, TPC-H, TPC-DS and TPCx-BB. He is very familiar with TPC processes and benchmark specifications and led teams that published numerous benchmark results. He also served as a member of the TAB, the TPC regulatory committee.
- Feifei Li: Feifei is a Tenured Professor of Computer Science at the University of Utah and a world's top scientist in the field of databases. For his academic and scientific achievements he has won the ACM SIGMOD 2016 Best Paper Award, ACM SIGMOD 2015 Best System Presentation Award, IEEE ICDE 2014 10 The Most Influential Papers Award, Hewlett-Packard's 2011 and 2012 Global R&D Awards, Google Faculty Award in 2015, Visa Faculty Award in 2017, ACM Distinguished Member in 2018, and the US NSF Career Award. He has hosted and participated in many important research projects and has served as a member of the editorial board and the chairman of many leading international academic journals and academic conferences and is a reviewer and panelists of many major projects.

© Springer Nature Switzerland AG 2020
R. Nambiar and M. Poess (Eds.): TPCTC 2019, LNCS 12257, pp. 133–138, 2020.
https://doi.org/10.1007/978-3-030-55024-0_9

- Meikel Poess: Meikel is Consulting Member of Technical Staff at Oracle Corporation's database performance group. He has a long history with the TPC and SPEC and have made significant contributions to industry standards. Has served as the chairman of TPC-H, TPC-DS and TPCx-IoT standards committees and is the chairman of the TPC Public Relation committee.
- Peter Boncz: Peter holds appointments as tenured researcher at CWI and professor at VU University Amsterdam. His academic background is in core database architecture, with the MonetDB the systems outcome of his PhD – MonetDB much later won the 2016 ACM SIGMOD systems award. He has a track record in bridging the gap between academia and commercial application, receiving the Dutch ICT Regie Award 2006 for his role in the CWI spin-off company Data Distilleries. In 2008 he co-founded Vectorwise around the analytical database system by the same name which pioneered vectorized query execution – later acquired by Actian. He is co-recipient of the 2009 VLDB 10 Years Best Paper Award, and in 2013 received the Humboldt Research Award for his research on database architecture. He also works on graph data management, founding in 2013 the Linked Database Benchmark Council (LDBC), a benchmarking organization for graph database systems.
- Raghunath Nambiar: Raghu is the Corporate Vice President and Chief Technology Officer of Datacenter Ecosystems and Application Engineering at AMD. He brings years of technical accomplishments with significant expertise in systems architecture, performance engineering, and creating disruptive technology solutions. Raghu has served in leadership positions on industry standards committees for performance evaluation and leading academic conferences. He chaired the industry's first standards committee for benchmarking big data systems, the industry's first standards committee for benchmarking Internet of Things, and is the founding chair of TPC's International Conference Series on Performance Evaluation and Benchmarking. Raghu has published more than 75 peer-reviewed papers and holds ten patents with several pending. He is the author of "Transforming Industry Through Data Analytics: Digital Disruption in Cities, Energy, Manufacturing, Healthcare, and Transportation".

2 State of the Union of the TPC and TPCTC

The Transaction Processing Performance Council (TPC) is a non-profit organization established in August 1988. Over the past three decades, the TPC has had a significant impact on the computing industry's use of industry-standard benchmarks. Vendors use TPC benchmarks to illustrate performance competitiveness for their existing products, and to improve and monitor the performance of their products under development. Many buyers use TPC benchmark results as points of comparison when purchasing new computing systems.

Over the years the TPC has created eighteen standards out of which eight are obsolete as the technologies and business landscape changed. See Fig 1.

The information technology landscape is evolving at a rapid pace, challenging industry experts and researchers to develop innovative techniques for evaluation, measurement and characterization of complex systems. The TPC remains committed to developing new benchmark standards to keep pace, and one vehicle for achieving this objective is

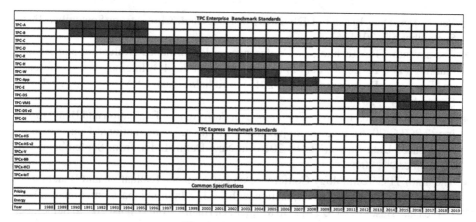

Fig. 1. TPC Timeline.

the sponsorship of the Technology Conference on Performance Evaluation and Benchmarking (TPCTC) since 2009 [1]. With this conference series, the TPC encourages researchers and industry experts to present and debate novel ideas and methodologies in performance evaluation and benchmarking. Over the past decade the TPCTC has emerged a leading forum for performance evaluation and benchmarking and the new benchmark standards.

- The first TPC Technology Conference on Performance Evaluation and Benchmarking (TPCTC 2009) was held in conjunction with the 35th International Conference on Very Large Data Bases (VLDB 2009) in Lyon, France from August 24th to August 28th, 2009 [1].
- The second TPC Technology Conference on Performance Evaluation and Benchmarking (TPCTC 2010) was held in conjunction with the 36th International Conference on Very Large Data Bases (VLDB 2010) in Singapore from September 13th to September 17th, 2010 [2].
- The third TPC Technology Conference on Performance Evaluation and Benchmarking (TPCTC 2011) was held in conjunction with the 37th International Conference on Very Large Data Bases (VLDB 2011) in Seattle, Washington from August 29th to September 3rd, 2011 [3].
- The fourth TPC Technology Conference on Performance Evaluation and Benchmarking (TPCTC 2012), held in conjunction with the 38th International Conference on Very Large Data Bases (VLDB 2012) in Istanbul, Turkey from August 27th to August 31st, 2012 [4].
- The fifth TPC Technology Conference on Performance Evaluation and Benchmarking (TPCTC 2013), held in conjunction with the 39th International Conference on Very Large Data Bases (VLDB 2013) in Riva del Garda, Trento, Italy from August 26th to August 30th, 2013 [5].
- The sixth TPC Technology Conference on Performance Evaluation and Benchmarking (TPCTC 2014), held in conjunction with the 40th International Conference on

Very Large Data Bases (VLDB 2014) in Hangzhou, China, from September 1st to September 5th, 2014 [6].

- The seventh TPC Technology Conference on Performance Evaluation and Benchmarking (TPCTC 2015), held in conjunction with the 41st International Conference on Very Large Data Bases (VLDB 2015) in Kohala Coast, USA, from August 31st to September 4th, 2015 [7].
- The eighth TPC Technology Conference on Performance Evaluation and Benchmarking (TPCTC 2016), held in conjunction with the 42nd International Conference on Very Large Data Bases (VLDB 2016) in New Delhi, India, from September 5th to September 9th, 2016 [8].
- The ninth TPC Technology Conference on Performance Evaluation and Benchmarking (TPCTC 2017), held in conjunction with the 43rd International Conference on Very Large Data Bases (VLDB 2017) in Munich, Germany, from August 28th to September 1st, 2017 [9].
- The tenth TPC Technology Conference on Performance Evaluation and Benchmarking (TPCTC 2018), held in conjunction with the 44th International Conference on Very Large Data Bases (VLDB 2017) in Rio de Janeiro, Brazil, from August 27th to August 31st, 2018 [10].

TPCTC conference series have emerged as a key forum in the performance benchmarking space and have contributed to several new industry standards and enhancements to existing standards by the TPC.

3   Panel Discussions

These are the main observations from the panel discussions on TPC and TPC benchmark result publications:

- More "Express Class" benchmarks publications than "Enterprise Class" benchmarks. Express Class Benchmarks are kit based and easier and more economical for companies to test, tune and publish than the specification-based Enterprise Class Benchmarks
- There are TPC benchmark result publications on public cloud instances which is new and very encouraging
- Big Data Analytics is a top area of interest and observed several publications of TPC Big Data benchmarks such as TPC Express Benchmark HS (TPCx-HS), TPC Express Benchmark IoT (TPCx-IoT), TPC Express Benchmark (TPCxBB), and TPC Benchmark DS (TPC-DS)
- Artificial Intelligence has been a hot topic in research and industry. In 2017 the Transaction Processing Performance Council (TPC) today announced the formation of a new Working Group (TPC-AI), tasked with developing industry standard benchmarks for both hardware and software platforms associated with running Artificial Intelligence (AI) based workloads
- In 2017 the TPC changed its Pricing Specification to accommodate TPC benchmark publications on clouds and observed the first TPC benchmark results on public clouds

- While there has been significant progress within TPC in creating new standards, many TPC standards were established decades ago, which have not been adapting towards the complex workloads from new business scenarios. For example, applications for large-scale applications on internet (such as Amazon.com and Tmall.com) usually require high read throughput, as well as excellent scalability and high availability, which do not match the existing TPC model
- The evaluation criteria and cost models in TPC are relatively obsolete, where the pursuit of a high score often results in a prohibitive hardware investment. Achieving a high score is hence an unnecessary burdensome for database vendors, while it brings in very little reference value to end customers. Therefore, in the era of cloud computing, the cost effectiveness will become a vital indicator, which would bring more values to customers and in turn re-incentivizing more database vendors to use TPC benchmarks
- The evaluation process and criteria should be refined to encourage broader partici-pations from various database vendors. Only in this way can the evaluation results provide useful insight values to customers during their process of database product selection, rather than being a "score game" among database vendors and hardware manufacturers.

Following the discussion above, here is a list of more specific recommendations:

- The TPC evaluation process should be simplified. It is complex and extremely time consuming, involving huge endeavor from vendors to participate in and follow through an evaluation.
- The cost model of TPC benchmarks should shift from the perspective of resource consumption to the perspective of cloud service and database system itself, paying more attention to availability and cost-effectiveness indicators.
- The cost-effectiveness indicator should take cloud-native architectures into consid-eration, such as disaggregated storage and compute (e.g., Aurora, PolarDB). In this scenario, we need to reformulate the cost model, rather than accumulating expenses on purchased machines, disks and switches.
- The definition of high availability should be revised. The traditional "Failing the local disk" should be replaced with node-level failures.

The panel discussed about TPC Benchmark C (TPC-C), one of the most popular bench-marks from the TPC. Based on a simple model, it is still very relevant in transaction processing workloads. But there are quite a few mismatched configurations/properties in its cost model against current application trends, which should be re-visited:

- Data distribution. Though the access distribution in TPC-C considers data skewness, it still fails to reflect the influence of real-world hot-spot issues, e.g., hot products and hot records are not considered in current model.
- Integrity constraints. Compared to simple benchmarking tools (e.g., sysbench and pgbench), TPC-C contains more complex query types and integrity constraints. How-ever, more comprehensive integrity constraints should be enforced from the need of enterprise applications.

- Read-Write Ratio. TPC-C leverages a write-intensive workload (i.e., read-write ratio is 1.9/1), which makes the evaluation of database capacity dominated by the I/O bandwidth. However, as we observe, increasingly many enterprise applications are read-intensive, leading to completely different performance observations.

4 Conclusion

Industry standard bodies like the TPC has to transform quickly in line with the technology and industry evaluations. TPCTC is a vehicle to achieve that. The pricing changes to accommodate benchmark result publications on the cloud is a major step. The standards under developments like artificial intelligence can be very useful to industry and academic community. To serve the growing demands of cloud providers and cloud customers the panel suggested to explore more complex benchmark workloads, changes to the pricing policies and evaluation criteria.

References

1. Nambiar, R., Poess, M. (eds.): TPCTC 2009. LNCS, vol. 5895. Springer, Heidelberg (2009). https://doi.org/10.1007/978-3-642-10424-4. ISBN 978-3-642-10423-7
2. Nambiar, R., Poess, M. (eds.): TPCTC 2010. LNCS, vol. 6417. Springer, Heidelberg (2011). https://doi.org/10.1007/978-3-642-18206-8. ISBN 978-3-642-18205-1
3. Nambiar, R., Poess, M. (eds.): TPCTC 2011. LNCS, vol. 7144. Springer, Heidelberg (2012). https://doi.org/10.1007/978-3-642-32627-1. ISBN 978-3-642-32626-4
4. Nambiar, R., Poess, M. (eds.): TPCTC 2012. LNCS, vol. 7755. Springer, Heidelberg (2013). https://doi.org/10.1007/978-3-642-36727-4. ISBN 978-3-642-36726-7
5. Nambiar, R., Poess, M. (eds.): TPCTC 2013. LNCS, vol. 8391. Springer, Cham (2014). https://doi.org/10.1007/978-3-319-04936-6. ISBN 978-3-319-04935-9
6. Nambiar, R., Poess, M.: TPCTC 2014. LNCS, vol. 8904. Springer, Cham (2015). https://doi.org/10.1007/978-3-319-15350-6. ISBN 978-3-319-15349-0
7. Nambiar, R., Poess, M. (eds.): TPCTC 2015. LNCS, vol. 9508. Springer, Cham (2016). https://doi.org/10.1007/978-3-319-31409-9. ISBN 978-3-319-31408-2
8. Nambiar, R., Poess, M. (eds.): TPCTC 2016. LNCS, vol. 10080. Springer, Cham (2017). https://doi.org/10.1007/978-3-319-54334-5. ISBN 978-3-319-54333-8
9. Nambiar, R., Poess, M. (eds.): TPCTC 2017. LNCS, vol. 10661. Springer, Cham (2018). https://doi.org/10.1007/978-3-319-72401-0. ISBN 978-3-319-72400-3
10. Nambiar, R., Poess, M. (eds.): TPCTC 2018. LNCS, vol. 11135. Springer, Cham (2019). https://doi.org/10.1007/978-3-030-11404-6. ISBN 978-3-030-11403-9

Benchmarking Database Cloud Services

Manfred Drozd[(⊠)]

Peakmarks Ltd., Zürcherstrasse 59, 8800 Thalwil, Switzerland
manfred.drozd@peakmarks.com

Abstract. Meanwhile, many database cloud services are available. The well-known providers are AWS (Amazon Web Service), Google Cloud, and Azure (Microsoft). Oracle and IBM offer cloud services for their in-house database products. In the past, the TPC organization has focused on performance measurement of database systems. Often, however, a database system is predefined, and the question arises as to the most efficient infrastructure and the best price/performance ratio - whether on-premise or as a cloud service. On the Internet, you can hardly find comparable and traceable information about the performance of database cloud services. Therefore, it is challenging to make corresponding price/performance comparisons [1]. The company Peakmarks was founded in 2011 to provide a robust and comprehensive benchmarking framework to identify representative performance indicators of database services. Peakmarks does not sell any hardware but runs benchmarks on behalf of users and manufacturers and thus guarantees absolute independence. Users can license Peakmarks benchmark software to perform their own performance tests. This presentation gives a rough overview of the Peakmarks benchmark software, its architecture, and workloads. Examples are used to show how understandable key performance metrics for database cloud services can be determined quickly and practically.

Keywords: Benchmark · Databases · Cloud services

1 Requirements to Benchmark Software

Huppler [3] described the five most important characteristics of a good benchmark: relevant, repeatable, fair, verifiable, and economical. Peakmarks[1] meets all these requirements.

However, other features are also crucial for customer acceptance of benchmark software:

Simplicity. It must be easy to install the benchmark software, perform the benchmark, and interpret the results. Peakmarks is implemented with the tools of the database without operating system scripts. Therefore, Peakmarks runs unchanged everywhere where the database software is available. Any DBA can easily manage the benchmark software without additional know-how.

---

[1] From now on, we use the word Peakmarks synonymously with Peakmarks benchmark software.

© Springer Nature Switzerland AG 2020
R. Nambiar and M. Poess (Eds.): TPCTC 2019, LNCS 12257, pp. 139–153, 2020.
https://doi.org/10.1007/978-3-030-55024-0_10

Speed. The installation, loading of the data, processing of the various workloads, and evaluation of the performance key figures should be fast. Peakmarks is installed in a few hours, including all adjustments of the database. The loading time of the database depends on the database size and the performance of the infrastructure. On powerful systems, loading times of 4 TByte per hour were measured. Complete benchmark runs with all workloads typically take between 12 and 24 h; the results are immediately available. A comprehensive benchmark project can be completed within a week. This is significantly faster than many proof-of-concepts, which may take several weeks and whose value is limited to the tested application.

Different Load Situations. Often it is not the maximum value of a performance metric that is of interest, but the optimal value. Peakmarks analyzes the performance of a database service in all load situations. A benchmark test starts with a low load and increases the load continuously until the system is saturated. In this way, the optimum performance range of a database service can be determined.

More Performance Metrics. Many benchmarks provide only a single performance metric. This dramatically simplifies the comparison of different systems. However, a single metric is difficult to understand [2]. Peakmarks provides a set of representative and easy-to-understand metrics for different aspects. Actual performance questions can be answered more easily. Performance bottlenecks and malfunctions can be detected more easily. Since several performance metrics are available, the user must decide with which priority the individual metrics are to be included in the decision-making process, when choosing the right cloud service.

Product Specific Workloads. When customers have to pay license fees for database software, they are interested in getting the highest performance out of their database service. That's why we've deliberately implemented workloads that can only be found on certain database products but are essential for the solution architecture. Currently, Peakmarks is available for Oracle 12.2 and upwards. There are considerations to port the software to other database systems as well. Peakmarks is not suitable to compare different database products; it only serves to compare the underlying infrastructure, on-premise or in the cloud.

2   Key Performance Indicators

Representative performance indicators of database services can be used for various tasks:

Quality Assurance. A database service is validated for its performance properties. Performance bottlenecks can be quickly identified; performance promises of the providers are easily checked.

Evaluation. Performance indicators are used for price/performance considerations of various database services, technologies, or configurations.

Capacity Planning. When systems migrate to new platforms or cloud services, performance indicators help with capacity planning.

License Cost Optimization. Our experience over many years has shown that many users can halve license costs for the same performance, only by optimizing the infrastructure. License costs often exceed infrastructure costs by far.

3   The Architecture of Peakmarks Benchmark Software

Peakmarks is written in the procedural SQL extension of the database system, in the case of Oracle in PL/SQL. The size of the database can be configured in a range from 250 GByte up to 64 TByte per database server. Clusters with multiple servers are supported. The record length of the benchmark tables can be configured between 80 bytes and 4'000 bytes. The redundancy of the benchmark data can be controlled via a parameter. The data can optionally be encrypted using a further configuration parameter. All encryption methods offered by the database system are supported. The scalable loading process of the benchmark data automatically adapts its parallelism to the performance capabilities of the database platform.

A workload generator generates the database load with database jobs, and a performance monitor collects all relevant performance statistics before and after each performance test. All workloads are generated within the database, and all performance statistics also originate from the database (Fig. 1).

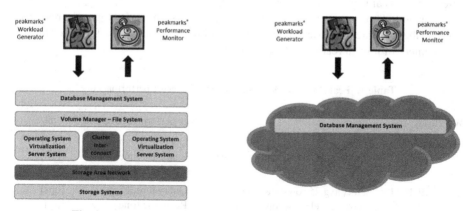

Fig. 1. Peakmarks benchmark software – on-premise and in the cloud

Peakmarks provides a library of workloads to determine the most important performance indicators of database services for:

- Server and storage systems in database operation.
- Critical database background processes, responsible for transaction management (log writer) and buffer management (database writer).
- Typical database operations such as data load, data analytics and transaction processing.
- PL/SQL application code.

4 Simple and Complex Workloads

Peakmarks distinguishes between simple and complex workloads. Simple workloads execute precisely one type of load (SQL statement). Complex workloads are hierarchically composed of different simple workloads to simulate complex load situations.

The runtime of the workloads is configurable. Runtimes between 5 and 10 min per test have proven to be representative. Let us take a closer look at some of the workloads.

4.1 Server Workloads

Server workloads determine the power of a server with its processors, main memory, and internal memory channels in database operation. These workloads are especially crucial if license cost must be optimized. License costs are often linked to the number of processors[2] used. In this case, a server with the highest performance per processor is searched for.

Server workloads also show the efficiency of multithreading and virtualization technologies and provide hints about scalability when high numbers of sockets and cores are used (NUMA effects). If database encryption is selected, its impact on the overall database performance can also be determined.

All server workloads access tables via SQL with different access patterns. The affected tables are fixed in the buffer cache. There are almost no I/O operations, so these workloads are entirely CPU-bound.

The essential primary performance metrics are queries per second (qps), the response time, and the scan rate of queries (memory bandwidth). A secondary performance metric is the number of logical reads per second (Table 1).

Table 1. Peakmarks workloads to determine server performance.

Workload	Action	Key performance metric	Unit
SRV-LIGHT	Select single row via index. Example: select account, product, order, invoice, etc.	• Query throughput • Response time	[qps] [μs]
SRV-MEDIUM	Select avg 25 rows via index. Example: select account postings last week; item list of order, etc.	• Query throughput • Response time	[qps] [μs]
SRV-HEAVY	Select avg 125 rows via index. Example: report of last month's call records, etc.	• Query throughput • Response time	[qps] [μs]
SRV-SCAN	Data search without index support	Buffer scan rate	[MBps]
SRV-MIXED	Complex workload with a mix of simple server workloads and concurrent table scan.	• Query throughput • Response time	[qps] [μs]

---

[2] A processor may be a core or a thread, dependent on processor architecture and the used multithreading technology.

The benchmark report in Fig. 2 shows the performance of a database service for workload SRV-LIGHT. This benchmark comprises 5 tests. The second column shows the workload name. The column *Nodes* indicate how many cluster nodes are used in the test. The column *Jobs* describes the number of processes that generate the load for the workloads. The next 4 columns describe the percentage CPU load in the different CPU modes. The column *Queries total* describes the total number of queries processed per second. The column *Queries per cpu* shows the performance per involved processor. This information is important for license cost considerations. The columns *Logical reads total* and *Logical reads per cpu* are the corresponding performance metrics for database accesses in the buffer cache. The column *BuCache read* displays the hit rate of all read accesses in the buffer cache and is only used to check that this workload has been optimally processed.

Test	Workload	Nodes	Jobs	CPU busy [%]	CPU user [%]	CPU sys [%]	CPU idle [%]	Queries total [qps]	Queries per cpu [qps]	Response time [ms]	Log reads total [dbps]	Log reads per cpu [dbps]	BuCache read [%]
1	SRV-LIGHT	1	1	13	12	1	87	62,241	62,241	0.016	186,890	186,890	100.0
2	SRV-LIGHT	1	2	25	24	1	75	115,499	57,750	0.017	346,601	173,301	100.0
3	SRV-LIGHT	1	4	50	48	2	50	198,302	49,575	0.020	595,053	148,763	100.0
4	SRV-LIGHT	1	8	99	95	4	1	284,839	35,605	0.028	854,567	106,821	100.0
5	SRV-LIGHT	1	12	99	95	4	1	283,995	35,499	0.041	848,451	106,056	100.0

Fig. 2. Benchmark report for a server system workload.

It is straightforward to see how, as the load increases, the response time also increases, but the number of queries per CPU decreases. The short response times of less than 30 μs show the exceptional efficiency of database queries when all the data is in the buffer cache. It is also noticeable that throughput and CPU utilization do not correlate above 50%; a typical characteristic of some processor architectures when multi-threading is enabled.

4.2 Storage Workloads

Conventional I/O benchmark tools such as vdbench, iometer, Orion often display performance values that are not achieved in real database operations. The reason for this is the complexity of database I/O operations.

If a data block is read, the buffer cache management of the database has to perform many tasks: a) find a free slot for the block; b) if there is no free slot, replace older blocks; c) synchronize all database processes that simultaneously try for free slots in the buffer cache; d) if a shared disk cluster architecture is used, the synchronization has to be cluster-wide; e) finally, blocks are checked for their integrity and consistency during I/O transfer.

Peakmarks, therefore, generates I/O load with so-called SQL-generated I/O operations to obtain representative performance metrics for the storage system (Table 2).

Table 2. Peakmarks workloads to determine storage performance.

Workload	Action	Key performance metric	Unit
STO-READ	SQL generated sequential block read	Sequential I/O throughput	[MBps]
STO-RANDOM	SQL generated random block read/write	• Random I/O throughput in database blocks per second • I/O service time	[dbps] [μs]

Storage workloads show the efficiency of the I/O stack (I/O scheduler, queues, multipathing, virtualization), the technologies used (HDD, SSD, Flash, SAS or PCI, NVMe, etc.) and storage specific functionalities (deduplication, compression, encryption, snapshots, mirroring, SQL offloading).

The benchmark report in Fig. 3 shows the performance of a database service for workload STO-RANDOM with 100% read operations.

Test	Workload	Wri [%]	Nodes	Jobs	CPU busy [%]	CPU user [%]	CPU sys [%]	CPU idle [%]	CPU iow [%]	Phys reads total [dbps]	Phys reads total [IOPS]	Service time [us]	Phys reads total [MBps]	BuCache read [%]	FlCache read [%]
6	STO-RANDOM	0	1	1	2	1	1	98	0	33,390	33,410	167	261	0.0	0.0
7	STO-RANDOM	0	1	2	3	1	1	99	0	63,570	63,590	175	497	0.0	0.0
8	STO-RANDOM	0	1	4	5	3	3	95	0	117,600	117,600	182	919	0.1	0.0
9	STO-RANDOM	0	1	8	10	5	5	90	0	209,800	209,800	194	1,640	0.1	0.0
10	STO-RANDOM	0	1	16	20	10	9	80	0	355,000	355,000	211	2,774	0.1	0.0
11	STO-RANDOM	0	1	32	37	21	17	63	0	549,700	549,700	243	4,295	0.1	0.0
12	STO-RANDOM	0	1	64	68	39	30	32	0	756,900	772,800	451	6,038	0.1	0.0
13	STO-RANDOM	0	1	96	88	48	39	12	0	801,900	825,200	945	6,447	0.2	0.0
14	STO-RANDOM	0	1	128	89	49	40	11	0	792,700	823,200	1,563	6,432	0.3	0.0

Fig. 3. Benchmark report for random read storage system workload.

This report shows the difference between the maximum and optimal range of performance. The storage system can read over 800,000 random single database blocks per second (dbps), but at a service time of just under one millisecond (Test 13). An all-flash storage system is used in this case study. We expect a service time of less than 500 microseconds per single database block read for this storage technology. The optimal performance is more like 750,000 dbps (Test 12). Higher values are possible, but only at the price of sharply increasing service times. It is a good advice to keep the storage utilization below this value.

4.3 Data Load Workloads

System architects and capacity planners need performance metrics from database services regarding their ability to load data. This is particularly important for Data Warehouse and Data Analytics systems, where data volumes are constantly growing as the time available for loading becomes smaller.

Oracle provides different technologies for loading data: conventional loading via buffer cache and direct loading bypassing the buffer cache. Peakmarks provides workloads for both data loading techniques (Table 3).

Table 3. Peakmarks workloads to determine data load performance.

Workload	Action	Key performance metric	Unit
DL-BUFFER	Buffered data load	Data load throughput	[MBps]
DL-DIRECT	Direct data load	Data load throughput	[MBps]

The benchmark report in Fig. 4 shows the performance of a database service for both data load workloads. The key performance metrics for data load is the amount of data that can be loaded within a certain timeframe in column *Loaded user data*.

Test	Workload	Nodes	Jobs	DOP	CPU busy [%]	CPU user [%]	CPU sys [%]	CPU idle [%]	CPU iow [%]	Loaded user data [rps]	Loaded user data [MBps]	REDO data [MByte]	BuCache read [%]	FlCache read [%]	FlCache write [%]
15	DL-BUFFER	1	1	1	2	1	1	98	0	29,935	9	30	100.0	56.7	89.7
16	DL-BUFFER	1	2	1	4	3	1	96	0	54,752	16	55	100.0	48.5	91.7
17	DL-BUFFER	1	4	1	7	6	1	93	0	105,138	32	107	100.0	49.4	91.8
18	DL-BUFFER	1	8	1	8	7	1	92	0	181,662	54	184	100.0	59.6	92.5
19	DL-BUFFER	1	16	1	12	10	1	88	0	284,286	85	288	100.0	63.0	93.9
20	DL-BUFFER	1	32	1	14	12	2	86	0	338,027	101	344	100.0	65.3	96.4
21	DL-BUFFER	2	64	1	30	26	3	70	0	786,876	236	798	100.0	59.4	96.1

Test	Workload	Nodes	Jobs	DOP	CPU busy [%]	CPU user [%]	CPU sys [%]	CPU idle [%]	CPU iow [%]	Loaded user data [rps]	Loaded user data [MBps]	REDO data [MByte]	BuCache read [%]	FlCache read [%]	FlCache write [%]
22	DL-DIRECT	1	1	1	5	4	1	95	0	46,254	14	22	98.6	66.1	84.0
23	DL-DIRECT	1	2	1	5	4	1	95	0	92,640	28	44	99.3	62.5	86.0
24	DL-DIRECT	1	4	1	6	5	1	94	0	202,426	61	79	99.3	63.3	84.0
25	DL-DIRECT	1	8	1	7	6	1	93	0	387,664	116	121	99.3	67.9	87.7
26	DL-DIRECT	1	16	1	10	8	1	90	0	714,476	214	179	99.3	68.8	92.2
27	DL-DIRECT	1	32	1	16	14	2	84	0	1,144,732	343	225	99.3	68.5	93.5
28	DL-DIRECT	2	64	1	28	24	3	72	0	2,398,864	720	485	99.3	66.8	92.4

Fig. 4. Benchmark report for data load workloads.

This case study was run on an Oracle Engineered System which uses flash cache technology. The buffered load generates more REDO data. The direct load in workload DL-DIRECT provides much higher throughput in data load. In the last test of each workload, the load is doubled but distributed over two database servers. In both cases, the system scales well.

4.4 Data Analytic Workloads

System Architects and capacity planners require performance metrics from database services regarding their ability to search for data. Data analytics applications are typically based on "full table scan" operations. The performance of "full table scans" depends on the position of the data in the storage hierarchy and the technology used to boost scanning performance.

Peakmarks provides workloads to test different data locations (storage, memory) and to test different boost technologies (smart scan, in-memory column store) (Table 4).

Table 4. Peakmarks workloads to determine data analytics performance.

Workload	Action	Key performance metric	Unit
DA-LOW	Full table scan with an aggregate of low complexity	Data scan throughput	[MBps]

The benchmark report in Fig. 5 shows the performance of a database service for data analytic workloads. The key performance metric for data analytics is the amount of data that can be scanned within a certain timeframe in column *Scanned user data.*

Test	Workload	Loc	Nodes	Jobs	DOP	CPU busy [%]	CPU user [%]	CPU sys [%]	CPU idle [%]	Scanned user data [rps]	Scanned user data [MBps]	BuCache read [%]	FlCache read [%]
29	DA-LOW	STO	1	1	1	3	2	1	97	2,957,446	1,009	0.0	99.9
30	DA-LOW	STO	1	2	1	3	2	1	97	6,504,650	2,220	2.9	99.9
31	DA-LOW	STO	1	4	1	2	1	1	98	11,139,254	3,802	0.0	100.0
32	DA-LOW	STO	1	8	1	5	4	1	95	16,622,389	5,674	0.0	100.0
33	DA-LOW	STO	1	16	1	5	4	1	95	16,620,501	5,673	0.0	100.0
34	DA-LOW	STO	1	24	1	4	3	1	96	16,841,046	5,748	0.0	100.0
35	DA-LOW	STO	2	48	1	5	4	1	95	33,858,898	11,557	0.0	100.0

Test	Workload	Loc	Nodes	Jobs	DOP	CPU busy [%]	CPU user [%]	CPU sys [%]	CPU idle [%]	Scanned user data [rps]	Scanned user data [MBps]	BuCache read [%]	FlCache read [%]
36	DA-LOW	EXA	1	1	1	2	1	1	98	38,705,238	13,211	0.0	100.0
37	DA-LOW	EXA	1	2	1	4	3	1	96	74,473,109	25,420	0.0	100.0
38	DA-LOW	EXA	1	4	1	5	4	1	95	121,551,795	41,490	0.0	100.0
39	DA-LOW	EXA	1	8	1	5	3	1	95	171,804,526	58,642	0.0	100.0
40	DA-LOW	EXA	1	16	1	6	4	2	94	221,632,126	75,650	0.0	100.0
41	DA-LOW	EXA	1	24	1	5	3	2	95	246,288,356	84,066	0.0	99.8
42	DA-LOW	EXA	2	48	1	7	5	2	93	272,648,654	93,064	0.0	99.9

Fig. 5. Benchmark report for data analytics workloads using storage.

"Full table scans" cause sequential storage reads on the storage system and are usually limited by the bandwidth between the storage system and server system, in this case around 6 GBps (test 34). When two database servers request sequential reads, the storage system scales well (2 cluster nodes are used in test 35 and test 42).

Test 36 to 42 show the performance when SQL offload technology can be used. Even one database server can use the full performance capabilities of the storage system, which is by factors higher than on a conventional storage system. But this technology requires specialized hardware and software (Oracle Engineered System).

The benchmark report in Fig. 6 shows the same workload, but data is stored in main memory using row store (test 43–51) or column store (test 52–60). The results are very different (by factors) and allow a fair comparison of different technologies to calculate the price-/performance ratio of each data analytics solution.

Test	Workload	Loc	Nodes	Jobs	DOP	CPU busy [%]	CPU user [%]	CPU sys [%]	CPU idle [%]	Scanned user data [rps]	Scanned user data [MBps]	BuCache read [%]	FlCache read [%]
43	DA-LOW	ROW	1	1	1	2	2	0	98	24,461,819	8,100	100.0	0.0
44	DA-LOW	ROW	1	2	1	4	4	0	96	46,686,828	15,459	100.0	0.0
45	DA-LOW	ROW	1	4	1	8	8	0	92	87,802,201	29,073	100.0	0.0
46	DA-LOW	ROW	1	8	1	17	16	0	83	76,070,044	25,188	100.0	0.0
47	DA-LOW	ROW	1	12	1	25	25	0	75	82,624,704	27,359	100.0	0.0
48	DA-LOW	ROW	1	16	1	33	33	0	67	113,429,349	37,559	100.0	0.0
49	DA-LOW	ROW	1	24	1	50	50	0	50	143,799,960	47,615	100.0	0.0
50	DA-LOW	ROW	1	32	1	66	66	0	34	145,733,328	48,255	100.0	0.0
51	DA-LOW	ROW	1	48	1	99	99	0	1	159,741,657	52,894	100.0	0.0

Test	Workload	Loc	Nodes	Jobs	DOP	CPU busy [%]	CPU user [%]	CPU sys [%]	CPU idle [%]	Scanned user data [rps]	Scanned user data [MBps]	BuCache read [%]	FlCache read [%]
52	DA-LOW	COL	1	1	1	2	2	0	98	161,621,061	53,516	100.0	0.0
53	DA-LOW	COL	1	2	1	4	4	0	96	321,493,739	106,453	100.0	0.0
54	DA-LOW	COL	1	4	1	8	8	0	92	638,947,218	211,569	100.0	0.0
55	DA-LOW	COL	1	8	1	17	16	0	83	1,190,488,863	394,195	100.0	0.0
56	DA-LOW	COL	1	12	1	25	25	0	75	1,830,025,038	605,959	100.0	0.0
57	DA-LOW	COL	1	16	1	33	33	0	67	2,478,718,508	820,755	100.0	0.0
58	DA-LOW	COL	1	24	1	50	50	0	50	3,579,861,738	1,185,366	100.0	0.0
59	DA-LOW	COL	1	32	1	66	65	0	34	4,064,304,827	1,345,775	100.0	0.0
60	DA-LOW	COL	1	48	1	99	99	0	1	4,830,584,944	1,599,506	100.0	0.0

Fig. 6. Benchmark report for data analytics workloads using main memory.

4.5 Transaction Processing Workloads

System architects and capacity planners need performance metrics from database services regarding their ability to run typical transaction processing applications. Peakmarks provides transaction processing workloads of varying complexity (light, medium, and heavy) (Table 5).

Table 5. Peakmarks workloads to determine transaction processing performance.

Workload	Action	Key performance metric	Unit
TP-LIGHT	Select/Update single row via index. Example: account, product, order, invoice, etc.	• Transaction throughput • Response time	[tps] [ms]
TP-MEDIUM	Select/Update avg 25 rows via index. Example: account postings last week; item list of order, etc.	• Transaction throughput • Response time	[tps] [ms]
TP-HEAVY	Select/Update avg 125 rows via index. Example: last month's call records of smartphones, etc.	• Transaction throughput • Response time	[tps] [ms]
TP-MIXED	Complex workload: mix of Select/Update/Insert transactions.	• Transaction throughput • Response time	[tps] [ms]

The following benchmark report in Fig. 7 shows the performance of a database service for workloads TP-LIGHT and TP-HEAVY with 80/20 select/update ratio. The percentage of update transactions can be configured from 0% to 100% in 10% steps (column *Upd*).

Test	Workload	Upd [%]	Jobs	CPU busy [%]	CPU user [%]	CPU sys [%]	CPU idle [%]	CPU iow [%]	Trans total [tps]	Trans per cpu [tps]	Resp time [ms]	Log reads per tx [dbptx]	Phys reads per tx [dbptx]	Log writes per tx [dbptx]	Phys writes per tx [dbptx]	BuCache read [%]
61	TP-LIGHT	20	1	13	10	3	87	0	21,535	21,535	0.046	5.22	0.18	2.81	0.13	96.6
62	TP-LIGHT	20	2	20	17	3	80	0	29,990	14,995	0.066	5.22	0.14	2.81	0.15	97.2
63	TP-LIGHT	20	4	39	32	7	61	0	47,151	11,788	0.084	5.21	0.18	2.81	0.18	96.6
64	TP-LIGHT	20	8	65	53	13	35	0	64,295	8,037	0.123	5.21	0.24	2.81	0.28	95.4
65	TP-LIGHT	20	12	69	52	17	31	0	52,553	6,569	0.225	5.21	0.44	2.81	0.51	91.6
66	TP-HEAVY	20	1	14	12	2	86	0	657	657	1.516	281.37	3.73	301.79	5.19	98.7
67	TP-HEAVY	20	2	28	22	6	72	0	1,011	506	1.967	281.53	7.37	301.84	9.43	97.4
68	TP-HEAVY	20	4	49	41	8	51	0	1,620	405	2.446	281.29	6.35	301.71	12.78	97.7
69	TP-HEAVY	20	8	64	51	14	36	0	1,505	188	5.264	281.42	11.83	301.88	24.07	95.8
70	TP-HEAVY	20	12	46	24	22	54	0	551	69	21.525	282.31	43.06	302.12	60.28	84.7

Fig. 7. Benchmark report for transaction processing, 20% updates.

The key performance metrics for these workloads are transactions per second (column *Trans total*) and the response time (column *Resp time*).

The performance of these workloads depends on various factors, including the ratio of database size to buffer cache size. The higher the hit rate of the buffer cache (column *BuCache read*), the higher the transaction rate and the lower the response time of the transactions column *Resp time*). This is particularly true for low update rates, where the proportion of write operations is low in relation to the number of read operations.

The following benchmark report in Fig. 8 shows the performance of a database service with the workload "TP-MIXED" with 20% update share. This complex workload is similar to a TPC-C workload, where queries, update, and insert transactions are processed simultaneously.

Test	Workload	Upd [%]	Jobs	CPU busy [%]	CPU user [%]	CPU sys [%]	CPU idle [%]	CPU iow [%]	Trans total [tps]	Trans per cpu [tps]	Resp time [ms]	Log reads per tx [dbptx]	Phys reads per tx [dbptx]	Log writes per tx [dbptx]	Phys writes per tx [dbptx]	BuCache read [%]
71	TP-MIXED	20	4	45	36	9	55	0	13,326	3,331	0.298	21.57	0.48	20.59	0.66	97.8
72	TP-MIXED	20	8	77	60	17	23	0	17,242	2,155	0.460	23.60	0.85	22.84	1.39	96.4
73	TP-MIXED	20	12	80	61	19	20	0	13,440	1,680	0.879	29.35	1.22	29.22	2.44	95.8

Fig. 8. Benchmark report for mixed transaction processing, 20% updates.

4.6 PL/SQL Application Performance

PL/SQL is the preferred programming language for complex transaction logic and algorithms. PL/SQL code is stored in the database server. Some large applications, e.g., core banking systems, are entirely implemented in PL/SQL.

Peakmarks provides workloads to test PL/SQL code efficiency on a particular processor. These workloads are entirely CPU-bound. The key performance metrics for PL/SQL application performance are the number of executed PL/SQL operations within a certain timeframe and the execution time of PL/SQL algorithms (Table 6).

Table 6. Peakmarks workloads to determine transaction processing performance.

Workload	Action	Key performance metric	Unit
PLS-ADD	Addition of numbers.	Throughput of PL/SQL operations	[Mops]
PLS-BUILTIN	Datatype-specific operations, including SQL built-in functions, based on core banking and telco billing applications.	Throughput of PL/SQL operations	[Mops]
PLS-PRIME	Calculation of first N prime numbers.	Algorithm processing time	[s]
PLS-FIBO	Calculation of Fibonacci number N using a recursive algorithm.	Algorithm processing time	[s]
PLS-MIXED	Datatype-specific operations, including SQL built-in functions.	Throughput of PL/SQL operations	[Mops]

The following benchmark report in Fig. 9 shows the performance of a database service with the workload "PLS_MIXED" with different numerical datatypes.

```
                                CPU  CPU  CPU  CPU  Operations  Operations  Elapsed
                                busy user sys  idle      total     per cpu     time
Test Workload    Type  N Nodes  Jobs [%]  [%]  [%]  [%]    [Mops]      [Mops]     [s]
---- --------    ----  ------- ----- ---- ---- ---- ----  --------- ----------- --------
  74 PLS-MIXED     0     0       1    4    50   50   0   50    337.07      84.27      180
  75 PLS-MIXED     0     0       1    8    99   99   0    1    401.76      50.22      180
  76 PLS-MIXED     0     0       1   12   100   99   0    0    418.11      52.26      181
```

Fig. 9. Benchmark report for PL/SQL code with mixed datatypes.

4.7 Database Service Processes

In the case of Oracle, the performance of the log writer background process is critical. It is responsible for transaction logging and database recovery after system failures. The latency of transaction logging can have a significant impact on the response time of user transactions.

Optionally, the log writer is also used for database replication to synchronize standby databases. This technology is very popular for disaster recovery solutions. Replication can take place in synchronous or asynchronous mode. The data transfer between primary and standby databases can optionally be encrypted and/or compressed. With synchronous replication, local transactions have to wait until the standby databases have also applied the transaction log. This may delay local transaction processing considerably.

To analyze the performance behavior of the log writer process in all possible situations, Peakmarks offers two different workloads. One workload analyzes log writer latency, and the other one's log writer throughput (Table 7).

Table 7. Peakmarks workloads to determine log writer performance.

Workload	Action	Key performance metric	Unit
LGWR-LAT	Small insert transactions with 1, 25 or 125 rows per transaction and commit wait	• Transaction throughput • Response time • REDO sync time	[tps] [ms] [µsec]
LGWR-THR	Large insert transaction with 2'000 rows per transaction and commit wait	Log writer throughput	[MBps]

The following benchmark report in Fig. 10 shows the performance of a database service with the workload "LGWR-LAT" and different transaction sizes (column *TX size*) of 1 and 25 rows per transaction.

Test	Workload	TX size [rpt]	Nodes	Jobs	CPU busy [%]	CPU user [%]	CPU sys [%]	CPU idle [%]	CPU iow [%]	Transactions total [tps]	Response time [ms]	REDO blocks [rbps]	REDO data [MByte]	REDO sync [ms]	FlCache write [%]
77	LGWR-LAT	1	1	1	12	9	3	88	0	6,762	0.147	29,240	13	0.058	0.0
78	LGWR-LAT	1	1	2	24	17	7	76	0	11,293	0.176	49,077	21	0.070	0.0
79	LGWR-LAT	1	1	4	41	31	10	59	0	15,719	0.253	66,757	30	0.118	0.0
80	LGWR-LAT	1	1	8	65	52	13	35	0	27,992	0.285	114,960	53	0.138	0.0

Test	Workload	TX size [rpt]	Nodes	Jobs	CPU busy [%]	CPU user [%]	CPU sys [%]	CPU idle [%]	CPU iow [%]	Transactions total [tps]	Response time [ms]	REDO blocks [rbps]	REDO data [MByte]	REDO sync [ms]	FlCache write [%]
81	LGWR-LAT	25	1	1	12	9	3	88	0	1,270	0.785	70,581	35	0.242	0.0
82	LGWR-LAT	25	1	2	25	21	4	75	0	2,573	0.769	143,785	70	0.154	0.0
83	LGWR-LAT	25	1	4	46	40	7	54	0	4,267	0.925	239,056	117	0.192	0.0
84	LGWR-LAT	25	1	8	84	76	8	16	0	6,089	1.298	339,946	167	0.232	0.0

Fig. 10. Benchmark report for log writer latency.

The following benchmark report in Fig. 11 shows the performance of a database service with the workload "LGWR-THR" with large transactions.

Test	Workload	TX size [rpt]	Nodes	Jobs	CPU busy [%]	CPU user [%]	CPU sys [%]	CPU idle [%]	CPU iow [%]	Transactions total [tps]	Response time [ms]	REDO blocks [rbps]	REDO data [MByte]	REDO sync [ms]	FlCache write [%]
85	LGWR-THR	2000	1	1	14	12	3	86	0	115	8.631	115,085	57	0.740	0.0
86	LGWR-THR	2000	1	2	27	23	4	73	0	205	9.615	205,126	102	0.802	0.0
87	LGWR-THR	2000	1	4	52	48	4	48	0	321	12.390	322,406	160	0.596	0.0
88	LGWR-THR	2000	1	8	95	88	6	5	0	449	17.545	450,739	223	0.914	0.0

Fig. 11. Benchmark report for log writer throughput.

4.8   Order in Which Workloads Are Executed

We run the workloads in a logical order and start with the server and storage workloads. For example, if the storage workloads do not perform satisfactorily, other workloads that are heavily dependent on storage performance will also deliver disappointing results.

The following order has proven workable

- Workloads for Server Systems.
- Workloads for Storage Systems.
- Workloads for Database Background Processes.
- Workloads for Data Load.
- Workloads for Data Analytics.
- Workloads for Transaction Processing.
- Workloads for PL/SQL application programs.

5   Case Study

The Peakmarks benchmark software offers a fast and comprehensive performance analysis of Database Cloud Services. The results are understandable key performance metrics for representative database operations and provide a reliable foundation for price/performance comparisons and capacity planning.

Here is a summary of performance metrics of a database service with 8 processors, 32 GByte main memory, flash storage, and a 250 GByte database. The min/max values describe the system behavior in all load situations (best case, worst case).

The whole benchmark took less than 24 h. The customer selected those workloads from all that are important to him. The parameters for the workloads were chosen to reflect the customer's current environment best (Tables 8, 9, 10, 11, 12, 13 and 14).

Table 8. Peakmarks key performance metrics for server component.

Workload	Description	Cloud service A
SRV-MIXED	Min/Max query throughput per CPU in [qps]	12,458/17,673
SRV-SCAN	Min/Max scan throughput per CPU in [MBps]	2,118/3,986

[qps] queries per second
[MBps] megabytes per second

Table 9. Peakmarks key performance metrics for storage component.

Workload	Description	Cloud service A
STO-READ	Max sequential read throughput in [MBps]	2,014
STO-RANDOM 100% read	Max random read throughput in [dbps] at service time in [μs]	180,632 @ 387
STO-RANDOM 50% read	Max random read throughput in [dbps] at service time in [μs]	55,043 @ 546

[dbps] database blocks per second
[MBps] megabytes per second
[μs] microseconds

Table 10. Peakmarks key performance metrics for data load.

Workload	Description	Cloud service A
DL-BUFFER	Buffered data load, max data load rate in [MBps]	68
DL-DIRECT	Direct data load, max data load rate in [MBps]	136

[MBps] megabytes per second

Table 11. Peakmarks key performance metrics for data analytics.

Workload	Description	Cloud service A
DA-LOW default storage	Max data scan rate in [MBps]	1,755
DA-LOW storage offload	Max data scan rate in [MBps]	–
DA-LOW row store	Max data scan rate in [MBps]	16,828
DA-LOW column store	Max data scan rate in [MBps]	96,078

[MBps] megabytes per second

Table 12. Peakmarks key performance metrics for transaction processing (80% read, 20% update).

Workload	Description	Cloud service A
TP-LIGHT 1 row per tx	Max transaction rate in [tps] at response time in [ms]	73,0976 @ 107
TP-MEDIUM 25 rows per tx	Max transaction rate in [tps] at response time in [ms]	8,041 @ 971
TP-HEAVY 125 rows per tx	Max transaction rate in [tps] at response time in [ms]	1,775 @ 4,570
TP-MIXED	Max transaction rate in [tps] at response time in [ms]	20,924 @ 708

[tps] transactions per second
[ms] millisecond

Table 13. Peakmarks key performance metrics for PL/SQL application code.

Workload	Description	Cloud service A
PLS-ADD PLS_INTEGER	Min/Max throughput per CPU in [Mops]	167/381
PLS-BUILTIN NUMBER	Min/Max throughput per CPU in [Mops]	6.10/11.46
PLS-BUILTIN VARCHAR2	Min/Max throughput per CPU in [Mops]	1.98/4.38
PLS-MIXED all data types	Min/Max mixed operations per CPU in [Mops]	50.22/84.27

[Mops] million operations per second

Table 14. Peakmarks key performance metrics for database service processes.

Workload	Description	Cloud service A
LGWR-LAT 1 row per tx	Max log writer transaction rate in [tps] at service time in [μs]	27,992 @ 285
LGWR-LAT 25 rows per tx	Max log writer transaction rate in [tps] at service time in [μs]	6,089 @ 1,298
LGWR-LAT 125 rows per tx	Max log writer transaction rate in [tps] at service time in [μs]	1,583 @ 4,969
LGWR-THR	Max log writer throughput in [MBps]	223
DBWR-THR	Max database writer throughput in [dbps]	67,592

[Mops] million operations per second
[μs] microseconds
[tps] transactions per second
[dbps] database blocks per second

References

1. Bermbach, D. (ed.): Cloud Service Benchmarking. Springer, Cham (2017). https://doi.org/10.1007/978-3-319-55483-9_15
2. Crolotte, A.: Issues in benchmark metric selection. In: Nambiar, R., Poess, M. (eds.) TPCTC 2009. LNCS, vol. 5895, pp. 146–152. Springer, Heidelberg (2009). https://doi.org/10.1007/978-3-642-10424-4_11
3. Huppler, K.: The art of building a good benchmark. In: Nambiar, R., Poess, M. (eds.) TPCTC 2009. LNCS, vol. 5895, pp. 18–30. Springer, Heidelberg (2009). https://doi.org/10.1007/978-3-642-10424-4_3

Use Machine Learning Methods to Predict Lifetimes of Storage Devices

Yingxuan Zhu[1(✉)], Bowen Jiang[3], Yong Wang[1], Tim Tingqiu Yuan[2], and Jian Li[1]

[1] Futurewei Techonologies, Boston, USA
{yingxuan.zhu,yong.wang,jian.li}@futurewei.com
[2] Huawei Techonologies, Shenzhen, China
ytq@huawei.com
[3] Boston, USA
bowenjiang1993@hotmail.com

Abstract. Erase count is a key performance indicator of hard drives, and it shows the lifetime of a device. Analysis of erase counts helps us understand the performance of a device and prevent the failure of it. In this paper, a machine learning based framework is proposed to predict the curves of erase counts. Specifically, probabilities and erase-count curves of different hard drives are first calculated from training data. The probabilities are for deciding disk type in testing data. The erase-count curves from training data serve as references to testing data. Long short-term memory is utilized to model the erase-count difference between a reference device and a testing device, and to predict the lifetime of the testing device. Preliminary results of synthetic data show that our method can follow references and precisely predict erase counts.

1 Introduction

Digitalization has become necessary to companies that take advantages of big data to improve performance and enhance competitiveness. In addition, personal devices become prevalent and generate tremendous data. The astronomical amount of data bring new challenges to data center, including the use of storage devices and the management of them. When a hard drive fails, data in the hard drive will be lost, which results in interruption of operation and financial losses of business [3]. Failure of storage device is a crucial issue that every data center needs to prevent and address [16]. In this paper, solid state drive (SSD) is used as an example of storage devices when we explain our methods.

A storage device usually works in a write-erase-write cycle. After data are written into the device, they will be erased before new data are written, either when the disk is full or the data are manually deleted by user. This cycle is called program-erase cycle (P/E cycle), which is a criterion for quantifying the endurance of a device. Generally speaking, each cycle consumes a tiny portion of the lifetime of a device. As the number of cycles increases, the remaining

---

B. Jiang—This work was performed while at Futurewei Technologies.

R. Nambiar and M. Poess (Eds.): TPCTC 2019, LNCS 12257, pp. 154–163, 2020.
https://doi.org/10.1007/978-3-030-55024-0_11

lifetime of a device decreases. Because erasing pairs with writing, thus erase count is simply used as a key performance indicator (KPI) in measuring lifetime of a storage device.

Figure 1 shows curves of erase counts generated by synthetic data, where x-axis is for time and y-axis indicates erase counts. In this figure, each curve shows the erase counts of a device, and different colors represent different disk types and patterns. In each curve, as time goes by, erase counts increase in variable speeds depending on how the device was used. At the end of life, the increase of erase counts slowly fades out. Erase-count curves change according to how devices are used. For instance, the erase-count curves of university users are different from those of bank users. Hard drive erasing and writing of bank users usually are frequent during business hours but rare after. On the other hand, students in universities run computers overnight to get experiment results, and the erasing and writing of those devices will not follow a 9–5 work schedule.

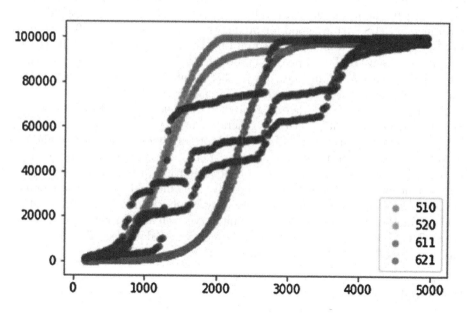

Fig. 1. Curves of erase counts from synthetic data. (Color figure online)

Predict the erase-count curve of a storage device is an interesting topic in device management. Knowing the curve will help us anticipate the lifetime of a device, adjust the use of it accordingly, and extend its life. In addition, analyze usage pattern can predict device failure.

The lifetime of a device depends on a variety of factors, including device specifications and how a device is being used [7,10]. In order to prevent device failure, a general solution is to replace a device at a specific time before the end of its life. However, it is difficult to anticipate when is the best time for replacement. Too early to replace a device will increase costs unnecessarily, while too late and the device fails before replacement will result in data losses [6]. Not to mention that not every hard drive is used in the same way, i.e., most devices do not fail at the same lifetime and do not have the same maximum erase counts. Schroeder *et al.* studied a wide range of reliability characteristics and found unexpected conclusions in flash reliability [13,14]. Narayanan *et al.* analyzed extensive data and provided the first comprehensive analysis of the characteristics of SSD failures [12].

Work has been done to predict device lifetime. Murray *et al.* developed a mi-NB algorithm based on naive Bayesian learning to predict failure of hard drive. They also compared their method with support vector machines, unsupervised clustering, and non-parametric statistical tests [11]. Some statistical techniques were employed in [2] to automatically detect which SMART parameters correlate with disk replacement and use them in predicting disk replacement. In addition, Shu *et al.* applied multiple machine learning methods to predict disk drive failures for timely replacement [15]. They also evaluated these methods by comparing prediction accuracy, recall and F-score. The methods of long short-term memory (LSTM) are good for predictions of time series data [9]. Recently, Lima *et al.* proposed a method based on LSTM and remaining useful life (RUL) binning to classify RUL and predict failure [4]. In [1], Anantharaman *et al.* compared LSTM with random forest on prediction of RUL, and suggested careful feature selection may help improving the performance of LSTM.

In this paper, machine learning methods are used in lifetime prediction. Specifically, erase-count curves are generated from training data and used as benchmarks to guide the prediction. Probability methods are applied to find the most possible curve from reference curves. Long Short-Term Memory (LSTM) is utilized to predict the parameters of a distribution instead of predicting the erase-count curve or device lifetime directly. This method catches the trend of curve, and is robust to changes. Preliminary results from synthetic data show that our methods can predict a erase-count curve even at an early stage of device usage. The ability to predict lifetime early reduces the data needed in prediction and increases the lifetime of a device.

2   Methods

The erase-count curves of a specific disk type usually follow the same pattern, and are differentiable from those of other disk types. Disk type here is a type of disks that have the same specifications and are used similarly.

Even though the erase-count curves of same disk type may not be exactly the same, they follow the same pattern and the difference between these curves can be seen as noise and modeled by functions. Accordingly, once the disk type is known, the shape of corresponding erase-count curve is approximately known, and the curve can be estimated by getting the parameters of a noise function, i.e., adding noise to the reference curve. Using disk type and corresponding erase-count curve from training data as benchmarks to predict lifetime of testing data can dramatically narrow down options and reduce the data needed for prediction.

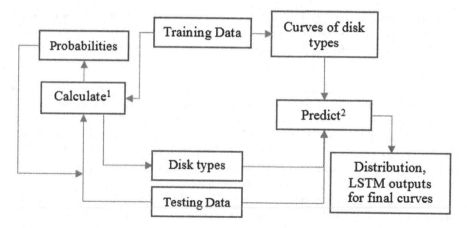

Fig. 2. The framework of our methods. (1. Include calculation of probabilities; 2. include obtaining parameters of distribution functions and fitting parameters into LSTM model.)

Figure 2 shows the framework. First of all, the probability of disk type given attributes are calculated using training data. The probability is used to determine disk types in testing data. Training data are also used to generate erase-count curves of different disk types. These curves serve as references to testing data. In order to approximate the curves of testing data, the reference curves are added with noise that is presented by noise function. One of the benefits doing so is to reduce the testing data needed for prediction so as to anticipate the lifetime as early as possible. Theoretically, without using parameters, it will take significant amount of data to predict a curve. Modeling the erase-count curve as reference and noise makes it possible to know the whole lifetime with a small amount of time points, as long as the noise function truly represents the difference. Once the parameters of a noise function are known, the noise function is predicted, so as the erase-count curve. Even though the disk type stays the same, parameters of a disk may change overtime because of changes in usage. In order to include these changes in our model and obtain the most recent set of parameters in prediction, LSTM is applied to predict the trends of parameters. There are advantages of using LSTM to predict function parameters. It enhances robustness in our model and reduces errors from fluctuation over time. It takes into account the overall dataset up to the last time point and predicts the most recent set of parameters. It provides flexibility in data needed. During prediction, the model can use as many data as the whole lifetime and as few as the first several time points.

2.1   Determination of Disk Type

In our method, there are two kinds of parameters that determine a disk type, disk specifications and usage factors. Disk specifications are set during manufacture, and they cannot be changed by users. Usage factors show how devices are used, and they can be changed by users. In this paper, we use attributes to describe all the parameters (disk specifications and usage factors) that determine a disk type. Let $\mathcal{D} = \{D_i | D_i \in \mathbb{N}_{\Bbbk}, i = 1, 2, ..., m\}$ represent the disk types, and let $\mathcal{A} = \{A_j | A_j \in \mathbb{R}, j = 1, 2, ... n\}$ be the disk attributes, i.e., attributes that are set once a disk is made, where m and n are the numbers of disk types and disk specifications, respectively. Each attribute has a pool of options, such as 0 and 1. In addition, let $\mathcal{H} = \{H_k | H_k \in \mathbb{R}, k = 1, 2, ..., p\}$ be the user attributes, i.e., attributes that can be changed by users and depend on how the devices are being used. Disk attributes affect user attributes because users tend to make proper use of a device according to its specifications. On the other hand, given user attributes, the disk attributes can be estimated. Therefore, there are casual relationships among disk attributes, user attributes, and disk types. A disk type can be decided by attributes using conditional probabilities, i.e., given attributes, the disk type is probably known.

Not every data center has all disk types, and not every user attribute is known in practice. The conditional probability of disk type given attributes can be calculated using training data. The most possible disk types are decided by conditional probabilities and testing data. As discussed above, disk types associate with specifications, i.e., given $\mathcal{D}$, probability $p(\mathcal{A}|\mathcal{D})$ is known. Disk type and specifications lead to how users use that type of disks, i.e., given $\mathcal{D}$ and $\mathcal{A}$, probability $p(\mathcal{H}|\mathcal{D}, \mathcal{A})$ is known. Thus, even without all the information in testing data as in a real situation, using training data, disk type can be decided by choosing the one with highest probability.

$$p(\mathcal{D}|\mathcal{A}, \mathcal{H}) \propto p(\mathcal{H}|\mathcal{D}, \mathcal{A})p(\mathcal{A}|\mathcal{D})p(\mathcal{D}) \tag{1}$$

The probabilities of $p(\mathcal{H}|\mathcal{D}, \mathcal{A})$, $p(\mathcal{A}|\mathcal{D})$, $p(\mathcal{D})$ are determined by training and testing data. The disk type that has the largest value of posterior probability will be decided as the disk type of that device. Data centers (users) can define user attributes according to the services they provide and the hardware they use. Thus, user attributes vary from disk type to disk type. In training, it is advantageous to define attributes to detail, so the calculation of probabilities will cover all possible disk types. Though, that means a large amount of data and time are needed in training. In practice, if the testing data do not have a specific attribute that is defined in training, than the probabilities relative to that attribute can be simply set to 0 or 1 depending on the situation.

2.2   Prediction of Lifetime

Presumably, every attribute affects the shape of erase-count curve. Even though two disks have the same disk type, their curves probably will not be the same, because the exact value of each attribute can be different. However, devices with same disk type usually have similar curves.

Once a disk type is decided, its reference erase-count curve is known. Let $\mathbf{y}$ represent the reference curve, and $\mathbf{y}'$ be the curve of a disk with the same disk type as $\mathbf{y}$. $\mathbf{y}'$ can be obtained by

$$\mathbf{y}' = \mathbf{y} + \mathbf{E}, \tag{2}$$

where $\mathbf{E}$ is noise. $\mathbf{E}$ changes according to the values of attributes, and are decided by a variety of conditions such as temperature and disk functionality.

In our method, $\mathbf{E}$ is modeled by a noise function. In order to find out function parameters of $\mathbf{E}$ in testing data, erase counts of given time points are fit into the curve combining reference and noise function. In our experiments, Gaussian distribution is applied to present noise $\mathbf{E}$. Though, $\mathbf{E}$ can be presented by other distribution functions.

Solve Gaussian function at time t provides a set of parameters at that time point. However, the parameters at a specific time point are not certain the optimal parameters. In addition, parameters change from time to time because attributes change. LSTM network is applied to extract the trend of changes from parameters. Specifically, parameters of different time points are sent to LSTM units to train and predict the best set of parameters for all the unknown time points. Note that, the testing data are used for both training and testing of LSTM network, because all the parameters are obtained from testing data. The model is robust to local changes because of LSTM network.

2.3   Change of Disk Type

Disk type can be changed during the lifetime of a disk. For example, in a data center, a hard drive can be assigned to bank users in the first half year but university users in the second. When disk type and usage pattern change, erase-count curve changes too. Thus, once disk type is changed, new prediction should be performed.

There are methods to detect changes in disk type. The easiest way is through detecting the changes in attributes. When the attributes of a disk change, its disk type changes. Change of disk type can also be detected by distinct changes in erase-count curve. If the shape of erase-count curve changes it is usually because the attributes change. However, decision based on curve changes should be made carefully, because a large number of factors can lead to curve changes, such as noise. The duration, frequency, and amount of curve changes should be considered.

After a change is detected, the erase-count curve of the corresponding new disk type will start being used as a reference for prediction. It is possible that a disk has multiple disk types in its lifetime. Because data consistency is important to training and testing, frequent changes in disk type jeopardize prediction accuracy.

3   Implementations

Our model is tested with synthetic data as shown in Fig. 1. The colors in this figure represent disk types. The formulas in [8] are utilized to solve the parameters of Gaussian distribution, Appendix A. Specifically, time points between $t-5$

and $t + 5$ are used to calculate the set of Gaussian parameters at t. The LSTM network in our method is based on [5], one LSTM for each parameter. If training data have multiple curves of one disk type, the reference curve of that disk type is generated by averaging all the curves.

Figure 3 and Fig. 4 show the preliminary results of our method. In these figures, the two curves in each figure have same disk type. The curves in blue are from training data and serve as references for prediction. The curves in orange are from testing data, and the curves in green are prediction results. From the results, we can see the predicted curves nicely follow the patterns of reference curves.

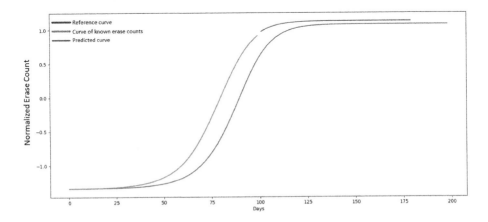

Fig. 3. Reference and prediction results of disk type 1. (Color figure online)

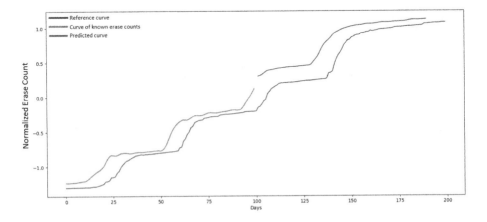

Fig. 4. Reference and prediction results of disk type 2. (Color figure online)

4   Discussions and Future Work

Because it takes thousands of P/C cycles for a device to fail, and there are a variety of devices in the market, thus it takes time and effort to create a database of erase-count curves as benchmarks. Some datasets are mentioned in the papers of different vendors, such as BackBlaze, Google, and Microsoft. However, the detail information, such as the attribute values of these data are not public. Some of the data are hard drive data instead of SSD data. Thus, synthetic data are used in the demonstration of our method. Methods and solutions need to be updated for real data.

Gaussian distribution is used empirically in our experiments. The difference between erase-count curve of training and that of testing may not follow Gaussian distribution. Investigation in other distributions is of interest to us, especially when real data are obtained.

Erase-count curves present combinations of attributes. It would be interesting to see how attributes affect erase-count curves, and how each attribute contributes to the curves. Knowing the contribution of attributes can generate an erase-count curve by combining the effects of attributes without using any data.

Future work includes investigation of other distribution models and how they affect prediction results, investigation of the same distribution model on other hard drives, comparison of state-of-the-art methods, and so on.

Appendix

A   Estimation of Gaussian Parameters

Equation (2) can be written as

$$x = \mathbf{y}' - \mathbf{y} = h + ce^{-\frac{(t-a)^2}{b}}, \tag{3}$$

where t is time, and a, b, c, h are the Guassian parameters to estimate.

Let

$$P_1 = 0 \tag{4}$$

$$P_m = P_{m-1} + \frac{1}{2}(x_m + x_{m-1})(t_m + t_{m-1}) \tag{5}$$

$$Q_1 = 0 \tag{6}$$

$$Q_m = Q_{m-1} + \frac{1}{2}(t_m x_m + t_{m-1} x_{m-1})(t_m + t_{m-1}) \tag{7}$$

where m is the index of each $\{t_m, x_m\}$.

In addition, let

$$
U = \begin{pmatrix}
\sum\limits_{m=1}^{n} P_m^2 & \sum\limits_{m=1}^{n} P_m Q_m \\
\sum\limits_{m=1}^{n} P_m Q_m & \sum\limits_{m=1}^{n} Q_m^2 \\
\sum\limits_{m=1}^{n} P_m(t_m^2 - t_1^2) & \sum\limits_{m=1}^{n} Q_m(t_m^2 - t_1^2) \\
\sum\limits_{m=1}^{n} P_m(t_m - t_1) & \sum\limits_{m=1}^{n} Q_m(t_m - t_1)
\end{pmatrix}
$$

$$
\begin{pmatrix}
\sum\limits_{m=1}^{n} P_m(t_m^2 - t_1^2) & \sum\limits_{m=1}^{n} P_m(t_m - t_1) \\
\sum\limits_{m=1}^{n} Q_m(t_m^2 - t_1^2) & \sum\limits_{m=1}^{n} Q_m(t_m - t_1) \\
\sum\limits_{m=1}^{n} (t_m^2 - t_1^2)^2 & \sum\limits_{m=1}^{n} (t_m^2 - t_1^2)(t_m - t_1) \\
\sum\limits_{m=1}^{n} (t_m^2 - t_1^2)(t_m - t_1) & \sum\limits_{m=1}^{n} (t_m - t_1)^2
\end{pmatrix} , \tag{8}
$$

$$
V = \begin{pmatrix}
\sum\limits_{m=1}^{n} P_m(x_m - x_1) \\
\sum\limits_{m=1}^{n} Q_m(x_m - x_1) \\
\sum\limits_{m=1}^{n} (t_m^2 - t_1^2)(x_m - x_1) \\
\sum\limits_{m=1}^{n} (t_m - t_1)(x_m - x_1)
\end{pmatrix} , \tag{9}
$$

and

$$
\begin{pmatrix} B \\ C \\ F \\ G \end{pmatrix} = U^{-1} V. \tag{10}
$$

The parameters a and b are obtained by

$$
a = -\frac{B}{C}, \tag{11}
$$

$$
b = -\frac{2}{C}. \tag{12}
$$

Finally,

$$
q_m = e^{-\frac{(t_m - a)^2}{b}}, \tag{13}
$$

and

$$
\begin{pmatrix} c \\ h \end{pmatrix} = \begin{pmatrix} \sum\limits_{m=1}^{n} q_m^2 & \sum\limits_{m=1}^{n} q_m \\ \sum\limits_{m=1}^{n} q_m & n \end{pmatrix}^{-1} \begin{pmatrix} \sum\limits_{m=1}^{n} q_m x_m \\ \sum\limits_{m=1}^{n} x_m \end{pmatrix} . \tag{14}
$$

References

1. Anantharaman, P., Qiao, M., Jadav, D.: Large scale predictive analytics for hard disk remaining useful life estimation. In: Proceedings of the IEEE International Congress on Big Data, July 2018
2. Botezatu, M.M., Giurgiu, I., Bogojeska, J., Wiesmann, D.: Predicting disk replacement towards reliable data centers. In: Proceedings of the 2016 ACM SIGKDD International Conference on Knowledge Discovery and Data Mining, August 2016, New York, NY. ACM Press (2016)
3. Copeland, M.: The cost of it downtime, June 2018. https://www.the20.com/blog/the-cost-of-it-downtime/
4. dos Santos Lima, F.D., Amaral, G.M.R., de Moura Leite, L.G., Gomes, J.P.P., de Castro Machado, J.: Predicting failures in hard drives with LSTM networks. In: Proceedings of the 2017 Brazilian Conference on Intelligent Systems, pp. 222–227, October 2017
5. Ganegedara, T.: Stock market predictions with LSTM in Python, May 2018. https://www.datacamp.com/community/tutorials/lstm-python-stock-market
6. Hamerly, G., Elkan, C.: Bayesian approaches to failure prediction for disk drives. In: Proceedings of the International Conference on Machine Learning, San Francisco, CA, June 2001, pp. 202–209. Morgan Kaufmann Publishers Inc. (2001)
7. Hughes, G.F., Murray, J.F., Kreutz-Delgado, K., Elkan, C.: Improved disk-drive failure warnings. IEEE Trans. Reliab. **51**(3), 350–357 (2002)
8. Jacquelin, J.: Rregressions and integral equations (2009). https://www.scribd.com/doc/14674814/Regressions-et-equations-integrales
9. Lipton, Z.C.: A critical review of recurrent neural networks for sequence learning. CoRR (2015). https://dblp.org/rec/bib/journals/corr/Lipton15
10. Meza, J., Wu, Q., Kumar, S., Mutlu, O.: A large-scale study of flash memory failures in the field. In: Proceedings of the 2015 ACM SIGMETRICS International Conference on Measurement and Modeling of Computer System, June 2015
11. Murray, J.F., Hughes, G.F., Kreutz-Delgado, K.: Machine learning methods for predicting failures in hard drives: a multiple-instance application. J. Mach. Learn. Res. **6**, 783–816 (2005)
12. Narayanan, I., et al.: SSD failures in datacenters: what? when? and why? In: Proceedings of the 9th ACM International on Systems and Storage Conference, June 2016
13. Schroeder, B., Lagisetty, R., Merchant, A.: Flash reliability in production: the expected and the unexpected. In: Proceedings of the 14th USENIX Conference on File and Storage Technologies (FAST 16), Santa Clara, CA, pp. 67–80. USENIX Association (2016). https://www.usenix.org/conference/fast16/technical-sessions/presentation/schroeder
14. Schroeder, B., Merchant, A., Lagisetty, R.: Reliability of nand-based SSDS: what field studies tell us. In: Proceedings of the IEEE, vol. 105, pp. 1751–1769. IEEE, September 2017
15. Shu, G., Jang, J.E.: Proactive storage health management to reduce data center downtime, December 2017
16. Zenlayer. Measuring data center downtime, January 2018. https://www.zenlayer.com/data-center-downtime/

Author Index

Printed in the United States
By Bookmasters